HIPPIAS MAJOR

Publication of this book was assisted
by a grant from the Publications Program
of the National Endowment for the Humanities,
an independent federal agency.

PLATO
HIPPIAS MAJOR

Translated,
with Commentary and Essay,
by
PAUL WOODRUFF

Hackett Publishing Company
Indianapolis | Cambridge

Printed in the United States of America
First Printing

Interior design by Jared Carter

For further information, please address
Hackett Publishing Company, Inc.
Post Office Box 44937
Indianapolis, Indiana 46204

Library of Congress Cataloging in Publication Data

Plato.
   Hippias major.

   Bibliography: p. 198
   Includes indexes.
   1. Values. I. Woodruff, Paul, 1943- . II. Title.
B391.H42E5   1982   184   81-7027
ISBN 0-915145-25-1   AACR2

For My Parents

Contents

Preface   ix | Introduction   xi

HIPPIAS MAJOR

Preliminaries   1 | The Question   7
A Fine Girl   9 | Gold   11
Burying Your Parents   14 | The Appropriate   16
The Able and Useful   18 | The Beneficial   20
Aesthetic Pleasure   22

COMMENTARY

Preliminaries   35 | The Question   43
A Fine Girl   46 | Gold   56
Burying Your Parents   59 | The Appropriate   62
The Able and Useful   67 | The Beneficial   70
Aesthetic Pleasure   77

ESSAY

One: DATE AND AUTHENTICITY   93
PLATONIC PARALLELS   104

Two: PLOT, HUMOR, AND SUBJECT   106

Three: MILIEU   113
The Older Sophists   114 | Socrates   117

Four: CHARACTERIZATION OF HIPPIAS   123
The Historical Hippias   123 | Rhetorical Mannerisms   125
Plato's Hippias   127 | Why Hippias?   131

Five: SOCRATES' QUESTION   136
Independence of the Question   136 | Priority of Definition   138
The Bounds of Ignorance   141 | Socrates' Use of Examples   146

Six: PRINCIPLES OF DEFINITION   149
Explanation and Logical Causes   151
Self-Predication as Strict Predication   153
Unity and Generality   156

Seven: ONTOLOGY   161
Forms   162 | Ontology   163
The Silence of Earlier Dialogues   165
The Modest Separation of Forms   168
One-over-Many   171
The Place of the *Hippias Major* in Plato's
Philosophical Development   175

Eight: THE FINE, THE GOOD, AND THE BENEFICIAL   181
The Bounds of Ignorance Revisited   182
The Fine Is Beneficial   183
The Fine Is Good   187

Bibliography   191
General Index   199
Index Locorum   203

Preface

My hope for this book is that it will open paths into the *Hippias Major* for scholars and general readers both. I began it as a scholarly commentary, but I could not let it end there. In order that Greekless readers might not miss Plato's comic and philosophical twists, I needed to make a fresh translation. In addition, to treat adequately the themes that run through the dialogue, I had to append a general Essay as long as the Translation and Commentary combined. The most interesting questions about the *Hippias Major* concern Socrates' method and Hippias' character, and these cannot be answered in commentary format.

Nevertheless, I have kept to my purpose of writing about the *Hippias Major*. Even the Essay does not consider wider questions about Plato and Socrates except insofar as the *Hippias Major* helps answer them. I try to be neutral on the interpretation of the rest of Plato's work.

The Introduction is a summary of the argument of the Essay; its claims are supported at length there. The Translation attempts to reproduce the dramatic vigor of Platonic dialogue without loss of philosophical clarity. So far as possible, each word is translated the same way throughout. The Commentary is keyed to the Translation by division into segments. Each segment begins with a general introduction and analysis of the argument, followed with line-by-line notes which treat problems of textual criticism, translation or interpretation, and also provide information on the people and places mentioned in the text.

Chapters Two through Four of the Essay are introductory. They discuss literary features of the *Hippias Major* in terms I believe are accessible to laymen. The remaining chapters treat subjects of interest mainly to Plato scholars. Some overlapping of Essay with Commentary is inevitable and saves the reader leafing back and forth.

ACKNOWLEDGEMENTS

I have been influenced in my thinking about Plato and helped in the writing of this book by a number of scholars. Alexander Nehamas not only was midwife to the project but inseminator of some of the main ideas. For his encouragement and thorough editorial help I am very grateful. After that my greatest debt is to Gregory Vlastos, who introduced me to Plato and whose work has guided me since. I must also acknowledge the influence in many ways of G. E. L. Owen and the generous advice of my colleagues A. P. D. Mourelatos and Edwin Allaire. I have Douglass Parker to thank for helping me hit Plato's comic tone in my translation. The main work of the project I carried out at the Center for Hellenic Studies, with the generous help of staff and fellows: Bernard Knox (Director), Jenö Platty (Librarian), Peter Rhodes, and Richard Patterson. Assorted anonymous referees have also been generous with advice.

Some of the ideas of Chapters Five through Seven were first mooted in my two articles of 1978, and ancestors of Chapters Five and Eight were originally presented at the Princeton University Colloquium for Ancient Philosophy in 1979. On that occasion Donald Zeyl gave useful critical comments.

My work on the *Hippias Major* has been supported by a grant from the Research Institute of the University of Texas, and by a junior fellowship at the Center for Hellenic Studies. I prepared the final draft while enjoying a visiting position at the University of Pittsburgh, where the Department of Philosophy made me comfortable and gave me time to work. Students and guests in my seminar made helpful suggestions for several chapters that were still in nascent form.

Thanks go to Trisha Stroud for accurately typing a balky manuscript, to Jim Lovelace for spotting my errors, and to Olga Vorloou for correcting them. I wish I knew how to thank my wife and daughters for putting up with me while I did all this.

Paul Woodruff

Introduction

Two dialogues of Socrates with Hippias come down to us under Plato's name. The *Hippias Major,* the longer of the two, is distinguished from other Platonic works by its richly comic and unusual vocabulary, and by its startling use of ridicule against Socrates' adversary. This aroused a suspicion in scholarly circles during the nineteenth century that the *Hippias Major* was not the work of Plato. Those who thought Plato would not have written two *Hippias* dialogues therefore chose the *Major* to strike from the canon. That has been a great loss, for the *Hippias Major* is likely to be authentic. It is rewarding as a uniquely comic dialogue, an intriguing piece of philosophy, and a clue to Plato's development.

AUTHENTICITY. Since the *Hippias Major* first came under suspicion, debate on its authenticity has flourished, overshadowing the many interesting features of the work itself. Those who would reject, or athetize, the work deemed it unworthy of Plato and were surprised by its unusual vocabulary. Defenders for the most part found the dialogue splendidly Platonic. Both sides are still at it. The issue depends too much on taste—and on taste in the shadowy realm of humor, at that—to be definitely resolved. Both sides, however, agree to date the *Hippias Major* during Plato's lifetime, and both set it apart from the ruck of pseudo-Platonica. I argue for accepting the *Hippias Major* provisionally. The presumption in its favor has not been upset by any compelling arguments. If we can interpret the dialogue smoothly as part of Plato's work, we shall have no remaining reason to reject it. That condition will be satisfied if the Essay of this book carries out such an interpretation successfully. The Essay as a whole, then, is my argument for authenticity.

CHARACTERS. Hippias was a traveling teacher of public speaking and various other subjects, including mathematics, astronomy, geometry, euphony, mnemonics, history, and ethics. He would give displays of oratory (or whatever else was wanted) for a substantial fee, which he thought he deserved. He was in his opinion especially qualified to enhance the virtues of his paying students. In Plato's eyes that made him a sophist; and though so far as we know Hippias taught nothing morally offensive, he was himself a moral offense to Plato, somehow making it worth Plato's while a half-generation later to lambaste him through the literary person of Socrates. The ridicule is personal, for Hippias' defect was not in his beliefs (if he had any to pin down) so much as in his personality. He was the most versatile of sophists. He could teach anything, and could be counted on to tell an audience what it wanted to hear. This flexibility, coming as it did with a promise of moral instruction, was morally alarming. It alarmed Plato enough to provoke him into writing not only the two Hippias dialogues, but numerous attacks on nameless sophists for their versatility, a despised quality which Hippias exemplified.

The *Hippias Major* shows Socrates mercilessly laying bare the empty core under Hippias' multi-faceted veneer. He is the annoying and fascinating Socrates of the *Apology* and dialogues of search. He has a little (an important little) in common with Xenophon's Socrates. How accurate a portrait he is of the man who hooked Plato on philosophy no one can definitely say. He is interesting enough, at any rate, to be the historical Socrates. But he is connected in the *Hippias Major* with the beginnings of Plato's theory of Forms, and that theory, according to consensus, is not Socratic.

SUBJECT. Plato's subject is as alarmingly slippery as Hippias himself. It is the important thing Socrates' other objects of search have in common: the *kalon*. Variously translated "beautiful," "noble," "admirable," and "fine," *kalon* is a general term of commendation. The virtues Socrates wants to know about elsewhere are each of them *kalon*. So are the lovely boys and young men with whom he spends his days. So are sound laws and good habits, fast horses and fierce fighting birds. So are true sentences and morally improving speeches. And so, surprisingly, is ugly old Socrates himself.

When the fashion was to translate *kalon* "beautiful," the *Hippias Major* was diminished to a disappointing treatise in aesthetics. Understood more broadly, with "fine" for *kalon* (as I translate it), the dialogue is an interesting inquiry into the foundation of all sorts of value judgments.

The slipperiness on which Socrates is trying to find ground for a firm stand is the liability of words like "fine," "good," and "large" to take on apparently different meanings in different contexts. A fine soldier may not have the qualities of a fine man, any more than a large diamond has the size of a large rock. Hippias seems content to slide with the usage of the word, but Socrates is not. Socrates wants to know the one nature that the fine is in every fine thing. Hippias does not want to know anything of the sort. He thinks he already knows how to get by, come what may, by making a crowd laugh at a person who asks questions, for example. Neither man has any part in the other's enterprise, so the contest that emerges is like what would happen if two skilled persons tried to play "Go" and Checkers against each other on the same board, using the same pieces, at the same time.

PRELIMINARY SKIRMISH. Socrates interrogates Hippias on his career— his earnings, his high opinion of himself, the subjects he teaches. Sparta, it turns out, refuses to admit Hippias as a teacher. His credentials in question, Hippias invites Socrates to hear and judge a speech Hippias gave in Sparta about what practices are fine training for young men. This reminds Socrates that the last time he tried to evaluate speeches as fine or foul, he was interrupted by someone asking him how he knew what sorts of things were fine or foul. Socrates still does not know how to answer him. Will Hippias help?

THE ARGUMENT. Through the undeceiving mask of the unnamed Questioner, Socrates asks what the fine is—what it is to be fine, or what it is that makes things fine. After showing how Hippias' three tries are all failures, he initiates a line of answers himself and drives it to an impasse. The fine turns out to be an elusive quarry. "What's fine is hard," says Socrates at the end, and that lesson appears to be the meager fruit of the dialogue. But that is neither meager nor the only accomplishment of the *Hippias Major*.

Quick learner that he is, Hippias had thought the fine would be an easy subject, like every subject for him. That was what was the matter with Hippias, that he took difficult matters to be trifles. And that, if Socrates is right in his high standards for definition, is the matter with a great many people. Showing the elusiveness of the fine, then, is of considerable importance for Socrates.

The *Hippias Major* is more than an exposure of Hippias and his overconfident kind, however. Its argument illustrates a conception of definition that was new in its time and is interesting in any time. Although so far as we know Socrates had no general theory of definition, he is clear in the *Hippias Major* about what conditions a definition of the fine should satisfy. These requirements for definition carry with them presuppositions about the nature of the fine. If the fine is to be definable by Socrates' rules, then it must turn out to be of a certain sort: it must be one and the same in every fine thing; it must always be fine, and it must be what makes fine things fine. To know such things about the fine is to know a great deal about it.

With these presuppositions comes the ghost of an ontology, the early beginnings of Plato's theory of Forms. That is what has made the *Hippias Major* important to recent scholarship on Plato's development. Socrates supposes that the fine is a form and that it is *something,* an unchanging nature. He does not go beyond this to ask how such natures fit into a general ontological theory; nor does he state or presuppose the most distinctive doctrines of the theory of Forms. That theory, nevertheless, is a natural development of the sort of thing Socrates says about the fine in the *Hippias Major*.

There is still another sort of belief about the fine that we may assign to Socrates, but more speculatively. He seems to have held that the fine is both good and beneficial, but not that it is defined as either *the* good or *the* beneficial. When Socrates knows what the fine is, he will probably know as well what both of those things are. But that is just what Socrates does not know. His ignorance is hard for him, but he is prepared to make the best of it.

On that note the dialogue ends. Hippias has learned nothing but to avoid Socrates; Socrates has only learned again how difficult a subject he has undertaken. And the reader—what should he learn? Socrates' lesson, at least, but also much about definition and something even about the fine itself.

NOTE ON THE TRANSLATION AND THE COMMENTARY

This is not a word-for-word translation of the original. Most of the *Hippias Major* is written in a conversational style. I have therefore tried to present it in English I would not be ashamed to speak. That meant that particles in particular, which are frequent in Greek but are rare in English, could not be brought over directly. Some speeches parody Hippias' style (p. 132); the effect is odd in Greek, and I have tried to make it odd in English.

I have followed Burnet's text, except where indicated in the notes. I have altered his punctuation freely, however.

Much of the dialogue's argument hangs on equivocation or other word play. To carry this into English I have adhered strictly to one translation for each Greek word that is played on. The result is unusual English in a few contexts.

Examples:

kalos is "fine" throughout, though some contexts taken alone would call for "beautiful" or "good." Its opposite, *aischros,* is "foul" throughout.

phainesthai is "to be seen." When it occurs, as often in the *Hippias Major,* alone with an adjective, it is ambiguous between "is plainly" (with a participle understood) and "is thought to be" (with an infinitive understood).

dunatos is "able," though one context calls for "powerful."

I have adopted two conventions for ease of translation: (1) Where the Greek has a neuter adjective as a substantive, I supply "thing" or "things." For example, *kalon* becomes "fine thing." I use "thing" here neutrally for anything that may be said to be fine, and I never have occasion to use "thing" to translate a Greek noun. (2) I use "this" to point to something about to be mentioned, and "that" for something mentioned earlier, as in "Let me say this about that."

The Commentary is divided like the tranlation into segments. Each segment of Commentary consists of a discursive introduction followed by notes on specific points of interpretation, translation, or textual criticism. These notes are keyed to the translation by Stephanus page, and are consecutively numbered as well for ease of reference.

CITATIONS AND ABBREVIATIONS

Citations are by date-paging. Page 4 of the work published by Marion Soreth in 1953 is cited: "Soreth, 1953: 4." Works cited in this manner are listed in the bibliography. In addition, I have used two abbreviations: "DK" for *Die Fragmente der Vorsokratiker,* ed. by Hermann Diels, the sixth edition ed. by Walter Kranz (Berlin/Zurich, 1952); and "LSJ" for the new edition of Liddell and Scott's *Greek English Lexicon* (Oxford, 1940).

Internal cross-references are by page or note number. All notes cited as, e.g., "note 52," are in the Commentary.

HIPPIAS MAJOR

Socrates. Here comes Hippias, fine and wise![1] How long   281a1
it's been since you put in to Athens!

Hippias. No spare time, Socrates. Whenever Elis[2] has business to work out with another city, they always come first to me   281a5
when they choose an ambassador. They think I'm the citizen
best able to judge and report messages from the various cities.   281b1
I've often been on missions to other cities, but most often and
on the most and greatest affairs to Sparta.[3] That, to answer
your question, is why I don't exactly haunt these parts.

S. That is what it is like to be truly wise, Hippias, a man of   281b5
complete accomplishments: in private you are able to make a
lot of money[4] from young people (and to give still greater
benefits to those from whom you take it); while in public you   281c1
are able to provide your own city with good service (as is
proper for one who expects not to be despised, but admired by
ordinary people).

But Hippias, how in the world do you explain this: in the
old days people who are still famous for wisdom[5]—Pittacus   281c5
and Bias and the school of Thales of Miletus, and later ones
down to Anaxagoras—that all or most of those people, we see,
kept away from affairs of state?[6]

1

H. What do you think, Socrates? Isn't it that they were
281d1 weak and unable to carry their good sense successfully into
both areas, the public and the private?

S. Then it's really[7] like the improvements in other skills,
281d5 isn't it, where early craftsmen are worthless compared to modern ones?[8] Should we say that your skill—the skill of the sophists—has been improved in the same way, and that the ancients
are worthless compared to you in wisdom?

H. Yes, certainly, you're right.

282a1 *S*. So if Bias came to life[9] again in our time, Hippias, he
would make himself a laughingstock compared with you people, just as Daedalus[10] also, according to the sculptors, would
be laughable if he turned up now doing things like the ones that
made him famous.

282a5 *H*. That's right, Socrates, just as you say.[11] However *I*
usually praise the ancients who came before us before and
more highly than I praise people of our own day, for while I
take care to avoid the envy of the living, I fear the wrath of
the dead.[12]

282b1 *S*. You're putting fine thoughts in fine words, Hippias;
that's what I think. I can support the truth of your claim; the
skill you people have has really been improved in its ability to
handle public business as well as private.

282b5 Why, Gorgias of Leontini,[13] the well-known sophist, came
here on public business as ambassador from his home-town—
because he was best qualified in Leontini to handle community
affairs. In the assembly, he won his case,[14] and in private, by
giving displays[15] and tutorials[16] to young people, he made a lot
282c1 of money and took it out of the city. Or, another case, our colleague Prodicus[17] came often enough on public business; but
just this last time, when he came on public business from
Ceos,[18] he made a great impression with his speech in the coun-
282c5 cil, and in private he earned a wonderful sum of money giving
displays and tutoring the young. But none of these early thinkers thought fit to charge a monetary fee or give displays of his
282d1 wisdom for all comers. They were so simple they didn't realize
the great value of money. But either Gorgias or Prodicus made
more money out of wisdom than any other craftsman made

from any skill whatever. And Protagoras[19] did the same even earlier. 282d5

H. Socrates, you haven't the slightest idea how fine this can be. If you knew how much money *I've* made, you'd be amazed. Take one case: I went to Sicily once, when Protagoras 282e1 was visiting there (he was famous then, and an older man); though I was younger I made much more than a hundred and fifty minas[20] in a short time—and from one very small place, Inycum,[21] more than twenty minas. When I went home with 282e5 this I gave it to my father, so that he and the other citizens were amazed and thunderstruck. And I almost think I've made more money than any other two sophists you like put together.

S. That's a fine thing you say, Hippias, strong evidence of your own and modern wisdom, and of the superiority of 283a1 men nowadays over the ancients. There was a lot of ignorance among our predecessors down to[22] Anaxagoras,[23] according to you. People say the opposite of what happened to you happened to Anaxagoras: he inherited a large sum, but lost every- 283a5 thing through neglect—there was so little *intelligence*[24] in his wisdom. And they tell stories like that about other early wise men. You make me see there's fine evidence, here, I think, for the superiority of our contemporaries over those who came be- 283b1 fore; and many will have the same opinion, that a wise man needs to be wise primarily for his own sake. The mark of being wise, I see, is when someone makes the most money.[25] Enough said about that.

Tell me this: from which of the cities you visit did you 283b5 make the most money? From Sparta, obviously, where you visited most often.

H. Lord no, Socrates.

S. Really? Did you make the least?

H. Nothing at all, ever. 283c1

S. That's weird, Hippias, and amazing! Tell me, isn't the wisdom you have the sort that makes those who study and learn it stronger in virtue?

H. Very much so, Socrates.

S. But while you were able to make the sons of Inycans 283c5 better, you were powerless for the sons of Spartans?

H. Far from it.

S. But then do Sicilians want to become better, but not Spartans?

283d1   *H.* Certainly the Spartans want to, as well, Socrates.

S. Well, did they stay away from you for lack of money?

H. No. They have enough.

S. How could it be that they have money and the desire,
283d5   and you have the ability to give them the greatest benefits, but they didn't send you away loaded with money? Could it be this, that the Spartans educate their own children better than you would? Should we say this is so, do you agree?

283e1   *H.* Not at all.

S. Then weren't you able to persuade the young men in Sparta that if they studied with you[26] they would make more progress in virtue than if they stayed with their own teachers?
283e5   Or couldn't you persuade their fathers they should entrust the matter to you, rather than look after it themselves, if they cared at all for their sons? Surely they didn't enviously begrudge their own sons the chance to become as good as possible.

H. I don't think they begrudged it.

S. But Sparta really is law-abiding.[27]

H. Of course.

284a1   *S.* And what's most highly prized in law-abiding cities is virtue.

H. Of course.

S. And you, you know most finely of men how to pass virtue on to other people.[28]

H. Very much so, Socrates.

S. Well, a man who knew most finely how to teach skill
284a5   with horses[29] would be most honored, and get the most money, in Thessaly, or wherever else in Greece that skill is seriously studied.

H. That's likely.

S. Then won't a man who can teach lessons of the great-
284b1   est value for virtue be given the highest honor, and make the most money, if he wishes, in Sparta, or in any other law-abiding Greek city? But you think it will be more in Sicily, more in Inycum? Should we believe all this, Hippias? If *you* give the
284b5   order, it has to be believed.

H. An ancestral tradition of the Spartans, Socrates, forbids them to change their laws, or to give their sons any education contrary to established customs.

S. What do you mean? The Spartans have an ancestral tradition of not doing right, but doing wrong? 284c1

H. I wouldn't say so, Socrates.

S. But they would do right to educate their young men better, not worse?

H. Right, indeed. But foreign education is not lawful for 284c5 them: because, mind you, if anybody else had ever taken money from there for education, I would have taken by far the most— they love my lectures and applaud—but, as I say, it's against the law.

S. Do you call law[30] harmful or beneficial to the city, 284d1 Hippias?

H. I think it is made to be beneficial, but sometimes it does harm, too, if the law is made badly.

S. But look here. Don't lawmakers make law to be the greatest good to the city? Without that, law-abiding civilized 284d5 life is impossible.[31]

H. True.

S. So when people who are trying to make laws fail to make them good, they have failed to make them lawful— indeed, to make them law.[32] What do you say?

H. In precise speech, Socrates, that is so. But men are not 284e1 accustomed to use words in that manner.

S. Do you mean those who know, Hippias, or those who don't?

H. Ordinary people.[33]

S. Are *they* the ones who know the truth—ordinary people?

H. Of course not. 284e5

S. But I suppose people who know, at least, believe that what is more beneficial is more lawful in truth for all men. Do you agree?

H. Yes, I grant it's that way in truth.[34]

S. Then it is and stays just the way those who know believe it to be?

H. Quite.

S. But, as you say, it would be more beneficial for the
Spartans to be educated by your teaching, though it's foreign—
more beneficial than the local education?

H. And what I say is true.

S. And that what is more beneficial is more lawful—do
you say that too, Hippias?

H. I did say it.

S. By your account it is more lawful for the sons of the
Spartans to be educated by Hippias and less lawful by their
fathers, if they will really be more benefited by you.

H. They certainly will be benefited, Socrates.

S. Then the Spartans are breaking the law by not giving
you money and entrusting their sons to you.

H. I grant that. I think you said your say on my behalf,
and there's no need for me to oppose it.

S. So we find the Spartans to be lawbreakers, and that on
the most important issue, though they appear to be most lawful.[35] So when they applaud you, really Hippias, and enjoy
your speech, what sort of things have they heard?[36] Surely
they're those things you know most finely, things about stars
and movements in the sky?[37]

H. Not at all. They can't stand the subject.

S. Then do they enjoy hearing about geometry?

H. No. Many of them can't even, well, *count.*

S. Then they're a long way from putting up with your
displays of arithmetic.

H. Good god, yes. A long way.

S. Well, do they like those things on which you know how
to make the sharpest distinctions of anybody—the functions of
letters, syllables, rhythms, and harmonies?[38]

H. Harmonies and letters, indeed!

S. Well just what is it they love to hear about from you,
and applaud? Tell me yourself; I can't figure it out.

H. The genealogies of heroes and men, Socrates, and the
settlements (how cities were founded in ancient times), and in
a word all ancient history—that's what they most love to hear
about.[39] So because of them I have been forced to learn up on
all such things and to study them thoroughly.

S. Good lord, Hippias, you're lucky the Spartans don't

enjoy it when someone lists our archons from the time of Solon. 285e5
Otherwise, you'd have had a job learning them.

H. How come, Socrates? Let me hear them once and I'll
memorize fifty names.

S. That's right. I forgot you had the art of memory.[40] So I
understand: the Spartans enjoy you, predictably, because you 286a1
know a lot of things, and they use you the way children use
old ladies,[41] to tell stories for pleasure.

H. Yes—and, good lord, actually about fine activities,
Socrates. Just now I made a great impression there speaking
about the activities a young man should take up. I have a 286a5
speech[42] about that I put together really finely, and I put the
words particularly well. My setting and the starting-point of
the speech are something like this: After Troy was taken, the
tale is told that Neoptolemus asked Nestor[43] what sort of ac- 286b1
tivities are fine—the sort of activities that would make someone most famous if he adopted them while young. After that
the speaker is Nestor, who teaches him a very great many very
fine customs.[44] I displayed that there and I expect to display it 286b5
here the day after tomorrow, in Pheidostratus' schoolroom—
with many other fine things worth hearing. Eudicus,[45] Apē-
mantus' son, invited me. But why don't you come too, and bring 286c1
some more people, if they are capable of hearing and judging
what is said?

S. Certainly, Hippias, if all goes well.

[2. The Question | 286c3–287e1]

Socrates. But now answer me a short question about that;
it's a fine thing[46] you reminded me. Just now someone[47] got 286c5
me badly stuck when I was finding fault with parts of some
speeches for being foul,[48] and praising other parts as fine.[49]
He questioned me this way, really insultingly: "Socrates, how
do *you* know what sorts of things are fine and foul? Look, 286d1
would you be able to say what the fine is?"[50] And I, I'm so
worthless, I was stuck and I wasn't able to answer him properly. As I left the gathering I was angry and blamed myself,
and I made a threatening resolve, that whomever of you wise 286d5

men I met *first,* I would listen and learn and study, then return to the questioner and fight the argument back.[51] So, as I say, it's a fine thing you came now. Teach me enough about what

286e1 the fine is itself, and try to answer me with the greatest precision possible, so I won't be a laughingstock again for having been refuted a second time. Of course you know it clearly; it would be a pretty small bit of learning out of the many things *you* know.[52]

286e5 *Hippias.* Small indeed, Socrates, and not worth a thing, as they say.

S. Then I'll learn it easily, and no one will ever refute me again.

H. No one will. Or what I do would be crude and amateurish.

S. Very well said, Hippias—*if* we defeat the man! Will it hurt if I act like him and take the other side of the argument

287a5 when you answer, so that you'll give me the most practice? I have some experience of the other side. So if it's the same to you I'd like to take the other side, to learn more strongly.

287b1 *H.* Take the other side. And, as I just said, the question is not large. I could teach you to answer much harder things than that so no human being[53] could refute you.

S. That's amazingly well said![54] Now, since it's your com-

287b5 mand, let me become the man as best I can and try to question you. If you displayed that speech to him, the one you mentioned about the fine activities, he'd listen, and when you stopped speaking he'd ask not about anything else but about

287c1 the fine—that's a sort of habit with him—and he'd say: "O visitor from Elis, is it not by justice[55] that just people are just?" Answer, Hippias, as if *he* were the questioner.

H. I shall answer that it is by justice.

S. "And is this justice *something?*"[56]

H. Very much so.

287c5 *S.* "And by wisdom wise people are wise, and by the good all good things are good?"[57]

H. How could they be otherwise?

S. ". . . by these each *being* something? Of course, it can't be that they're not."

H. They are.

S. "Then all fine things, too, are fine by the fine,[58] isn't that so?"

H. Yes, by the fine.   287d1

S. ". . . by that being *something?*"

H. It is. Why not?[59]

S. "Tell me then, visitor," he'll say, "what is that, the fine?"

H. Doesn't the person who asks this want to find out   287d5 what is a fine thing?[60]

S. I don't think so, Hippias. What is *the* fine.

H. And what's the difference between the one and the other?

S. You don't think there is any?

H. There's no difference.[61]

S. Well, clearly your knowledge is finer. But look here, 287d10 he's asking you not what is a fine thing, but what is the fine.   287e1

[3. A Fine Girl | 287e2–289d5]

Hippias. My friend, I understand. I will indeed tell him what the fine[62] is, and never will I be refuted. Listen, Socrates, to tell the truth, a fine girl is a fine thing.[63]

Socrates. That's fine, Hippias; by Dog[64] you have a glori-   287e5 ous answer.[65] So you really think, if *I* gave that answer, I'd be answering what was asked, and correctly, and never will I   288a1 be refuted?

H. Socrates, how could you be refuted when you say what everyone thinks, when everyone who hears you will testify that you're right?

S. Very well. Certainly. Now, look, Hippias, let me go   288a5 over what you said for myself. *He* will question me somewhat like this: "Come now, Socrates, give me an answer. All those things you say are fine, will they be fine if the fine itself is *what?*"[66] Shall I say that if a fine girl is a fine thing, those things 288a10 will be fine because of that?[67]

H. Then do you think that man will still try to refute you   288b1 —that what you say[68] is not a fine thing—or if he does try, he won't be a laughingstock?[69]

288b5   *S.* You're wonderful! But I'm sure he'll try. Whether trying will make him a laughingstock—we'll see about that. But
I want to tell you what he'll say.

H. Tell me.

S. "How sweet you are, Socrates," he'll say. "Isn't a fine
mare[70] a fine thing? The god praised mares in his oracle."[71]
288c1   What shall we say, Hippias? Mustn't we say that the mare is
a fine thing? At least if it's a fine one. How could we dare deny
that the fine thing is a fine thing?[72]

H. That's true, Socrates. And the god was right to say
288c5   that too. We breed very fine mares in our country.

S. "Very well," he'll say, "What about a fine lyre? Isn't
it a fine thing?" Shouldn't we say so, Hippias?

H. Yes.

S. Then after that he'll ask—I know fairly well, judging
from the way he is—"Then what about a fine pot,[73] my good
fellow? Isn't it a fine thing?"

288d1   *H.* Who is the man, Socrates? What a boor he is to dare
in an august proceeding to speak such vulgar speech that way![74]

288d5   *S.* He's like that, Hippias, not refined. He's garbage,[75] he
cares about nothing but the truth. Still the man must have an
answer; so here's my first opinion: *If* the pot should have been
turned by a good potter, smooth and round and finely fired,
like some of those fine two-handled pots that hold six choes,[76]
288e1   very fine ones—*if* he's asking about a pot like that, we have to
agree it's fine. How could we say that what is fine is not a
fine thing?

H. We couldn't, Socrates.

S. "Then is a fine pot a fine thing too? Answer me!"
he'll say.

288e5   *H.* But I think that's so, Socrates. Even that utensil is
fine[77] if finely made. But on the whole that's not worth judging
fine, compared to a horse and a girl and all the other fine
things.[78]

289a1   *S.* Very well. Then I understand how we'll have to answer
him when he asks this question, here: "Don't you know that
what Heracleitus said holds good—'the finest of monkeys is
foul put together with another[79] class,' and the finest of pots

is foul put together with the class of girls, so says Hippias the 289a5
wise." Isn't that so, Hippias?

H. Of course, Socrates. Your answer's right.

S. Then listen. I'm sure of what he'll say next. "What?
If you put the class of girls together with the class of gods, 289b1
won't the same thing happen as happened when the class of
pots was put together with that of girls? Won't the finest girl
be seen to be[80] foul? And didn't Heracleitus (whom you bring
in) say the same thing too, that 'the wisest of men is seen to
be a monkey compared to god in wisdom and fineness and 289b5
everything else?' " Should we agree, Hippias, that the finest
girl is foul compared to the class of gods?

H. Who would object to that, Socrates?

S. Then if we agreed to that, he'd laugh and say, "Socra- 289c1
tes, do you remember what you were asked?"[81] "Yes," I'll say:
"Whatever is the fine itself?" "Then," he'll say, "when you were
asked for the fine, do you answer with something that turns
out to be no more fine than foul,[82] as you say yourself?" "Ap- 289c5
parently," I'll say. Or what do you advise me to say, my friend?

H. That's what I'd say. Because compared to gods, anyway, the human race is not fine—that's true.

S. He'll say: "If I had asked you from the beginning what 289d1
is both fine and foul,[83] and you had given me the answer you
just gave, then wouldn't you have given the right answer? Do
you *still* think that the fine itself by which everything else is
beautified[84] and seen to be fine when that form is added to it[85]
—that *that* is a girl or a horse or a lyre?" 289d5

[4. Gold | 289d6–291c9]

Hippias. But if *that's* what he's looking for, it's the easiest
thing in the world to answer him and tell him what the fine
(thing)[86] is by which everything else is beautified and is seen
to be fine when it is added. The man's quite simple; he has no 289e1
feeling at all for fine possessions. If you answer him that this
thing he's asking for, the fine, is just *gold,* he'll be stuck and
won't try to refute you. Because we all know, don't we, that

289e5 wherever that is added, even if it was seen to be foul before, it will be seen to be fine[87] when it has been beautified with gold.

Socrates. You have no experience of this man, Hippias. He stops at nothing, and he never accepts anything easily.

290a1 *H.* So what? He *must* accept what's said correctly, or, if not, be a laughingstock.

S. Well, *that* answer he certainly will not accept, my

290a5 friend. And what's more, he'll jeer at me, and say, "Are you crazy?[88] Do you think Pheidias is a bad workman?"[89] And I think I'll say, "No, not at all."

H. And you'll be right about that.

S. Right enough. Then when I agree that Pheidias is a

290b1 good workman, this person will say, "Next, do you think Pheidias didn't know about this fine thing you mention?" "What's the point?" I'll say. "The point is," he'll say, "that Pheidias didn't make Athena's[90] eyes out of gold, nor the rest of her face, nor her feet, nor her hands—as he would have done if

290b5 gold would really have made them be seen to be finest—but he made them out of ivory. Apparently he went wrong through ignorance; he didn't know gold was what made everything fine, wherever it is added." What shall we answer when he says that, Hippias?

290c1 *H.* It's not hard. We'll say he made the statue right. Ivory's fine too, I think.[91]

S. "Then why didn't he work the middles of the eyes out

290c5 of ivory? He used stone, and he found stone that resembled ivory as closely as possible. Isn't a stone a fine thing too, if it's a fine one?" Shall we agree?

H. Yes, at least when it's appropriate.[92]

S. "But when it's not appropriate[93] it's foul?" Do I agree or not?

H. Yes, when it's not appropriate anyway.

290d1 *S.* "Well," he'll say. "You're a wise man![94] Don't ivory and gold make things be seen to be fine when they're appropriate, but foul when they're not?" Shall we be negative? Or shall we agree with him that he's right?

290d5 *H.* We'll agree to *this:* whatever is appropriate to each thing makes that particular thing fine.[95]

S. "Then," he'll say, "when someone boils the pot we just mentioned, the fine one, full of fine bean soup, is a gold stirring spoon or a figwood one more appropriate?"

H. Herakles![96] What kind of man is this! Won't you tell me who he is? 290e1

S. You wouldn't know him if I told you the name.

H. But I know right now he's an ignoramus.

S. Oh, he's a real plague,[97] Hippias. Still, what shall we say? Which of the two spoons is appropriate to the soup and 290e5 the pot? Isn't it clearly the wooden one? It makes the soup smell better, and at the same time, my friend, it won't break our pot, spill out the soup, put out the fire, and make us do without a truly noble meal, when we were going to have a banquet.[98] That gold spoon would do all these things; so *I* think 291a1 we should say the figwood spoon is more appropriate than the gold one, unless you say otherwise.

H. Yes, it's more appropriate. But *I* wouldn't talk with a man who asked things like that.

S. Right you are. It wouldn't be appropriate for you to 291a5 be filled up with words like that, when you're so finely dressed, finely shod, and famous for wisdom all over Greece.[99] But it's nothing much for me to mix with him. So help me get pre- 291b1 pared. Answer for my sake. "If the figwood is really more appropriate than the gold," the man will say, "wouldn't it be finer? Since you agreed, Socrates, that the appropriate is finer than the not appropriate?"[100]

Hippias, don't we agree that the figwood spoon is finer 291b5 than the gold one?

H. Would you like me to tell you what you can say the fine is—and save yourself a lot of argument?

S. Certainly. But not before you tell me how to answer. 291c1 Which of those two spoons I just mentioned is appropriate and finer?

H. Answer, if you'd like, that it's the one made of fig. 291c5

S. Now tell me what you were going to say. Because by *that* answer, if I say the fine is gold, apparently I'll be made to see that gold is no finer than wood from a figtree.[101] So what do you say the fine is this time?

[5. Burying Your Parents | 291d1–293c8]

291d1   *Hippias.* I'll tell you. I think you're looking for an answer that says the fine is the sort of thing that will never be seen to be foul for anyone, anywhere, at any time.[102]

291d5   *Socrates.* Quite right, Hippias. Now you've got a fine grasp of it.

H. Listen now, if anyone has anything to say against *this*, you can certainly say I'm not an expert on anything.

S. Tell me quickly, for god's sake.

H. I say, then, that it is always finest, both for every man and in every place, to be rich, healthy, and honored by the

291e1   Greeks, to arrive at old age, to make a fine memorial to his parents when they die, and to have a fine, grand burial from his own children.

S. Hurray, Hippias! What a wonderful long speech,

291e5   worthy of yourself! I'm really delighted at the kind way[103] in which—to the best of your ability—you've helped me out. But we didn't hit the enemy, and now he'll certainly laugh at us harder than ever.

H. That laughter won't do him any good, Socrates. When he has nothing to say in reply, but laughs anyway, he'll be

292a1   laughing at himself, and he'll be a laughingstock to those around.

S. That may be so. But maybe, as I suspect, he'll do more than laugh at me for that answer.

292a5   *H.* What do you mean?

S. If he happens to have a stick, and I don't run and run away from him, he'll try to give me a thrashing.[104]

H. What? Is the man your owner or something? Do you mean he could do that and not be arrested and convicted? Or

292b1   don't you have any laws in this city, but people are allowed to hit each other without any right?

S. No, that's not allowed at all.

H. Then he'll be punished for hitting you without any right.

292b5   *S.* I don't think so, Hippias. No, if I gave *that* answer he'd have a right—in *my* opinion anyway.

H. Then I think so too, seeing that you yourself believe it.

S. Should I tell you why *I* believe he'd have a right to hit 292b10
me if I gave that answer? Or will you hit me without trial too?
Will you hear my case?

H. It would be awful if I wouldn't. What do you have 292c1
to say?

S. I'll tell you the same way as before. I'll be acting out
his part—so the words I use are not directed against you;
they're like what he says to me, harsh and grotesque. "Tell me, 292c5
Socrates," you can be sure he'll say, "do you think it's wrong
for a man to be whipped when he sings such a dithyramb[105] as
that, so raucously, way out of tune with the question?" "How?"
I'll say. "How!" he'll say. "Aren't you capable of remembering
that I asked for the fine itself? For what when added to any- 292d1
thing—whether to a stone or a plank or a man or a god or any
action or any lesson—*anything* gets to be fine? I'm asking you
to tell me what fineness is itself, my man, and I am no more
able to make you hear me than if you were sitting here in stone 292d5
—and a millstone at that, with no ears and no brain!"

Hippias, wouldn't you be upset if I got scared and came
back with this: "But that's what Hippias said the fine was. And 292e1
I asked him the way you asked me, for that which is fine always
and for everyone."[106] So what do you say? Wouldn't you be upset if I said that?

H. Socrates, I know perfectly well that what I said is fine 292e5
for everyone—everyone will think so.

S. "And *will* be fine?" he'll ask. "I suppose the fine is always fine."

H. Certainly.

S. "Then it *was* fine, too," he'll say.

H. It was.

S. "For Achilles as well?"[107] he'll ask. "Does the visitor
from Elis say it is fine for *him* to be buried after his parents?
And for his grandfather Aeacus?[108] And for the other children 293a1
of the gods? And for the gods themselves?

H. What's that? Go to blessedness.[109] These questions the
man asks, Socrates, they're sacrilegious!

S. What? Is it a sacrilege to say that's so when someone
else asks the question?

293a5   *H.* Maybe.

S. "Then maybe you're the one who says that it is fine for everyone, always, to be buried by his children, and to bury his parents? And isn't Herakles[110] included in 'everyone' as well

293a10   as everybody we mentioned a moment ago?"

H. But I didn't mean it for the *gods*.

293b1   *S.* "Apparently you didn't mean it for the heroes either."

H. Not if they're children of gods.

S. "But if they're not?"

H. Certainly.

293b5   *S.* "Then according to your latest theory, I see, what's awful and unholy and foul for some heroes—Tantalus and Dardanus and Zethus—is fine for Pelops and those with similar parentage."[111]

H. That's my opinion.

S. "Then what you think is what you did not say a moment ago—that being buried by your children and burying

293c1   your parents is foul sometimes, and for some people. Apparently it's still more impossible for that to become and be fine for everyone; so that has met the same fate as the earlier ones, the girl and the pot, and a more laughable fate besides:[112] it is

293c5   fine for some, not fine for others. And to this very day, Socrates, you aren't able to answer the question about the fine, what it is."

That's how he'll scold me—and he's right if I give him such an answer.

[6. *The Appropriate* | 293c8–294e10]

Socrates. Most of what he says to me is somewhat like

293d1   that. But sometimes, as if he took pity on my inexperience and lack of education, he himself makes me a suggestion.[113] He asks if I don't think such and such is the fine, or whatever else he happens to be investigating and the discussion is about.

293d5   *Hippias.* How do you mean?

S. I'll show you. "You're a strange man, Socrates," he'll say, "giving answers like that,[114] in that way. You should stop

293e1   that. They're very simple and easy to refute. But see if you think this sort of answer is fine. We had a grip on it just now when we replied that gold is fine for things it's appropriate to, but not for those it's not. And anything else is fine if *this* has been added to it: this, the appropriate itself—the nature of the appropriate itself.[115] See if it turns out to be the fine."

293e5

I'm used to agreeing with such things every time, because I don't know what to say. What do you think? Is the appropriate fine?[116]

H. In every way, Socrates.

S. Let's look it over. We'd better not be deceived.[117]

H. We have to look it over.

S. See here, then. What do we say about the appropriate: is it what makes—by coming to be present—each thing to 294a1 which it is present *be seen to be fine,*[118] or *be fine,* or neither?

H. I think it's what makes things be seen to be fine. For example, when someone puts on clothes and shoes that suit him, even if he's ridiculous, he is seen to be finer. 294a5

S. Then if the appropriate makes things be seen to be finer than they are, it would be a kind of deceit about the fine, and it wouldn't be what we are looking for, would it, Hippias? I thought we were looking for that by which all fine things are 294b1 fine. For example, what all large things are large by is *the projecting.*[119] For by that all large things—even if they are not seen to be so—if they project they are necessarily large. Similarly, we say the fine is what all things are fine by, whether or 294b5 not they are seen to be fine. What would it be? It wouldn't be the appropriate. Because that makes things be seen to be finer than they are—so you said—and it won't let things be seen to be as they are. We must try to say what it is that makes things 294c1 fine, whether they are seen to be fine or not, just as I said a moment ago. That's what we're looking for, if we're really looking for the fine.

H. But Socrates, the appropriate makes things both be fine and be seen to be fine, when it's present.[120]

S. Is it impossible for things that are really fine not to 294c5 be seen to be fine, since what makes them be seen is present?

H. It's impossible.

S. Then shall we agree to this, Hippias: that everything really fine—customs and activities both—are both thought to 294d1 be, and seen to be, fine always, by everybody? Or just the opposite, that they're unknown, and individuals in private and cities in public both have more strife and contention about them than anything?[121]

H. Much more the latter, Socrates. They are unknown.

294d5   *S.* They wouldn't be, if "being seen to be" had been added to them. And that would have been added if the appropriate were fine and made things not only be but be seen to be fine. Therefore, if the appropriate is what makes things fine, it would be the fine we're looking for, but it would not be what makes

294e1   things be seen to be fine. Or, if the appropriate is what makes things be seen to be fine, it wouldn't be the fine we're looking for. Because *that* makes things be; but by itself it could not make things be seen to be and be, nor could anything else.[122]

294e5   Let's choose whether we think the appropriate is what makes things be seen to be, or be, fine.

H. It's what makes things be seen to be, in my opinion, Socrates.

S. Oh dear! It's gone and escaped from us, our chance to know what the fine is, since the appropriate has been seen to be something other than fine.

294e10   *H.* God yes, Socrates. And I think that's very strange.[123]

[7. The Able and Useful | 295a1–296d3]

295a1   *Socrates.* But we shouldn't let it go yet, my friend. I still have some hope that the fine will make itself be seen for what it is.

Hippias. Of course it will. It's not hard to find. I'm sure if

295a5   I went off and looked for it by myself—in quiet—I would tell it to you more precisely than any preciseness.[124]

S. Ah,[125] Hippias! Don't talk big. You see how much trouble it has given us already; and if it gets mad at us I'm afraid it

295b1   will run away still harder. But that's nonsense. You'll easily find it, I think, when you're alone. But for god's sake, find it in front of me, or look for it with me if you want, as we've been doing.[126] If we find it, that would be the finest thing; but

295b5   if not, I will content myself with my fate, while you go away

and find it easily. And if we find it now, of course I won't be
a nuisance to you later, trying to figure out what it was you
found on your own. Now see what you think the fine is: I'm   295c1
saying that it's—pay attention now, be careful I'm not raving
—let this be fine for us: whatever is useful.[127] What I had in
mind when I said that was this. We say eyes are fine not when
we think they are in such a state they're unable to see, but   295c5
whenever they *are able,* and are useful for seeing.[128] Yes?

H. Yes.

S. And that's how we call the whole body fine, sometimes for running, sometimes for wrestling. And the same goes
for all animals—a fine horse, rooster, or quail[129]—and all uten-   295d1
sils and means of transport on land and sea, boats and war-
ships, and the tools of every skill, music and all the others;
and, if you want, activities and laws—virtually all these are   295d5
called fine in the same way.[130] In each case we look at the
nature it's got, its manufacture, its condition; then we call
what is useful "fine" in respect of *the way* it is useful, *what* it is
useful *for,* and *when* it is useful; but anything useless in all   295e1
those respects we call "foul."[131] Don't you think that way too,
Hippias?

H. Yes, I do.

S. So then are we right to say now that the useful more   295e5
than anything turns out to be fine?[132]

H. Right, Socrates.

S. So what's *able*[133] to accomplish a particular thing is useful for that for which it is able; and what's unable is useless.[134]

H. Certainly.

S. Then is ability fine, but inability foul?

H. Very much so. Many things give us evidence for the   296a1
truth of that, especially politics. The finest thing of all is to be
able politically in your own city, and to be unable is the foulest
of all.

S. Good! Then doesn't it follow from these points that, by
god, wisdom[135] is really the finest thing of all, and ignorance   296a5
the foulest?

H. What are you thinking?

S. Keep quiet, my friend. I'm frightened. What on earth
are we saying now?

296b1   *H.* Why should you be frightened now? The discussion has gone really well for you this time.[136]

S. I wish it had! Look this over with me: could anyone do something he doesn't know how to do, and isn't at all able to do?

296b5   *H.* Not at all. How could he do what he isn't able to do?

S. Then when people make mistakes, do bad work, even when they do it unintentionally—if they aren't able to do things, they wouldn't ever do them, would they?

H. That's clear.

296c1   *S.* But people who are able are able by ability?[137] I don't suppose it's by inability.

H. Of course not.

S. And everyone who does things is able to do the things he does.

H. Yes.

S. And all men do much more bad work than good, start-
296c5   ing from childhood—and make mistakes unintentionally.[138]

H. That's right.

S. So? We don't call that ability and that sort of useful
296d1   thing fine, do we? The sort that's useful for doing some bad piece of work? Far from it.

H. Far indeed, Socrates. That's what I think.

S. Then this able and useful of ours is apparently not the fine, Hippias.

[8. The Beneficial | 296d4–297d9]

Hippias. It is, Socrates, if it's able to do good, if it's useful for that sort of thing.

296d5   *Socrates.* Then here's what got away from us: the able-and-useful without qualification is fine. And this is what our mind wanted to say, Hippias:[139] The useful-and-able for mak-
296e1   ing some good[140]—*that* is the fine.

H. I think so.

S. But that is beneficial. Isn't it?

H. Certainly.

S. Then that's the way fine bodies and fine customs and wisdom and everything we mentioned a moment ago are fine— because they're beneficial.

H. That's clear.   296e5

S. So the beneficial appears to be the fine we wanted.

H. Certainly, Socrates.

S. But the beneficial is the maker of good.

H. It is.

S. And the maker is nothing else but the cause, isn't it?[141]

H. That's so.

S. Then the fine is a cause of the good.

H. It is.   297a1

S. But the cause is different from what it's a cause of. I don't suppose the cause would be a cause of a cause.[142] Look at it this way: isn't the cause seen to be a maker?

H. Certainly.   297a5

S. Then what is made by the maker is the thing that comes to be; it's not the maker.[143]

H. That's right.

S. Then the thing that comes to be and the maker are different things.

H. Yes.

S. So the cause isn't a cause of a cause, but of the thing   297b1 that comes to be from it.

H. Certainly.

S. So if the fine is a cause of the good, the good should come to be from the fine.[144] And apparently this is why we're eager to have intelligence and all the other fine things: because their product, their child—the good[145]—is worth being eager   297b5 about. It would follow that the fine is formally a kind of father[146] of the good.

H. Certainly. You're talking fine, Socrates.

S. Then see if this is fine as well: the father is not a son and the son is not a father.[147]   297c1

H. Fine.

S. The cause is not a thing that comes to be, and the thing that comes to be is not a cause.

H. That's true.

S. Good god! Then the fine is not good, nor the good
297c5   fine.[148] Or do you think they could be, from what we've said?

H. Good god, no. I don't think so.

S. So are we happy with that? Would you like to say that
the fine is not good, nor the good fine?

H. Good god, no. I'm not at all happy with it.

297d1   *S.* Good god, yes, Hippias. Nothing we've said so far
makes me less happy.

H. So it seems.

S. Then it doesn't turn out to be the finest account, as we
297d5   thought a moment ago, that the beneficial—the useful and the
able for making some good—is fine. It's not that way at all,
but if possible it's more laughable than the first accounts,[149]
when we thought the girl, or each one of those things mentioned earlier,[150] was the fine.

H. Apparently.

[9. Aesthetic Pleasure | 297d10–303d10]

Socrates. And *I* don't know where to turn, Hippias. I'm
stuck. Do you have anything to say?

297e1   *Hippias.* Not at present; but as I said a little while ago,[151]
I'm sure I'll find it when I've looked.

S. But I don't think I can wait for you to do that, I have
297e5   such a desire to know. And besides I think I just got clear.
Look. If whatever makes us be glad, not with all the pleasures,
but just through hearing and sight—if we call *that* fine, how do
you suppose we'd do in the contest?[152]

298a1   Men, when they're fine anyway—and everything decora-
tive, pictures and sculptures—these all delight us when we see
them, if they're fine. Fine sounds and music altogether, and
298a5   speeches and storytelling have the same effect. So if we answered that tough man,[153] "Your honor, the fine is what is
pleasant through hearing and sight,"[154] don't you think we'd
curb his toughness?

H. This time, Socrates, I think what the fine is has been
well said.

S. What? Shall we say that fine activities and laws are fine   298b1
by being pleasant through hearing and sight? Or that they have
some other form?

H. Those things might slip right past the man.[155]   298b5

S. By Dog, Hippias, not past the person I'd be most
ashamed to babble at, or pretend to say something when I'm
not saying anything.[156]

H. Who's that?

S. Sophroniscus' son.[157] He wouldn't easily let me say
those things without testing them, any more than he'd let me   298c1
talk as if I knew what I didn't know.

H. Well for my part, since you say so, I think that's something else in the case of the laws.[158]

S. Keep quiet, Hippias. We could well be thinking we're   298c5
in the clear again, when we've gotten stuck on the same point
about the fine as we did a moment ago.

H. What do you mean, Socrates?

S. I'll show you what's become obvious to me, if I'm saying anything. In the case of laws and activities, those could   298d1
easily be seen not to be outside the perception we have through
hearing and sight.[159] But let's stay with this account, that what
is pleasing through them is fine, and not bring that about the   298d5
laws into the center. But if someone should ask—whether he's
the one I mentioned or anyone else—"What, Hippias and Socrates? Are you marking off the sort of pleasant you call fine
from the pleasant, and not calling what is pleasant to the other
senses fine—food and drink, what goes with making love, and   298e1
all the rest of that sort of thing? Aren't they pleasant? Do you
say there's altogether no pleasure in such things? Not in anything but seeing and hearing?"

What shall we say, Hippias?

H. Of course we'll say there are very great pleasures in   298e5
those others, Socrates.

S. "What?" he'll say. "Though they're no less pleasures
than these, would you strip them of this word,[160] and deprive
them of being fine?"   299a1

"Yes," we'll say, "because anyone in the world would
laugh at us if we called it not *pleasant to eat* but *fine,* or if

we called a pleasant smell not *pleasant* but *fine*. And as for making love, everybody would fight us; they'd say it is most pleasant, but that one should do it, if he does it at all, where no one will see, because it is the foulest thing to be seen." When we've said that, Hippias, he'd probably reply, "I understand that too. You're ashamed, you've been ashamed a long time, to call those pleasures fine, because men don't think they are. But I didn't ask for that—what ordinary people think is fine—but for what *is* fine.

I think we'll repeat our hypothesis:[161] "This is what we say is fine, the part of the pleasant that comes by sight and hearing." What else would you do with the argument? What should we say, Hippias?

H. We must say that and nothing else, in view of what's been said.[162]

S. "That's fine," he'll say. "Then if the pleasant through sight and hearing is fine, whatever is not pleasant in that way clearly would not be fine."[163]

Shall we agree?

H. Yes.

S. "Then is the pleasant through sight pleasant through sight and hearing? Or is the pleasant through hearing pleasant through hearing and through sight?"

"By no means," we'll say. "In that case what comes through one would be what comes through both—I think that's what you mean—but *we* said that each of these pleasant things taken itself by itself is fine, and both are fine as well."

Isn't that our answer?

H. Certainly.

S. "Then," he'll say, "does one pleasant thing differ from another in *this:* in being pleasant? I'm not asking whether one pleasure can be greater or lesser than another, or more or less, but whether one can differ in this very way—in being a pleasure —and one of the pleasures not be a pleasure."[164]

We don't think so, do we?

H. We don't think so.

S. "So," he'll say. "You selected those pleasures from the other pleasures because of something different from their being

pleasures. You saw some quality[165] in the pair of them, something that differentiates them from the others, and you say they
are fine by looking at that.[166] I don't suppose pleasure through
sight is fine because of *that*—that it is through sight. Because
if that were the cause[167] of its being fine, the other—the one
through hearing—wouldn't ever be fine. It's not a pleasure
through sight."

 That's true. Shall we say that's true?

 H. We'll say it.

 S. "And again, pleasure through hearing turns out not to
be fine because of *that*—that it is through hearing. Otherwise,
pleasure through sight would never be fine, because it is not
a pleasure through hearing."

 Shall we say that the man who says this is saying the
truth, Hippias?

 H. It's true.

 S. "But both are fine, as you say." We do say that.

 H. We do.

 S. "Then they have some thing that itself makes them be
fine, that common thing[168] that belongs to both of them in
common and to each privately. Because I don't suppose there's
any other way they would both and each be fine."

 Answer me as you would him.

 H. I think it's as he says, and that's my answer.

 S. Then if something is attributed[169] to both pleasures but
not to each one, they would not be fine by that attribute.

 H. And how could that be, Socrates? That any state of
being whatever could be attributed to neither, since that attribute, which is attributed to neither, is attributed to both?[170]

 S. Don't you think it could happen?

 H. If it did I'd be in the grip of a lot of inexperience about
the nature of these things and the terms of the present termi-
nology.

 S. Pleasantly put, Hippias. But maybe I'm turning out to
think I can see something that's the way you say it can't be,
or I'm not seeing anything.

 H. It turns out that you're not, Socrates. You're quite
readily mis-seeing.

299e1

299e5

300a1

300a5

300b1

300b5

300c1

300c5

S. And yet a lot of things like that are seen plainly in my mind; but I don't believe them if they're not imagined in yours, since you're a man who's made the most money[171] by wisdom of anyone alive, and I'm one who never made anything. And I wonder, my friend, if you're not playing with me and deliberately fooling me, so many and so clear are the examples I see.

H. Socrates, no one will know finer than you whether I'm playing or not, if you try to say what these things are that are seen by you plainly. You'll be seen to be saying nothing. Because never shall you find what is attributed to neither me nor you, but is attributed to both of us.

S. What do you mean, Hippias? Maybe you're saying something I don't understand. But listen more clearly to what I want to say. Because I see what is not attributed to me to be, and what neither I am nor you are, and this can be attributed to both of us. And there are others besides, which are attributed to both of us to be, things neither of us is.

H. Your answers seem weird again, Socrates, more so than the ones you gave a little earlier. Look. If both of us were just, wouldn't each of us be too? Or if each of us were unjust, wouldn't both of us? Or if we were healthy, wouldn't each be? Or if each of us had some sickness or were wounded or stricken or had any other tribulation, again, wouldn't both of us have that attribute? Similarly, if we happened to be gold or silver or ivory, or, if you like, noble or wise or honored or even old or young or anything you like that goes with human beings, isn't it really necessary that each of us be that as well?

S. Of course.

H. But Socrates, *you* don't look at the entireties of things,[172] nor do the people you're used to talking with.[173] You people knock away at the fine and the other beings by taking each separately and cutting it up with words.[174] Because of that you don't realize how great they are—naturally continuous bodies of being.[175] And now you're so far from realizing it that you think there's some attribute or being[176] that is true of these both but not of each, or of each but not of both. That's how unreasonably and unobservantly and foolishly and uncomprehendingly you operate.

S. That's the way things are for us, Hippias. "They're not the way a person wants"—so runs the proverb people often quote—"but the way he can get them." But your frequent admonitions are a help to us. This time, for example, before these admonitions from you about the stupid way we operate . . . Shall I make a still greater display, and tell you what we had in mind about them? Or not tell?

301c5

301d1

H. You're telling someone who already knows, Socrates. I know how everybody who's involved in speeches operates. All the same, if it's more pleasant for you, speak on.

S. It really is more pleasant. We were so foolish, my friend, before you said what you did, that we had an opinion about me and you that *each* of us is *one,* but that we wouldn't *both* be one (which is what *each* of us would be) because we're not *one* but *two*—we were so stupid-like. But now, we have been instructed by you that if two is what we both are, two is what each of us must be as well; and if each is one, then both must be one as well. The continuous theory of *being,* according to Hippias, does not allow it to be otherwise; but whatever both are, that each is as well; and whatever each is, both are. Right now I sit here persuaded by you. First, however, remind me, Hippias. Are you and I one? Or are you two and I two?

301d5

301e1

301e5

H. What do you mean, Socrates?

S. Just what I say. I'm afraid of you, afraid to speak clearly, because you get angry at me whenever you think you've said anything. All the same, tell me more. Isn't each of us one, and *that*—being one—is attributed to him?

302a1

H. Certainly.

S. Then if each of us is one, wouldn't he also be odd-numbered? Or don't you consider *one* to be odd?[177]

H. I do.

302a5

S. Then will both of us be odd-numbered, being two?

H. It couldn't be, Socrates.

S. But both are even-numbered. Yes?

H. Certainly.

S. Then because both are even-numbered, on account of *that,* each of us is even-numbered as well. Right?

H. Of course not.

302b1

S. Then it's not entirely necessary, as you said it was a moment ago, that whatever is true of both and each, is true of each and both as well.

H. Not that sort of thing, but the sort I said earlier.

302b5 *S.* They're enough, Hippias. We have to accept them too, because we see that some are this way, and others are not this way.[178] I said (if you remember how this discussion got started) that pleasure through sight and hearing was not fine

302c1 by *this*—that each of them turned out to have an attribute but not both, or that both had it but not each—but by that by which both and each are fine, because you agreed that they are both

302c5 and each fine. That's why I thought it was by the being that adheres to both, if both are fine—it was by *that* they had to be fine, and not by what falls off one or the other.[179] And I still think so now. But let's make a fresh start. Tell me, if the

302d1 pleasure through sight and the one through hearing are both and each fine, doesn't what makes them fine adhere in both and in each of them?

H. Certainly.

S. Then is it because each and both are *pleasure*—would

302d5 they be fine because of that? Or would that make all other pleasures no less fine than these? Remember, we saw that they were no less pleasures.[180]

H. I remember.

S. But is it because they are through sight and hearing—

302e1 are they called *fine* because of that?

H. That's the way it was put.

S. See if this is true. It was said, I'm remembering, that the pleasant was fine this way: not all the pleasant, but what-

302e5 ever is through sight and hearing.

H. True.

S. Doesn't that attribute adhere in both,[181] but not in each? I don't suppose each of them is through both (as we said earlier), but both through both, not each. Is that right?

H. Yes.

302e10 *S.* Then *that's* not what makes each of them fine; it doesn't adhere in each (because "both" doesn't adhere in each). So the hypothesis[182] lets us call both of them fine, but it doesn't let us call each of them fine.

What else should we say? Isn't it necessarily so? 303a1

H. So we see.

S. Then should we call both fine, but not call each fine?

H. What's to stop us?[188]

S. *This* stops us, friend, in my opinion. We had things 303a5
that come to belong to particular things in this way: if they
come to belong to both, they do to each also; and if to each,
to both—all the examples you gave. Right?

H. Yes.

S. But the examples *I* gave were not that way. Among
them were "each" itself and "both."[184] Is that right?

H. It is.

S. With which of these do you put the fine, Hippias? With 303b1
those you mentioned? If I am strong and so are you, we're both
strong too; and if I am just and so are you, we both are too.
And if both, then each. In the same way, if I am fine and so are 303b5
you, we both are too; and if both, then each. Or does nothing
stop them from being like the things I said I saw clearly:[185] (303c1)
when both of anything are even-numbered, each may be either
odd- or possibly even-numbered.[186] And again, when each of
them is inexpressible, both together may be expressible, or possibly inexpressible.[187] And millions of things like that. With 303c1
which do you place the fine? Do you see the matter the way
I do? I think it's a great absurdity for both of us to be fine,
but each not; or each fine, but both not, or anything else like 303c5
that.

Do you choose the way I do, or the other way?

H. That's *my* way, Socrates.[188]

S. Well done, Hippias! We've saved ourselves a longer 303d1
search. Because if the fine is with *those,* then the pleasant
through sight and hearing is not fine anymore. "Through sight
and hearing" makes both fine, but not each. But that's impossible, as you and I agree, Hippias.

H. We do agree. 303d5

S. Then it's impossible for the pleasant through sight and
hearing to be fine, since if it becomes fine it presents one of the
impossibilities.

H. That's right.

S. "Tell me again from the beginning," he'll say;[189] "since

303e1   you were quite wrong with that. What do you say that is—the fine in both pleasures, which made you value them above the others and call them fine?"[190] Hippias, I think we have to say
303e5   that they are the most harmless pleasures[191] and the best, both and each as well. Or can you mention something else that distinguishes them from the others?

H. Not at all. They really are best.

S. He'll say, "Then this is what you say is the fine—beneficial pleasure?"

"Apparently so," I'll say. And you?

303e10   *H*. Me too.

S. He'll say: "The maker of good is beneficial, but we just saw that the maker and what is made are different. Your ac-
304a1   count comes down to the earlier account. The good would not be fine, nor the fine good, if each of these were different."

"Absolutely," we'll say, if we have any sense. It's not proper to disagree with a man when he's right.

304a5   *H*. But Socrates, really, what do you think of all that?[192] It's flakings and clippings of speeches, as I told you before, divided up small. But here's what is fine and worth a lot: to be able to present a speech well and finely, in court or council
304b1   or any other authority to whom you give the speech, to convince them and go home carrying not the smallest but the greatest[193] of prizes, the successful defense of yourself, your property, and friends. One should stick to that.

He should give up and abandon all that small-talking,[194]
304b5   so he won't be thought a complete fool for applying himself, as he is now, to babbling nonsense.[195]

S. Hippias, my friend, you're a lucky man, because you know which activities[196] a man should practice, and you've
304c1   practiced them too—successfully, as you say. But I'm apparently held back by my crazy luck. I wander around and I'm always getting stuck. If I make a display of how stuck I am to you wise men, I get mud-spattered by your speeches when
304c5   I display it.[197] You all say what you just said, that I am spending my time on things that are silly and small and worthless. But when I'm convinced by you and say what you say, that it's much the most excellent thing to be able to present a speech
304d1   well and finely, and get things done in court or any other gath-

ering, I hear every insult from that man (among others around
here) who has always been refuting me. He happens to be a
close relative of mine, and he lives in the same house. So when
I go home to my own place and he hears me saying those   304d5
things, he asks if I'm not ashamed that I dare discuss fine
activities when I've been so plainly refuted about the fine,
and it's clear I don't even know at all what *that* is itself![198]
"Look," he'll say. "How will you know whose speech—or any   304e1
other action—is finely presented or not, when you are ignorant
of the fine? And when you're in a state like that, do you think
it's any better for you to live than die?" That's what I get, as
I said. Insults and blame from you, insults from him. But I   304e5
suppose it is necessary to bear all that. It wouldn't be strange
if it were good for me. I actually think, Hippias, that associ-
ating with both of you has done me good.[199] The proverb says,
"What's fine is hard"[200]—I think I know *that*.

COMMENTARY

[*1. Preliminaries* | *281a1–286c3*]

The *Hippias Major* begins abruptly, like the *Ion,* with a greeting. But though the early conversation is studded with *kalos* and its cognates, Socrates does not turn to his main subject until relatively late, after he has made Hippias look foolish on a number of seemingly irrelevant topics. The preliminary conversation is about Hippias himself, his versatility and earning power, his ability to accommodate himself to the taste of his audience. Though Socrates is polite on the surface, his irony is intense from the first line, more consistently scathing than in any other of Plato's works. Readers inevitably wonder how Hippias could be so stupid as not to recognize what Socrates is doing to him, and this incredibility in characterization is one of the defects cited by those who reject the dialogue's authenticity (below, p. 97). We shall see that Hippias probably does appreciate Socrates' irony, but makes the best of a bad situation by not responding to it.

Purpose. These preliminaries are given over to the discussion and display of Hippias' talents. Why should that exiguous subject take up more than a fifth of the dialogue? Elsewhere, Plato is stingy in characterizing Socrates' interlocutors, even when they appear to be more interesting and important than Hippias. Critics of the dialogue find this preliminary conversation a major fault. Hippias, they believe, is presented by it as the type of an arrogant and stupid sophist. The author shows him to be that on the first page, and then makes the same point again and again. Why should an author of Plato's quality find Hippias' stupidity worth so much literary effort? (Horneffer, 1895; Tarrant, 1928.) My answer is that the preliminaries serve to illustrate Hippias' versatility, which requires a passage of considerable length.

35

We can have no doubt that the subject of the dialogue is not Hippias but the fine, though this appears only indirectly in the opening segment. The word "fine" is used strikingly in the first line, and recurs frequently (282b1, 282d6, 282e9, 285b8, 286a4, 286b4), wherever anything is to be commended. Still, as surely as the main part of the dialogue is about the fine, the opening segment is about Hippias. Hippias is interesting because of his incredible range and adaptability. That is something that can be described, but it must be illustrated to be believed. First we are told of Hippias' ability to combine public service (as a diplomat) with private gain (as a teacher), and we see something of Hippias' fascination with money (282de). At the same time, we see him ostensibly agreeing with Socrates to an outrageous falsehood (281c), and we understand that Hippias is a man who adapts his views to harmonize with those of his audience. That impression is strengthened when Hippias pretends (with a quibble) to accept a theory of law that must have been anathema to him (284e). As a teacher, Hippias is versatile as well. He will add to his repertoire whatever his public wants. All this the opening segment shows without redundancy.

For the connection between Hippias' versatility and Socrates' inquiry into the fine, see p. 130.

1 | 281a1, "Here comes": supplied to make an idiomatic translation. "fine": *kalos*. See the general note, p. xv, and the discussion of *kalos* at p. 109. Here the word probably means "good-looking"; elsewhere its sense is more general. The opposite of *kalos* is *aischros* ("foul").

2 | 281a3, Elis: A city in the northwest Peloponnesus. Eleans were close allies of Sparta until events threw them into the Athenian camp in 420 B.C. The dramatic date of this dialogue is most likely between 421 and 413 B.C. (p. 94).

3 | 281b3, "Sparta": *Lakedaimōn*. So throughout this translation. See note 27.

4 | 281b7–283b4, Hippias' earning power: Socrates' irony is especially heavy-handed in this demonstration that Hippias is wiser than the venerable sages of antiquity, wiser because his wisdom turns a profit. "The mark of being wise," says Socrates in conclusion, slipping out of syntax, "is when someone makes the most money" (283b2–3). Hippias has been trapped in this absurdity. Socrates gives Hippias several times a choice between agreeing with some extravagant irony, or moderating his professional claims. Hippias always agrees. He was professionally intent on agreeing with people, both as philosopher and diplomat (p. 125).

Although Socrates playfully exploits Hippias' agreeability in this argument, he has a serious case. At issue is the idea of human progress, the idea that human beings are getting better and better through invention and study. That idea was naturally associated with the sophists as teachers and innovators; Hippias was probably as strongly committed to it as Protagoras. (For a discussion of the idea and our sources for it, see Guthrie, 1969: 60, ff.) Sophists, like everyone else, must be better than their predecessors on this view; and the improvement must lie in what chiefly distinguishes them— their earning power. The conclusion is absurd and would count against any unrestricted claim that humans make progress.

5 | 281c5, "wisdom": *sophia. Sophia* is also used for "skill" or "craft," as in the comparison at 281d3–7. I have rendered it "wisdom," however, throughout this translation, and *technē* as "skill."

6 | 281c8, the wise men who abstained from the affairs of state: The men Socrates mentions did not abstain from affairs of state, but Hippias chooses to proceed as if this absurdity were true, rather than to refuse Socrates' praise. Socrates has set directly to making a fool of Hippias.

Pittacus ruled in Mytilene for ten years, about 600 B.C., and was famous as a lawgiver. Bias was famous as a statesman of Priene, about 570 B.C. Thales, who is said to have predicted the eclipse of 585 B.C., was the foremost of the seven sages, and at least a forerunner of pre-Socratic philosophy. He also was famous for practical statesmanship (Herodotus I, 170). On Anaxagoras, see note 23 below.

What these examples actually show is that ancient wise men *did* use their wisdom in aid of their cities. What they did not do (as becomes clear at 282b ff.) was use their wisdom to make money by giving displays and tutorials. The joke, as usual in this dialogue, is on Hippias.

7 | 218d3, "really": *Pros Dios* ("by Zeus"). Where appropriate, I have chosen such idiomatic translations as this for Greek oaths.

8 | 281d4, "craftsmen": Socrates probably has in mind the sort of analogy between sophists and artisans rejected by Callicles at *Gorgias* 491a. Cf. *Symposium* 221e.

9 | 281d9, "if Bias came to life": *Bias anabioiē.* A play on words.

10 | 282a1, Daedalus: Elsewhere Socrates treats Daedalus as a model of unapproachable human skill. Cf. *Euthyphro* 11bc, 15b, *Meno* 97d, and *Republic* 529e. As at 281c5, he must be speaking here with heavy irony, unless, as is unlikely, he has changed models.

11 | 282a4, Hippias' ready agreement: See p. 125, and compare 284e1–2, 285b1, and 292b7, where Hippias accepts propositions we would except him to reject.

12 | 282a6–8, "for while I take care to avoid the envy of the living, I fear the wrath of the dead": The antithesis is balanced in the style of Gorgias, but forced. See p. 126.

13 | 282b5, Gorgias: Gorgias took Athens by storm on his first visit in 427 B.C. (Diodorus Siculus XII, 53 = DK 82 A4). On his contributions to rhetoric and philosophy, see p. 116.

14 | 282b7, "won his case": could equally well be translated as, "was thought to speak most eloquently."

15 | 282b7, "displays": Sophists gave display speeches to paying audiences. Afterwards they would take questions (Gorgias 447c5–8). Hippias invites Socrates to such a display at 286ab; the *Hippias Minor* represents a question-and-answer period, probably after the same display. Two display speeches by Gorgias have survived (the *Helen* and the *Palamedes*), as has one by Prodicus (Xenophon, *Memorabilia* II.i.21,ff.), and possibly one by Protagoras (*Protagoras* 320c8, ff.). Socrates is not fond of such speeches, presumably because they afford him no break-in with questions (*Protagoras* 329a, cf. 334cd and 347e; *Hippias Minor* 364b, and *Gorgias* 447c). His distaste for displays may also be caused by the facile versatility of their authors. Both Gorgias and Hippias would offer to give speeches on topics proposed by their audiences (DK 82A1a and Cicero, *De Finibus*, 2.1; *Hippias Minor* 363d; cf. *Meno* 70c). Socrates did not believe anyone could be expert on as many topics as these men were willing to display (*Sophist* 232a, 234a, cf. *Ion* 537c, ff., *Republic* 370ab, and below, p. 115). On display speeches, see Dodds, 1959: 188–190.

16 | 282b8, "tutorials": the Greek says merely that he *was with* young men. "Being with" (*sunousia*) seems to have been a technical term for what sophists did for their pupils. For Gorgias' teaching method, see p. 117. Greeks of the period for the teacher-student relationship. Gorgias' fans are called "lovers" (*erastai*) at *Meno* 70b3, for example. Such usages were not always sexually charged. See Dover, 1978: 157.

17 | 282c2, "our colleague Prodicus": Prodicus, who was a contemporary of Socrates and Hippias, seems to have found special favor (not entirely ironical) in Socrates' eyes. Cf. *Laches* 197d, *Charmides* 163d, and *Cratylus* 384b. For a parody of his style, see *Protagoras* 337a–c and cf. 315d.

18 | 282c4, Ceos: An Aegean island not far from Attica.

19 | 282d5, Protagoras: See below, p. 115, ff. Protagoras was the first sophist to charge for his teaching (*Protagoras* 349a) and made a substantial income (*Meno* 91d), even though he would allow a dissatisfied student to pay what he declared under oath the lessons were worth (*Protagoras* 328bc).

20 | 282e3, *mina:* a hundred drachmas. One hundred and fifty *minas* was a substantial sum. A single drachma would pay a man for a day's skilled labor at that time (421–416 B.C.).

21 | 282e4, Inycum: a place of no importance whatever.

22 | 283a2, "down to": reading *mechri* for *peri,* with Grube (1926A: p. 189).

23 | 283a3, Anaxagoras: Anaxagoras (c. 500–c. 428), a philosopher in whom Socrates took special interest (*Phaedo* 97c), gave a preeminent position in his system to *nous* ("intelligence"). For the tradition about his financial acumen, see Diogenes Laertius II.7, who reports that Anaxagoras gave his wealth to his relatives when they complained he was neglecting it.

24 | 283a6, "intelligence": Socrates uses a cognate of *nous* (see note 23). To appreciate the full force of this witticism, see *Phaedo* 97b8, ff., where Socrates finds Anaxagoras' work lacking in *nous*—on very different grounds.

25 | 283b3, "The mark of being wise . . . is when someone makes the most money": The syntax is similarly fractured in the Greek. Socrates picks up the thought at 300d1.

26 | 283e3, "studied with you": were *being* with you. See note 16.

27 | 283e9, "But Sparta really is law-abiding": a cliché in ancient times. The Greek word translated "law-abiding" (*eunomos*) has wider connotations and a special connection with Sparta. *Eunomia* is originally "the state of affairs which prevails in a polity with good laws and law-abiding citizens" (Tigerstedt: 73; cf. 380, n. 578). In the later fifth century it came to be opposed to democratic *isonomia* as a code word for aristocracy (see Pseudo-Xenophon, *The Constitution of Athens,* I, 9). For Socrates to ask if Sparta is *eunomos* is tantamount to his asking if Sparta is governed by aristocracy. Of course the answer must be affirmative, even from one like Hippias, who, we may presume, was no great supporter of the Spartan system.

I have translated *eunomos* "law-abiding" because that is the sense in which Socrates uses it here (although Hippias no doubt understands it simply as "aristocratic"). For Socrates the goodness of Spartan laws is not at issue: all laws are good (248d6–7). The question is whether Sparta obeys the laws. On this point, Hippias is made to contradict himself (285b1 ff. with 283e9). For this use of *eunomos* see *Laws* 815b6. For the idea, cf. Xenophon, *Memorabilia* IV.iv.15.

Socrates probably approved of Sparta's restrictions on teaching. See *Euthyphro* 2c9, ff., *Crito* 53b, and *Hippias Major* 292a7, with my note 104. Significantly, Socrates does not object in the *Crito* or anywhere else to the principle on which he was condemned. He does not, apparently, believe in the freedom of speech. Socrates was notorious in Athens for his love of Spartan *eunomia* (*Crito* 52e5–6). For ancient attitudes towards Sparta, see Rawson (1969) and Tigerstedt (1965).

28 | 284a3, the teaching of virtue: cf. 283c. With the exception of

Gorgias, sophists generally claimed the ability to teach virtue to their pupils (*Meno* 95c; cf. *Euthydemus* 274e8, ff., and *Apology* 19e–20c).

In agreeing that he teaches virtue, Hippias may mean: (a) that he makes his students excellent at the various special skills he imparts, such as astronomy and arithmetic (see note 36); or (b) that he teaches them the rhetorical skills that bring power in a democracy; or (c) that he teaches them moral virtue. No doubt (a) is part of his meaning; *Protagoras* 318e suggests that when students came to learn political virtue, Hippias taught them astronomy, etc. But clearly Hippias had an interest in teaching rhetoric (b) as well; he claims a high place for it at 304ab. But these cannot have exhausted his catalogue, for the fine activities on which he speaks at Sparta are none of the special skills in (a), and for political reasons cannot have been the sort of rhetoric useful in a democracy (286ab; cf. Xenophon, *Memorabilia* IV.iv.7). It should follow that Hippias did profess to teach a sort of moral virtue(c). (See note 196.) Indeed, he probably would not have distinguished the three possibilities. Gorgias apparently distinguishes moral virtue from rhetoric, but other sophists did nothing of the sort. Protagoras says he teaches "sound administrative judgment" (*euboulia peri tōn oikeiōn—Protagoras* 318e5). For this he accepts Socrates' characterization as "political virtue," and later, in the Great Speech (320c7, ff.), he seems to identify it with justice and respect (or soundmindedness). The modern distinction between disinterested Kantian morality and the skills required for success in life was alien to the Greek fifth century. Probably Hippias, like Protagoras, thought that teaching people how to succeed in politics was not separate from imparting moral virtue to them. (For a different account of Protagoras' profession, see Adkins, 1973).

29 | 284a4, "skill with horses": the analogy between moral virtue and practical skill or crafts is a familiar device of Socrates' arguments. See Irwin, 1977A:71–86, for a helpful discussion of the craft analogy. Sophists such as Protagoras resisted the analogy (*Protagoras* 322d3–4). Because knowledge of a craft belongs to a few gifted experts, the craft analogy has the undemocratic implication that each city has a small élite, whose members are uniquely qualified by their moral gifts and training to engage in public affairs.

30 | 284d1, "law": *nomos*. See notes 27 and 32. By the late fifth century the word is used commonly for statues but often retains the older sense of that on which people generally agree (chiefly values). Hence, it is sometimes translated "convention"; but the values on which people generally agree may be thought to have an absolute basis (e.g., in divine decree), so that *nomos* would carry the prescriptive sense on which Socrates here depends. The adjective *nomimos* ("lawful") has a more straightforwardly moral sense.

31 | 284d5, "without that, law-abiding civilized life is impossible": Cf. *Protagoras* 322d.

32 | 284d6–7, "when people who are trying to make laws fail to make them good, they have failed to make them . . . law": Could also mean, "When would-be lawmakers fail to achieve good, . . ."; either way, this is a statement of the doctrine of ideal or natural law (as opposed to positive law—cf. *Cratylus* 429b and *Minos* 314e). The theme is repeated at 284e5–7. See Guthrie, 1969: 117–131, for a survey of fifth-century thinking on this point. Compare Antigone's speech in Sophocles' play, lines 450 ff., where she distinguishes between Cleon's edicts (*kērugmata*) and the unwritten law of divine justice; contrast Aristotle's use of this speech at *Rhetoric* I.13, 2.

Socrates probably did believe that all genuine laws are beneficial, and that the law is therefore not always what courts decree or lawmakers enact. The *Crito* treats law as not a human artifact (53c1), and as worthy of much greater respect than Socrates accorded the products of human opinion.

Hippias must have held a positive conception of law. For Plato represents him in the *Protagoras* saying, "the law, being a tyrant over humankind, overpowers them often, contrary to nature" (337d2–3). Xenophon, too, represents Socrates and Hippias in disagreement over whether law is essentially just and worthy of obedience (Socrates' view) or a human product to be changed at will (Hippias' view—*Memorabilia* IV.iv.5–25). Xenophon misunderstands the conversation he recreates; he thinks Socrates is recommending justice, but Socrates' theme is obedience to law.

33 | 284e4, "ordinary people": *hoi polloi*. Often used with anti-democratic scorn; here used primarily of non-philosophers. Cf. the argument at *Crito* 47a2 ff., and the discussion at *Laches* 184d5. Hippias, apparently, ordinarily speaks the way ordinary people are accustomed to speak.

34 | 284e8, "Yes, I grant it's that way in truth": Hippias probably regards "in truth" as a saving reservation, for he would not have agreed to this without qualification (see note 32). Compare this with the similarly grudging agreement at 285b3–4, which can only be explained on the hypothesis that Hippias' custom is to avoid confrontation so far as possible. See p. 124.

35 | 285b5, "So we find the Spartans to be lawbreakers . . . ": Hippias yielded this outrageous point at 285b2–3 because, he said, it was in his favor. He thus resisted the blow of an argument that had been meant to be a *reductio ad absurdum;* but he left no doubt that the absurd conclusion belonged to Socrates ("I think you said your say . . ."). Plato's audience, believing that Sparta was law-abiding (note 27), would nevertheless conclude that Hippias' claims as a teacher (284a) had been made ridiculous. Although the argument played on Hippias' agreeable reluctance to quarrel, there was a shred of justice in it. Hippias did not volunteer to advertise the benefits of his teaching, but he no doubt sincerely believed that his teaching was good for people. But if it was, and the Spartan laws were justly admired, why did they make no room in their curriculum for Hippias? Underneath the surface of this conversation, a political issue probably divided Hippias and Socrates, an issue Hippias diplomatically avoided: Socrates does not believe people should be free to teach what they want; Hippias as a traveling speaker and teacher must be committed to that freedom. (The issue comes nearer the surface at 292ab. See my note 104.)

36 | 285b7–285e2, the catalogue of subjects Hippias teaches: astronomy, geometry, arithmetic, and euphony. Cf. *Protagoras* 318e for a similar list. There Protagoras, giving Hippias a look, says that he—Protagoras—does *not* teach skills such as arithmetic, astronomy, geometry and music, but just what his students come to learn—"sound administrative judgment, so the pupil may manage best his own business, and be best-fitted for government service, both in action and speech." Cf. also Socrates' inquiry into what it is that Gorgias teaches, at *Gorgias* 447c, ff.

Hippias thought he taught virtue (283c, 284a). Whether this was supposed to be moral virtue, or merely excellence at the skills listed above, is a difficult question. See note 28. On Hippias' polymathy and scope as a teacher, see pp. 114, 130.

37 | 285c1, astronomy: cf. *Protagoras* 315c, where Hippias is discovered answering questions ex cathedra, mainly about astronomy.

38 | 285d2, euphony: Hippias was expert on the effects of rhyme and rhythm on an audience. See p. 126, and the examples of his style on p. 132.

39 | 285e1, ancient history: the origins of civilization were of considerable interest to Hippias' generation, and particularly to sophists. See Guthrie, 1969: 63–84.

40 | 285e10, "I forgot": The joke is repeated in the *Hippias Minor,* at 368d6.

41 | 286a2, "old ladies": an insult only slightly mitigated by the use of *presbutis* for *graus*. Thrasymachus levels the stronger insult at Socrates (*Republic* 350e2).

42 | 286a5, "I have a speech": possibly the "Trojan Dialogue" mentioned by Philostratus (DK 86 A2). Hippias has lots of speeches (cf. *Protagoras* 347ab and Xenophon *Memorabilia* IV.iv.7).

43 | 286b1, Nestor and Neoptolemus: Neoptolemus (Achilles' son) and Nestor are types of the young hero and the old sage respectively.

44 | 286b4, "customs": *nomima*. A substantival use of the adjective formed from *nomos* ("law"—see note 30). *Nomima* are good things to do regularly.

45 | 286b7, Eudicus: probably Hippias' host in Athens. Cf. *Hippias Minor* 363b, where Socrates has presumably just heard this "Trojan" speech.

[2. The Question | 286c3–287e1]

Socrates says he is reminded of a question that arose when he recently pronounced judgment on speeches. Someone rudely asked him how he knew what sorts of things were fine or foul. Would he be able to say what the fine is? The "someone" who asks this is clearly another Socrates. We shall call him the Questioner. (On this device, see p. 107 and note 47.)

The question raises two issues about Socrates: Why does Socrates ask it? What would satisfy him as an answer? These I take up at length in Chapters Five and Six below.

Hippias' response to the question is puzzling. Apparently he understands it, for he answers Socrates' catechism at 287cd without hesitation; but apparently he does not, for he assures Socrates that the matter is a trifle and proceeds to trivialize the question by substituting "something fine" (*kalon*) for "the fine" (*to kalon*). On this maneuver, see note 61; on Hippias' misunderstanding, see pp. 168 and 178.

The *Hippias Major* creates an unusually artificial context for Socrates' question. Unlike other interlocutors in dialogues of search, Hippias does not directly provoke the question. Socrates sets him up as an expert on the fine. Socrates then provides an imaginary context for the question, and an imaginary Questioner. So whereas Euthyphro needed to show that he knew enough to be assured he did no impiety (4e4–5a2), Hippias is pressed merely to show that he can stand up to a questioner. Euthyphro is held to seriously answering the question by his own boasts; Hippias commits himself only to not being refuted and to making a laughing-stock of the Questioner. This is all the more interesting in light of the opportunity Hippias has presented to Socrates: when he says he tells the Spartans what activities and customs are fine for young men, he gives Socrates a chance to ask how Hippias knows that they are fine. Socrates' deliberate neglect of that opportunity is among the dialogue's most interesting dramatic features, adopted, no doubt, to give the sophist free rein to display his evasive talents (but note the use of activities and customs as examples late in the dialogue: 294c9, 295d5, 298b2, and, with special irony, 304b8).

46 | 286c4, "it's a fine thing": *eis kalon*. The idiom means "at the right time," but I have rendered it with "fine" to preserve the pun. (Cf. 286d8.)

47 | 286c5, "someone": This device of an imaginary disputant is the occasion for a major dispute about the authenticity of the *Hippias Major*. Horneffer (1895: 30) and Tarrant (1928: xiii) find fault with the author for not keeping it up consistently (the Questioner disappears at 293e–298a and 300a–303d), and further complain that the device is not Platonic.

Grube (1926B: 136) defends it with parallels; Tarrant (1927: 83, ff.) replies that Plato's other imaginary disputants appear in different sorts of contexts. I defend it below on its literary merits (p. 107). The two main difficulties with the Questioner are: (1) why Hippias does not see through him; and (2) why he is dropped twice and picked up again late in the dialogue. The first difficulty is easily remedied: Hippias does recognize Socrates in the Questioner (see below, p. 108). As for the second, I think it enough to observe that the Questioner would be a cumbersome device in just those passages where he is dropped; for those passages are given over to dense argumentation, which the Questioner would only obstruct (see also note 170).

Tarrant is right that Plato nowhere else uses such a device. The Questioner is in fact the most original feature of the *Hippias Major,* and the least likely to have been supplied by an imitator of Plato.

48 | 286c6, "foul": *aischra:* so translated throughout. *Aischron* is the polar opposite of *kalon,* having both aesthetic and moral uses: "ugly," "shameful." It does not, however, have quite the range of application of *kalon.*

49 | 286c7, "praising other parts as Fine": fine speaking is a matter of great importance for Plato. Cf. *Theaetetus* 185e4: "He who speaks finely is fine and good." For *Socrates,* fine speaking is true speaking; for Hippias, as for Gorgias, it probably need only be persuasive (*Phaedrus* 267a, below, p. 121, n. 12 and p. 124). On Hippias' and Socrates' different standards of fine speaking, see notes 53, 54, 68, 74, 75, 117, and 136.

50 | 286c8–286d2, "how do *you* know what sorts of things are fine and foul? Look, would you be able to say what the fine is?": Cf. 304d8–e2. On the question, see Chapter Five.

"the fine": *to kalon.* This expression refers to the logical cause that makes all fine things fine. On logical causes, see p. 151. *To kalon* is a neuter single adjective used substantively with the article. It could refer (a) to the fine in general, fineness (Smyth, 1920: 1023); or (b) to some fine thing mentioned earlier. Here, (a) is certainly intended; but Hippias understands the expression differently, as referring to anything that is fine (287d9, see note 61). On the uses of such expressions, see Guthrie 1975: 120, and Allen, 1969: 24.

51 | 286d3–7, "as I left . . . fight the argument back": anacoluthon. Socrates never picks up the clause with "whomever." The device is meant, no doubt, to reflect his distress at failing to answer the Questioner.

52 | 286d8–e4, "Teach me . . .": cf. *Euthyphro* 5a3, ff., and 15e5, ff. Hippias' response, too, is like Euthyphro's.

53 | 287b, "no human being could refute you": Cf. Parmenides, DK 28B8, *l.* 61: in the "deceitful ordering" of her words, the goddess tells the youth what is not strictly the truth, so that "no mortal thought will ever overtake you." In echoing this phrase, wittingly or not, Hippias aligns himself with deceit.

54 | 287b4, "That's amazingly well-said":*Pheu hōs eu legeis*. We have no English equivalent for the mock-tragic *pheu*. That Socrates is commending Hippias here on his style is apparent from the parallel expressions at *Phaedrus* 263d5 and 273c6. The joke, I suggest, is that Socrates is more impressed with the style of Hippias' sentence than with the boast it expresses. His target is probably the pleonasm *mēdena anthrōpōn* ("no one of men").

55 | 287c2, "by justice": the noun "justice" is used in the dative case. Cf. *Euthyphro* 6d11 ("that form by which all pious things are pious") and *Phaedo* 100d7 ("by the fine all fine things are fine").

This is usually called the "instrumental" dative, but there is nothing straightforwardly instrumental about its use in such contexts. This is the first of a number of ways in which Socrates will treat the fine as a kind of cause. I shall say that justice, wisdom, the fine, etc. are *logical* causes. I consider what that might mean below (p. 151).

Tarrant argues that this use of the dative is borrowed from the *Phaedo* (1928), *ad loc.*). I think it more likely that the *Phaedo* passage reflects on a Socratic practice illustrated already in such dialogues as the *Hippias Major*. (Socrates in the *Phaedo* says he is up to "nothing new"—100b1; see below, p. 170). Moreau suggests that the *Hippias* here borrows from *Gorgias* 497e (1941: 26, n. 3), but the two passages have very little in common.

56 | 287c4, "is this justice *something*": See p. 167. In context, this means that there is something that justice *is* (i.e., that there is something for a definition of justice to identify). It trivially entails the existence of justice, but does not carry with it any ontological doctrine (see p. 163).

57 | 287c5, "by the good all good things are good": Note the change from virtues of persons to qualities of things. As is his custom in arguments of this sort, Socrates moves from more to less plausible examples. People are no doubt made wise by having a certain quality; but that *things* are made good in the same way is not obvious. For the good, as Protagoras noted, appears to be complex (*Protagoras* 334b, see p. 116). For an argument that makes a similar move, see *Republic* 335bc. (On the *Hippias* passage, see Soreth, 1953: 17, n. 2).

58 | 287c8, "all fine things are fine by the fine": On the dative, see note 55. Nehamas argues that in this passage Socrates has Hippias explicitly admit the reality of universals (1975: 303, n. 20). See p. 169.

59 | 287d2, "why not?": *ti gar mellei*. Cf. *Republic* 349d12 (Grube, 1926B: 139).

60 | 287d5, "what is a fine thing": On Hippias' misunderstanding here, see p. 168. Hippias has agreed at 287c8 that the fine is a logical cause;

now he appears to be withdrawing from that position (*pace* Nehamas, 1975: 299 ff.). The present tense: Hippias suspects whose question this is.

61 | 287d9, "there's no difference": Though Hippias probably knows better, he hereby establishes the way in which *he* is using *to kalon* in answering the question. He intends to take it as meaning "the fine thing," and proposes to identify a fine thing. When he says, at 287e2, that he understands Socrates' distinction, he is probably sincere. What he does here and at 287e is to reject the distinction.

[3. A Fine Girl | 287e2–289d5]

Hippias' answer starts a series of seven proposed definitions, an unusually high number for such dialogues. The *Laches* and *Euthyphro* consider only three each, and the *Charmides* four. The sequence of proposals in the *Hippias* has struck some critics as repetitious and disorderly, adding to their suspicion that the work is not authentic (e.g., Gauss, 1954: 207–8).

The Sequence of Proposed Definitions

1. A fine girl is a fine thing (287e2–289d5).
2. Gold makes things fine, when added to them (289d6–291d5).
3. To live a certain sort of life (including burying your parents) is fine for everyone (291d6–293c8).

*   *   *

4. The appropriate is fine (293c8–294e10).
5. The able is fine (295a1–296d3).
6. The beneficial is fine (296d4–297d9).
7. Pleasure through sight and hearing is fine (297d10–303d10).

(Note that none of these is in the proper form. In Hippias' proposals, this is no surprise. For the form of Socrates' proposals, see note 116.)

This sequence is divided into two stages. The first consists of Hippias' own answers, or rather, evasions (1–3). The second (beginning at 293c8) follows a more appropriate line of reasoning initiated by Socrates' imaginary Questioner (4–7). Similar divisions occur at *Euthyphro* 11e4, *Laches* 194c2, and *Charmides* 161b3, with the introductions of Socratic or Socratic-sounding definitions. Each proposal in the *Hippias* sequence grows from ground prepared earlier. Except for the major shifts from numbers 3 to 4 and 6 to 7, each proposal attempts to correct for the errors that come to light in its predecessor.

Stage One: Hippias' Answers (287e–293c8). Hippias' three answers to Socrates' questions are all of the same kind, as the imaginary Questioner observes when he calls them "very simple and easy to refute" (293d8). Simple they may be; but each has a virtue on which Hippias hopes to capitalize: no one can deny it without looking ridiculous, for as qualified it is certainly true. Hippias says that a fine girl is a fine thing (287e4—here in the sense of "beautiful" or "sexually attractive"). What could be safer than that? It is, as it stands, undeniable. It is an answer that is supposed to embarrass and silence the Questioner. In the other cases too, Hippias mentions things that are undeniably fine.

Although Hippias plainly does not care to address Socrates' question, he does take pains to establish a connection between his irrefutable "answer" and Socrates' latest formulation of the question. He accomplishes this by playing on words. At 287d3 Socrates asks, "What is the fine?" And though the context makes Socrates' intention unmistakable (he wants to know what makes things fine), Hippias insists on understanding "the fine" in another way—as equivalent to "a fine thing" (287d4–9). So a fine thing is what he proceeds to mention. Again, at 289d, Socrates asks what makes things fine when it is *added* to them. And again, the context is clear. Socrates asks for the *character* (*eidos*) that makes things fine, but Hippias supplies the *substance* whose addition makes things fine, taking "add" physically. In the last case, Hippias observes that Socrates wants to know what will be fine "for all," and defends the fine life he describes by taking "for all" in the sense of "in everyone's opinion" (292e4–5).

Why does Hippias repeatedly misunderstand Socrates' question? Socrates' other partners in such discussions usually blunder in this manner only once (as at *Euthyphro* 5de and *Laches* 190e; but see *Meno* 71e–72a with 79ab). The repetition in this stage of the *Hippias* may seem dramatically and philosophically unnecessary.

These explanations for Hippias' repeated errors have been advanced:

1. He is meant to be incredibly stupid (p. 97).
2. His mistakes illustrate ways in which the theory of Forms may be misunderstood (Moreau, 1941: 27, ff.).
3. He does not misunderstand the question, but simply answers it incorrectly. His proposals must be read, "Being a fine girl (or being gold, or being such-and-such a life) is what it is to be fine" (Nehamas, 1975).

None of these explanations is convincing. (1) Misunderstanding Socrates' question is not a sign of stupidity (p. 127 ff.). (2) The mature theory of Forms is not clearly presupposed by the *Hippias* (Chapter Seven). And (3) Hippias' answers are probably not intended seriously as definitions (note 63).

I propose to explain this stage of the discussion as an illustration of the variety of ploys Hippias has for evading questions (p. 125).

Philosophical Significance of Hippias' Answers. The proposals are not repetitious, though they do fail in similar ways to answer Socrates' question. (On their common defects, see p. 168, ff.) They represent different sorts of things that may be thought to be fine, and different respects in which things may fail to be strictly fine.

Of the three things Hippias proposes, the first is any of a kind of particulars (a fine girl); the second is a mass substance (gold); and the third is a universal (to live a certain kind of life). The first fails because it is not fine in every comparison; the second because it is not fine in every use, and the third because it is not fine in every instance. The sequence illustrates three respects in which something strictly fine must always be fine (see p. 59).

Stage One: Socrates' Arguments (287e2–293c8). In each case, Socrates' Questioner responds by identifying a respect in which Hippias' fine thing is not fine. The girl, for example, be she ever so fine, is foul compared to goddesses (289b2). But why should Hippias be bothered by that? If Socrates calls her foul by herself, he will be the one who looks the fool. And if she is foul *in one comparison,* why, there are a great many other comparisons in which she is fine. She is fine "on the whole"—that is the implication of 288e.

Not surprisingly, Hippias never admits defeat in these cases. What is surprising is that Socrates' Questioner claims victory. Certainly he is right that Hippias' fine things do not answer the question; none of them could be what makes all fine things fine (288a), if for no other reason than because none of them occurs wherever fineness occurs. But Hippias recognizes that (288ab); he never claims to be stating *the* definition of fineness. What he claims steadfastly is that what he has said is true: the fine girl (or whatever) *is* a fine thing. That is what the Questioner undertakes to refute. His conclusion in each case must be that what Hippias proposes is not strictly or by itself fine or foul. Hippias' statement that it is a fine thing is not simply false; it is incomplete. It is not so much a fine thing as merely fine *for* a certain kind of thing, or *for* a certain purpose, or *in* a certain context. Hippias does not recognize this incompleteness as a defect; but the Questioner does. That is because a necessary condition of Socratic definition is that one identify something strictly or completely fine (p. 153).

Of Socrates' earlier arguments with Hippias, we may say simply that they are not by themselves compelling. They depend on an undefended assumption about the fine: that true sentences with "fine" in it are true by themselves, strictly and without qualifications. Because Hippias refuses to consider his sentences apart from their understood qualifications, he is unperturbed by Socrates' results. Only later, when Socrates directly attacks this issue, does Hippias complain of the other's inability to see things whole (301b, 304a; see p. 125, and note 172 below, and cf. 288e7 and *Hippias Minor* 369bc). What Hippias means by this is controversial. I think he means at least this: Socrates should not try to refute statements by cutting them off from the wider contexts in which they are made, and in which they are true.

Arguments Against the First Proposal (287e2–289d5). Hippias' answer and Socrates' reply to it together raise several problems for the interpreter. Hippias evidently confuses the fine (*to kalon*) with something else— *kalon*—and we shall need to determine what sort of confusion that is. On the received interpretation, Hippias confuses a universal (beauty) with particular (a girl). Nehamas has argued (1975) that no one could be that confused. He proposes to understand Hippias as seriously appealing to the nature of a fine girl in order to state the nature of the fine, and in this Irwin follows him (1977B:8, n.11). It is more likely, however, that Hippias is neither confused nor seriously attempting to state the nature of the fine, but that he substitutes *kalon* for *to kalon* merely as a debating tactic, saying what he thinks is by its nature fine (a fine girl) instead of what is the nature of the fine (the fine itself). See p. 125.

A second problem concerns the structure of Socrates' argument. There appear to be two arguments. The first is expressed in the rhetorical question at 288a8–11, which is repeated in different form at the end of the passage, 289d2–5. The argument there is that one cannot consider a fine girl to be what makes everything fine that is fine. The obvious suppressed premise is that no fine girl is general enough: there is not a fine girl in every fine law or every fine activity recommended for the young. The second argument (note 69) follows Hippias' challenge at 288b1–3 and comprises most of Socrates' reply. Its conclusion is stronger: that the fine girl fails to be strictly fine (289c5).

62 | 287e3, "what the fine is": Hippias proceeds to tell Socrates of something he supposes is irrefutably fine (288b1–3), instead of *the* logical cause of the fine. He apparently plays on the meaning of *to kalon* (see note

50). For a different account of Hippias' misunderstanding, see Nehamas, 1975: 299 ff., with my note 63.

63 | 287e4, "a fine girl is a fine thing": *parthenos kalē kalon*. Hippias' answer is puzzling: what does he think it has to do with Socrates' question?

Syntax. The predicate adjective *kalon* is neuter, and does not agree with its feminine subject. On such constructions, see Kühner-Gerth, 1898: II.1, 58–60 (§360). In such cases, the subject must be taken generally. Hippias has no particular girl in mind; he means that any fine girl is fine.

Translation. Grote (1888: II, 40) and Guthrie (1975: 179, n. 4) give translations similar to mine. Unfortunately, the sentence cannot be translated with exactly the right ambiguities into an uninflected language such as English. "A fine girl is fine" would be incorrect; the Greek for that tautology would be *parthenos kalē kalē*. *Parthenos* and *kalē* are feminine, but *kalon* is neuter singular. Jowett's "a beautiful maiden is a beauty" is elegant and quite close to the Greek, but "a beauty" fails to capture the play between *kalon* and *to kalon,* or to pick up the echo of *kalon* from 287d5: "Doesn't the person who asks this want to find out what is *kalon* (a fine thing)?" Our translation—"a fine girl is *a fine thing*"—is also flawed, because it suggests that Hippias is confusing a particular *thing* (Cassandra, say, or the young Helen) with a universal (the fine, or fineness). Although most commentators understand the passage in that way, evidence weighs heavily against it, as we shall see. My translation comes with the warning that "thing" here carries no metaphysical burden; it may or may not turn out to be a *particular* in the metaphysician's sense.

The most attractive alternative translation is that proposed by Nehamas (1975: 299, ff.): "being a fine girl is what it is to be fine." On this translation, which is a possible reading of the Greek, Hippias would probably be offering a partial or Gorgian definition of the fine: *one* way of being fine (the way for girls, in fact) is to be a fine girl. (On such definitions, see p. 77 and p. 117). Hippias would be answering in the right form (cf. 293e8, and my note on that passage). His mistake would be in giving only a partial definition. After the rhetorical question at 288a, he cannot suppose that he has given a complete definition; no fine girl could be what makes all fine things fine. Socrates, we may infer from 287c9, supposes that there is one logical cause for the fine. But Hippias would on this kind of interpretation be giving a specific logical cause that works for a specific set of fine things—in this case, girls. What Hippias does not realize, or does not accept, is that only one thing is supposed to be fine in the way that the fine is fine. He is prepared to give a list of things that are fine (290c1–2), each one of which would be part of what it is to be fine.

I do not believe that this is right. Certainly, Socrates does not understand Hippias' answer in that way. And what Hippias says calls for a different, and much simpler, explanation. If Socrates had taken Hippias' answer as an attempt at Gorgian definition, as the first item on a list of different ways to be fine for different things, he would have had two objections to make, neither of which appears in this part of the *Hippias Major*. First, and most obvious, he would have indicated that the definition is circular: it includes the term to be defined (cf. *Meno* 79d). Second, he would have shown that being a fine girl is not fine for everything or everybody. It would not be fine for Socrates to be any kind of girl, nor would it be fine for a god. But Socrates says neither of those things. Instead, he proposes to put the classes of girls and goddesses together, in order to see that the finest girl is foul compared with the class of goddesses (289b). He does not imply that it would be finer to be a goddess (she doesn't have a chance to be a goddess). What he says is that *the* finest girl is foul compared to the class of goddesses.

Hippias does not present his answer as anything so sophisticated as a partial definition. It is a trifle, he says at 286e5, and he means to trivialize the question. He does so by mentioning something he believes to be irrefutably fine, and something, besides, that was probably supposed to provoke nudges and titters from his audience. For the rhetorical tradition of using laughter against serious opponents, see p. 134, n. 5, and 288b2 ("laughing-stock").

64 | 287e5, "by Dog": This peculiar oath is commonly used by Socrates.

65 | 287e5, "a glorious answer": *eudoxōs apekrinō*. The adverb occurs in no Greek text but this. See p. 99.

66 | 288a9, "if the fine itself is *what?*" Cf. the Jowett editors' translation: "What must beauty by itself be in order to explain why we apply the word to them?" *Ti* ("what," "something"), though interrogative here, refers as in 287d1 to whatever it is that the fine should be said to be. For the syntax, cf. *Phaedo* 105b8, with Gallop's note *ad loc.* (1975: 237, n. 75).

67 | 288a11, "those things are fine because of that?": Most translators follow Schanz in supplying a *ti* after *esti,* so that the question would read, "there *exists something* through which those things are fine." The passage is understood so by Allen (1970:147), on whom see Rist (1975).

The best reading is Burnet's, which gives *di' ho* where the manuscripts read *dio*. This allows the translation I have given. It makes good Greek, and is easily justified: the "h" does not show as a letter in Greek.

Grube's alternative gives a similar sense (1926A: 189).

Socrates' point is not that the fine exists, but that it is the logical cause for fine things' being fine. That it exists is obvious. See p. 163.

68 | 288b2, "that what you say is not a fine thing": "what you say" is ambiguous, and may refer equally to the *sentence* Hippias has given Socrates *or* to the fine girl mentioned in the sentence. Hippias thinks both are fine. Cf. 292e4–5.

69 | 288b5–289d2, the second argument: Hippias has challenged the Questioner to show that "what I say is not a fine thing" (288b2) and Socrates is sure the Questioner will try. The challenge is deliberately ambiguous between:

1. ". . . that what I said is incorrect," and
2. ". . . that what I mentioned (=*parthenos kalē*) is not a fine thing (*kalon*)."

The Questioner must undertake to prove 1, and probably to prove 2 as well, for as Hippias puts the challenge, nothing but 2 would establish 1. Now the Questioner has cleverly provoked Hippias to introduce the Heracleitean view that what is fine in one comparison class may be foul in another; and indeed there is a comparison class in which the finest girl is foul. This, apparently, is enough to refute Hippias; for although he does not concede that the Questioner has met his challenge, he proceeds to another answer—as if he now understood Socrates to have asked a different question ("But if *that*'s what he's looking for . . ."—289d6).

Why does the comparison with gods refute Hippias? The Questioner puts the problem in two ways:

3. ". . . you answer with something that turns out to be *no more fine than foul*" (289c5).
4. "If I had asked from the beginning what is *both fine and foul* . . . then wouldn't you have given the right answer?" (289c9–d2)

This requires interpretation. As it stands, 4 would not refute Hippias. What is both *F* and *G* is by any plausible logic certainly *F* as well. If the girl is both fine and foul, she is fine, and Hippias is vindicated. So we must understand 4 as shorthand for:

4a. . . . what is fine in one comparison class and foul in another comparison class . . .

which, after all, is exactly what has been proved in the argument. But 4a by itself does not refute Hippias, unless Socrates assumes that what is fine only with a qualification (e.g., "in a certain comparison class") is not strictly fine. I suggest, as a hypothesis for interpreting such passages, that Socrates makes that assumption (see p. 153). Then 3 becomes clear: what is fine only with a qualification fails to be strictly either fine or foul. It is no more the one than the other, because, appropriately qualified, it can be either. So the girl is *neither fine nor foul* without qualification. From that, the defeat of Hippias—the proposition that no fine girl is fine without qualification—follows immediately. The conclusion of the argument, then, is most likely 3, interpreted naturally to mean ". . . neither strictly fine nor strictly foul." The Questioner has shown, albeit elliptically, that Hippias' first answer can successfully be denied.

70 | 288b8, "a fine mare": fine, presumably, for the breeding of chariot horses. All the examples in this passage are feminine, presumably to keep distinct the substantival use of *kalon* ("a fine thing"). If *kalon* were used of a neuter subject (as at 288e6) it could be understood as an adjective. Fine horses were bred in Hippias' country and raced at Olympia.

On the connection between reproduction and the fine in the Socratic tradition, see p. 188.

71 | 288b9, the oracle: Tarrant suggests that the reference is to a Delphic reply to the Megarians (v. Schol. ad Theocr. XIV.48) in which horses are praised, but not called fine (Tarrant, 1928, *ad loc.*).

72 | 288c3, "that the fine thing is a fine thing": cf. 288e1–2, which gives the sense more clearly: "that what is fine . . . is a fine thing."

73 | 288c10, "what about a fine pot?": *chytra*. On *chytrai* see *The Athenian Agora,* XII, Part I, p. 224 ff. They were big round pots used in everyday life for cooking and serving. Unwanted infants were exposed in them, and they seem on particularly riotous occasions to have been put to vulgar uses.

74 | 288d1–3, ". . . such vulgar speech . . . ": What is vulgar about the word *chytra*? Apparently, its only fault is that it refers to a household utensil. Gorgias, who probably influenced Hippias, was given to noble-sounding euphemisms ("living tomb" for "vulture"—DK 82 B5a), and no doubt would have used a more elegant example.

75 | 288d4, "not refined": cf. Xenophon, *Oeconomicus* VIII. 19, a passage that makes the best sense if understood as an allusion either to this episode in the *Hippias Major,* or to a commonly remembered episode in the life of Socrates (Chaintraine, 1947). Cf. also his *Memorabilia* III.viii, 6, where Socrates is represented agreeing that even a *kophinos koprophoros* ("shitbasket") is *kalos,* presumably because it is useful.

"garbage": *surphetos.* An unusual usage. See p. 99.

For the contrast between elegant speakers and Socrates (who speaks only the truth) see *Ion* 532d6–9 and *Apology* 17a. Compare the Socratic contrast between rhetoric and instruction (*Gorgias* 455a and *Phaedrus* 267a6–b2).

76 | 288d9, six choes: about two gallons.

77 | 288e6, "even that utensil is fine": *skeuos* in the singular for utensil is rare (Tarrant, 1928, *ad loc.*).

78 | 288e9, "But on the whole that's not worth judging fine, compared to a horse and a girl and all the other fine things": Hippias apparently likes to look at such matters "on the whole." Cf. 301b ("You don't look at the entireties of things"). But it is hard to pin down what, if anything, he means by this. Here, he seems to mean that a judgment of fineness should take into account all possible comparisons. Socrates, by contrast, presupposes that if anything is strictly fine in a single given context, then it is fine. (On strict predication, see below, p. 153.)

"on the whole": cf. 295c8.

"compared to": *pros*.

79 | 289a4, "another class": this is the reading of the manuscripts, and I see no reason to change it. Various editors have conjectured readings with forms of *anthrōpos* ("human being"), and most translators follow them: "the class of human beings" (DK 22 B82).

80 | 289b3, "be seen to be": *phaneitai*. Ambiguous between "is plainly" and "is thought to be." I have translated the verb consistently in this way.

81 | 289c2, "do you remember": such reminders are regular features of Socrates' arguments about definitions. Cf. *Euthyphro* 6d9, for example, and see p. 137.

82 | 289c5, "no more fine than foul": cf. *Republic* 479b9–10 and 538d9–e1. Both passages probably allude to the *Hippias Major;* both presuppose the reader's familiarity with arguments of the type given here in the *Hippias Major* (p. 178). For the thought, see note 69.

83 | 289d1, "if I had asked you from the beginning what is both fine and foul": cf. *Euthyphro* 8a10, ff. The *Hippias Major* appears to be more sophisticated than the *Euthyphro* on this point (p. 177). On conclusions of this kind, see Guthrie, 1975: 184, n. 1. Other comparable passages are:

a. *Charmides* 161b1, where respect is rejected as a definition for sound-mindedness on the grounds that it is "no more good than bad."

b. *Laches* 192e–193e, where prudent and imprudent endurance are shown to have equal claim to being courage; each, when shown to be foul, makes the other look fine.

[Both these arguments presuppose what the *Hippias* presupposes: that what is strictly fine or good is so in every context (p. 153, ff).]

c. *Phaedo* 74b8–9, 78d10–e4, with the contrasts at 74a9–12 and

78d3–7. Here Socrates seeks to distinguish Forms from, e.g., the many fine things, on the ground that any of the latter is seen to be both fine and foul (such at least is the implication of the passages taken together). The *Hippias Major* does not distinguish Forms from their namesakes in this way (p. 165 ff.). With the *Phaedo* doctrine, see *Parmenides* 129ab–d6 and *Republic* 479a.

d. *Philebus* 51b3, which distinguishes shapes and colors that are always fine from those fine only in relation to something. This distinction is, I think, much closer to the one presupposed in the *Hippias Major* and other early dialogues than it is to the distinction of the *Phaedo*.

e. Xenophon, *Memorabilia* III.viii. 6–9, where Socrates argues that the same things are both fine and foul, but that a fine house is fine for all seasons. Xenophon's report of Socrates is at odds here with Plato's in one respect: Xenophon's Socrates is not scornful of the things that are both fine and foul (see pp. 183 and 186).

84 | 289d3, "beautified": *kosmeitai*. The verb connotes orderly arrangement. Jowett translates it, "ordered in loveliness." The simpler translation is more appropriate in view of the way Hippias understands the word at 289d8.

85 | 289d4, "when that form is added to it": cf. *Phaedo* 100d4–6, "nothing else makes [a fine thing] fine but the fine I mentioned, whether by its presence or its participation or in whatever way or however it is added." Which passage is echoing which? Tarrant thinks the *Hippias* follows the *Phaedo* and supposes that both passages invoke Plato's mature theory of Forms (1928: *ad loc.*). Soreth defends the priority of the *Hippias* (1953: 25–28).

The view I defend in the Essay is that the two passages represent the same idea, which could be held independently of the mature theory of Forms: that the fine is the logical cause of things being fine (p. 151 and p. 168). The *Phaedo* passage reflects on earlier practices of Socrates (100b), which are represented nowhere so clearly as in the *Hippias Major*. Most likely, then, the *Phaedo* alludes here to the *Hippias*.

"that form": *ekeino to eidos*. The word *eidos* has a technical role in Plato's mature theory of Forms, but a nontechnical use as well. Cf. *Euthyphro* 6d10–11: "that form itself by which all the pious things are pious." Neither passage need be read as importing Plato's mature theory. On the theory and its relation to earlier dialogues such as the *Hippias* and *Euthyphro,* see Guthrie, 1969: 351–5 and 1975: 114–121; Shiner, 1974: 26–29; and below, Chapter Seven.

By "form" is meant an *ousia* (essence) or *physis* (nature). Socrates supposes that such a form is always the same, and that it is independent of our beliefs, conceptions, and habits of usage. But he does not have a developed theory of its ontological status, and he does not commit himself to the "two-world" theory associated with mature Plato (p. 163).

For the nontechnical use of *eidos* before Plato, see Guthrie, 1969: 430 and Allen, 1970: 28, ff. For the distinction between mature Platonic Forms and conceptions, see Shiner (1974: 19–21).

"is added to it": see p. 166. Socrates apparently speaks loosely, not having a definite theory of how a form is related to its instances. But Hippias takes him literally, and casts about for a kind of stuff that is physically added to things to make them fine.

[4. Gold | 289d6–291c9]

The Questioner sets out his object of search in provocatively new terms: the fine is something that can be added to other things in such a way that they are then beautified and seen to be fine. He is asking, in other words, after the character a thing must acquire if it is to become fine. Hippias ignores the word *eidos* ("character," or "form"), which makes the Questioner's meaning clear, and plays on the Questioner's expression "is added." (For a similar play on words by a rather different sophist, see *Euthydemus* 301a.)

Hippias now gives an answer that is true, and connected with the question by the play on words: anything is finer ("more valuable") by the addition to it of gold. (That Hippias has value in mind here is clear from 289e1–2: "he has no feeling at all for fine possessions.") Hippias does not suppose that gold is the only stuff with that property (ivory also is value-conferring, 290c1–2); but he thinks what he has said is irrefutable.

Socrates' counterargument (delivered through the Questioner) follows the same pattern as before. He uses examples to provoke Hippias into qualifying his answer (and incidentally shifting from the use of *kalon* for "valuable"). Different materials are fine for different parts of a statue, depending on where they are appropriate. But then, if being fine depends on being appropriate to something, gold is no finer than figwood; because as there is something for which gold is appropriate, there is something for which figwood is appropriate and therefore fine as well. Hippias rightly does not concede defeat. What he said has not been shown to be false, but incomplete. He should have said not that the addition of gold makes anything fine, but that the addition of gold makes anything a fine *investment*. Socrates has implicitly shown that sentences with "fine" tend to be incomplete in this way. They tend to omit the comparison class (on which the girl's fineness depended) and also the function of the object to be commended. Before you agree that something is fine, you will have to ask what it is used for, as well as what it is compared to.

The conclusion, that gold is no finer than figwood, is obviously distasteful to Hippias. It is also probably false: gold is fine for more purposes than figwood is. But that is not what Socrates means to deny. His point is that gold is fine with precisely the same sort of limitation as applies to figwood. It is fine only for a specified function.

86 | 289d7, "the fine thing": Hippias continues to understand *to kalon* in this way. That is a legitimate construal of the phrase, but perverse in view of Socrates' use of *eidos* ("character" or "form") at 289d4. Cf. 287d5, 287e4, and my notes 60 and 63.

87 | 289e6, "it will be seen to be fine": *kalon phaneitai*. I give no antecedent for "it" because the verb has no stated subject. The verb *phaneitai* is ambiguous between "will be plainly fine" and "will be thought to be fine." At 289d3 Socrates uses it in the first (objective) way; here, Hippias uses it subjectively: "is thought to be fine," in this context, "is valued."

88 | 290a5, "Are you crazy?": *ō tetuphōmene su*. The expression is challenged by athetizers. See Thesleff, 1976: 106 and Grube 1926B: 139. Thesleff thinks this is a mid–fourth century idiom, but I cannot see why. All we really know is that it is rare. Probably our author borrowed it from comedy of the fourth century (cf. pp. 99–100). Since the comedy of the 390's is almost entirely lost, we have no reason to think the borrowing could not have been from that period, which would be consistent with assigning the *Hippias Major* to Plato.

On the translation, see note 94.

89 | 290a5, Pheidias: Athenian sculptor, born about 490 B.C., best known as designer of the Parthenon sculptures. He fled to Elis (Hippias' home town) after 432 B.C., after allegedly embezzling construction funds. The charge may have been political, owing to Pheidias' association with Pericles (Plutarch, *Pericles* 31).

90 | 290b2, "Athena's eyes": Socrates refers to the Athena Parthenos made of ivory and gold for the Parthenon. The statue survives only in the form of miniature Roman copies. For a description, see Pausanias I, xxiv. 5–7.

The passage is parallel to *Republic* 420cd, where Socrates explains why statues' eyes are to be made not purple but black, "if by giving what is fitting to the particular [parts], we make the whole fine." Here I think it impossible to determine which passage is an echo of which. The contexts are quite different. Probably the use of black stone in statues' eyes was a commonplace example of how anything can be fine if put in the right place.

91 | 290c2, "Ivory's fine too, I think": Hippias is prepared to identify a number of different things that make things fine, in the Gorgian tradition (p. 117). The same tendency shows itself at 298c3–4, where he suggests that some things (laws, etc.) require a different (necessarily partial) account of the fine.

92 | 290c8, "when it's appropriate": Cf. the proposal at 293e, that the appropriate is fine. Hippias and Socrates appear to be using this word differently. See note 120.

93 | 290c8, "not appropriate": could be understood (a) as the contrary of "appropriate," or (b) as its contradictory, or (c) as its polar opposite. A pair of contrary predicates cannot be true of the same subject at the same time; of a pair of contradictories, one must be true and the other false of a given subject; polar opposites (e.g., "hot" and "cold") stand at opposite ends of a spectrum of judgment. Since "fine" and "foul" appear to be polar opposites, the same is most likely intended for "appropriate" and "not appropriate." This intention would be expressed by translating *mē prepōn* as "inappropriate."

Cf. *Euthyphro* 5d and 7a for an example of a similar opposition between "pious" and "impious."

94 | 290d1, "You're a wise man!": *ō sophe su*. Cf. 290a5. Because such apostrophes are not idiomatic in English, or used in comic insults, I have rephrased them throughout this translation in various appropriate ways.

95 | 290d5, "whatever is appropriate to each thing makes that particular thing fine." A good suggestion, taken up by the Questioner as a possible definition for the fine at 293e. Cf. Hippias' suggestion at 296d4.

96 | 290d10, "Herakles!": a comic oath.

97 | 290e4, "plague": *mermeros*. See p. 99.

98 | 290e9, "when we were going to have a banquet": athetizers make this an echo of *Republic* 372c1–2; but the contexts are quite different. See Grube, 1926B: 138.

99 | 291a8, "so finely dressed, etc.": Hippias, given to wearing clothes and shoes of his own making (*Hippias Minor* 368bc), is in no position to sneer at cookery. Shoemaking was no more a gentleman's avocation in classical Greece than was cooking. Hippias objected, probably, merely to embarrass the Questioner; but Socrates turns the joke against him.

"to mix with him": *phuresthai*. A metaphor from cooking. The pun is probably intended.

100 | 291b5, "you agreed, Socrates, that the appropriate is finer than the not appropriate": the agreement must be that of 290d5. But there

Hippias agrees to something different: "whatever is appropriate to each thing makes that particular thing fine." The Questioner should say, "what is appropriate for *x* makes *x* finer," which is indeed a consequence of the agreement.

101 | 291c8, "gold is no finer than wood from a figtree": the air of paradox this conclusion wears is due to the absence of the appropriate qualifications. Figwood is finer than gold *for making kitchen spoons,* but from that it should not follow that, generally speaking, gold is no finer than figwood (see p. 57).

[5. Burying Your Parents | 291d1–293c8]

Hippias' third answer is that it is fine for everyone to live a certain sort of life, a life in which (among other things) one buries one's parents with honor. Once more Hippias has said something with which no reasonable person will quarrel. But the Questioner is not reasonable; he is likely to beat Socrates with a stick for giving such an answer.

Again Socrates refutes Hippias with a reminder of the original question (292cd, cf. 289c2). The life Hippias describes is obviously one among many fine things (cf. note 91), and fine only for human beings. Socrates wanted to know what would make *any*thing whatever fine. But again, as at 288a9–10, Socrates does not pursue this point. Hippias' fine life was supposed to be fine at least for any human being (291d10); but the Questioner has only to turn to myth for a counterexample. Most of the mythical heroes have gods for parents; it would be a sacrilege for such men to bury *their* parents. So Hippias' fine life is not fine for everybody. Though, as Hippias said at 292e4–5, everyone would think such a life generally fine, there are certain people who ought not to live it to the hilt.

This argument comes closer than any in the *Hippias Major* to violating the principle of the priority of definition, which says that you cannot claim to know of anything that it is fine or foul till you know what the fine is (p. 138). But here no one claims to *know* that burying a god is foul, though both speakers accept it as obvious (293b5–7). And, more important, the search for a definition of the fine does not depend on knowing that such acts are foul. Hippias' third answer could be easily rejected on different grounds; for what he describes cannot occur in all the sorts of things that can be fine (see p. 156).

Socrates has now illustrated three ways in which a sentence of the form "*a* is fine" may be incomplete. Before agreeing that *a* is fine, we shall have to ask, depending on context:

1. . . . a fine what? (The lesson of the fine girl.)
2. . . . fine for what function? (The lesson of the golden spoon.)
3. . . . fine for whom to do? (The lesson of burying one's parents.)

Little is made of this incompleteness in the *Hippias Major*. At the time he wrote it, Plato was probably merely intrigued by the problem of incompleteness. Later, in the middle dialogues, it assumes new importance (Woodruff, 1978B).

102 | 291d2, "that will never be seen to be foul for anyone, anywhere at any time": in view of Hippias' proposed definition at 291d9, ff., this must be understood as, "that will never be plainly foul for anyone *to be* (or *to do*)." *Phaneitai* here has the objective use (with the participle *on* understood), and the dative *mēdeni* is taken with *aischron:* "foul for no one to be or do." Under pressure at 292e4–5 Hippias will speak as if he had all along meant something different: the phrase at 291d2 could be translated, "that no one anywhere will ever *think* to be foul," taking *phaneitai* subjectively and the dative with the verb. Reading back from 292e4–5, we would suppose that that was what Hippias had meant. He probably meant from the start to take advantage of the verb's ambiguity.

103 | 291e5, "the kind way": *eunoïkōs*. Thesleff considers this evidence of a mid-fourth-century date for the *Hippias Major* (1976: 107). His argument is essentially the same as the one he uses for *tetuphōmene* (290a5), and fails for the same reason (note 88).

104 | 292a7, "he'll try to give me a thrashing": cf. *Clouds* 1321, ff. Thrashing people with sticks was apparently a frequent topic of Attic comedy. The present passage alludes to *Iliad* II, 188, ff., where Odysseus thrashes Thersites and makes a joke of his attempt to speak out. Socrates was notorious in democratic Athens for quoting the opening lines of this élitist passage from Homer (Xenophon, *Memorabilia* I.ii. 58; the connection was suggested to me by I. F. Stone). See Stone (1979: 66) and my note 27.

The sophist Gorgias was supposed to have delivered a jocular threat of a thrashing in response to an impertinent question (DK 82A 24). Hippias' response at 292b7 is in the Gorgian tradition. Cf. also *Menexenus* 236c1.

105 | 292c8, dithyramb: a sort of choral ode in which the interest derived chiefly from music. Hippias is said to have written dithyrambs (*Hippias Minor* 368d1), and we shall see that his rhetorical style is designed to give acoustic pleasure (p. 125). The speech to which Socrates refers (291d9, ff.) is indeed replete with musical rhythms and rhymes.

Gorgias also was said to have a dithyrambic style (DK 82 A4). Cf. *Phaedrus* 238d3, where, in retrospect, Socrates' dithyrambic enthusiasm is a signal that he is about to speak false.

106 | 292e2, "that which is fine always and for everyone": *ho pasi kalon kai aei esti.* Cf. *Symposium* 210e–11b, with my comments below, p. 173.

The "always" here is not temporal, but picks up the "anything" at 292d1. The dative "for everyone" should be taken in the same way as the datives in 292d1: "that which is fine in every instance." Hippias has failed again to satisfy the principle his second answer violated. Gold is not fine either, *in every instance* (291c). Hence arises the vehemence of the present speech (esp. 292d3–6). Cf. 293c3–5, where the datives must range more widely, over the comparisons used in refuting the first answer.

107 | 292e8, "for Achilles as well": as the son of a minor immortal goddess, Achilles would never be in a position to bury his parents with propriety. Also, Achilles' choice of short-lived glory is supposed to be a paradigm of the fine, and disagrees with Hippias' definition.

The Questioner exaggerates his argument for rhetorical effect. Hippias' proposal was that it was fine to bury parents *when they die;* but since divine parents will never die, it will never, by Hippias' account, be fine to bury them. Socrates still has a case against Hippias, however; for Hippias' idea is that it is fine to outlive your parents and to be honored by the Greeks. But clearly that is not always possible. For counterexamples, we do not need to go as far as mythology. Achilles' case illustrates the choice some men must make between "being honored by the Greeks" and "arriving at an old age."

108 | 292e10, Aeacus: Achilles' parental grandfather. As a son of Zeus, Aeacus would commit the greatest impiety by burying his father.

109 | 293a2, "Go to blessedness!": an unusual and comic euphemism. As with other comic expressions cited by the athetizers (mainly Tarrant, 1928: lxxix) and defended by Grube (1926B), this expression is singularly appropriate in Plato's most comic dialogue. Hippias is represented trying for a laugh here.

110 | 293a9, Herakles: another child of Zeus.

111 | 293b8, Tantalus, Dardanus, and Zethus: each is, according to at least one tradition, a son of Zeus.

Pelops: son of Tantalus, a man of human (though heroic) parentage.

112 | 293c3–4, "the same fate . . . and a more laughable fate besides": For the common defect of Hippias' answer, see p. 168, ff.; for the common strategy of Socrates' arguments, see p. 48. Why is the result more laughable in the case of Hippias' third proposal (that the good life is always fine)? (1) The conclusion that heroes should bury their immortal parents is funnier than the awkward consequences of earlier proposals. (2) Hippias' failure here is more laughable because it is his third, and because at this point he could be expected to know better. But Hippias has not repeated precisely the same mistake; and in each case he has prepared for himself a different rhetorical evasion. Here he could, if he wished, safely maintain that the life he described is fine to everyone, i.e., *in everyone's opinion* (see note 102). So *he* has not been made ridiculous (not, at least, by his own standards), and is right not to admit defeat.

[6. The Appropriate | 293c8–294e10]

Socrates will not let Hippias continue in the same vein. He has the Questioner pick up Hippias' earlier suggestion, that the appropriate is what makes things fine (290d5). This inaugurates the second stage of the search.

Stage Two: The Socratic Approach (293c8–303d10)

1. The appropriate is fine (293c8–294e10).
2. The able is fine (295a1–296d3).
3. The beneficial is fine (296d4–297d9).
4. Pleasure through sight and hearing is fine (297d10–303d10).

The proposals are plausible; at least they could be made in the form of definitions. They culminate, moreover, in a statement the historical Socrates undoubtedly believed: that the fine is the beneficial (296e5, see p. 183). Yet none of the proposals is allowed to stand. In the end, we have learned more about the rules of definition from these arguments than we have about what it is to be fine.

What we have in Stage Two is essentially an exercise in the logic of Socratic definition. Socrates tries to take the incompleteness of "fine" into account (p. 110), proposing to define it by such similarity incomplete predicates as "the appropriate" and "the able." But both of these appear to be the logical causes of too many different sorts of things, and both need to be tied down, or completed, in such a way that the general commendatory use of "fine" is preserved and explained. The governing assumption of Stage Two is that it is a good thing to be fine (294b8–c2, 296d4–5, 297c3–d1, 303e4–5; see p. 188). The logical problem, of course, is to provide a definition that accounts for this *without circularity,* without, that is, using "fine" or an expression too closely related to it (as "good" turns out to be—note 148). This problem is illustrated by the refutation of the dialogue's best proposed definition: that the fine is a cause of good (296e9, ff.). The difficulty is underlined by the way in which the discussion is driven back to that very definition at 303e. Such difficulties inevitably beset attempts to define Socratically our most basic terms, and that may well be part of the lesson Socrates learns, that "what's fine is hard" (304e).

The first three proposals of Stage Two all turn out to be attempts to say the same thing, that the fine is the beneficial (note 150). The fourth proposal of this series represents an altogether fresh start: pleasure through hearing and sight is the fine (298a). This is a possibility that needs to be considered (p. 77), but Socrates makes no attempt to link it with earlier proposals until the very end, when its failure suggests marking off the fine pleasures as the beneficial ones, and so in effect returning to the next-to-last definition. This return gives an aesthetic closure to the dialogue and, at the same time, emphasizes the virtues of defining the fine as the beneficial. Of all the bad answers that, apparently, was the best.

Unlike Hippias' answers, the Questioner's proposals identify things that could be supposed to occur in every fine thing (p. 156). The first two fail because, apparently, they can also occur in foul things (p. 155). The third fails because it would be uninformative in the final analysis (p. 156 and p. 153). The last fails because it violates the unity of definition (p. 110 and p. 78).

THE ARGUMENT AGAINST THE QUESTIONER'S FIRST PROPOSAL (293d6–294e10). The obvious difficulty with the Questioner's first proposal is that different things are appropriate in different contexts. Though it is usually fine to do the appropriate thing, in some situations what is appropriate might not be fine at all, generally speaking. Like "fine," "appropriate" (*prepon*) is used to commend; but also like "fine," "appropriate" is used incompletely (see p. 110). Its meaning seems to shift from context to context, so that after conceding that gold is appropriate for parts of Pheidias' statue, we should still ask whether it is strictly fine. If the appropriate is to be what makes things fine, it must be tied firmly to a safe evaluative usage (at least, so Socrates apparently believes).

The point is hard to make, however, in view of the positive connotation of "appropriate." So Socrates tackles the proposal in another way. He provokes Hippias to say that the appropriate is what makes things both be and be seen to be fine (294c3–4). From that, and two premises that govern Socratic definition (see below), he obtains the impossible conclusion that if anything is fine it necessarily is seen to be fine. That is false for any interpretation of "is seen to be" (*phainesthai*). (On the two possibilities, see note 80.) Since Hippias maintains that the appropriate is what makes things be seen to be fine, whatever else it does, he must give up his suggestion that the appropriate is what makes things fine. The argument is elegant, and neatly presented. Guthrie treats it as a sophistic fallacy (1975: 185). The same argument, he says, could be used to disqualify any definition of the fine. That is not quite correct. The argument would discredit any definition of the fine that was intended to suffice for some other definiendum as well. Two different things cannot have the same logical cause (294e2–4) unless the two always occur together, because otherwise the cause would not safely carry with it each of the things it is intended to define. Hippias could defend his suggestion by choosing to make the appropriate define the fine and nothing else. He chooses not to do that (294e6). So the argument is not a trick; it serves to show that Hippias himself conceptually separates the appropriate from the fine.

The two premises that govern Socratic definition are explicitly stated, and are of some interest:

1. If anything is fine, the logical cause of the fine is present in it (294b2, 287c9, and *passim*).
2. If the logical cause of the fine is present in a thing, then *necessarily* that thing is fine (294b3–4).

The trouble with the appropriate is that as the cause of the fine it would be present in fine things whether or not they are seen to be fine; but as the cause of being seen to be fine it must make those things be seen to be fine. But we know that not everything fine is seen to be fine.

113 | 293d2, "he himself makes me a suggestion": compare *Euthyphro* 11e4, *Laches* 194c2, and *Charmides* 161b3, where either Socrates or someone under Socratic influence raises the level of the proposals. Is it irony here that the true source of the suggestion (not acknowledged by the Questioner) is Hippias himself, at 290d5–6?

114 | 293d7, "answers like that": The Questioner does not tell us exactly what weakness the answers have in common. See p. 168 for a discussion of this point.

115 | 293e4, "the nature of the appropriate itself": probably the earliest suggestion in Plato's works that Socrates is investigating the *natures* of things when he asks for definitions. This is a significant step towards ontological theory. See p. 171.

116 | 293e8, "Is the appropriate fine?": From the exchange at 287d4, ff., we would expect Socrates to ask, "Is the appropriate *the* fine?" The definite article is similarly missing frequently in the remainder of the dialogue: 294d6, 294e9, 295e6, 297e7, 298d4, 299c1, 303d2, cf. 293e1. This occurs too often to be a mocking acceptance of Hippias' pun on the fine.

As Stallbaum points out, the article is not necessary. The *Hippias Major* is not the only dialogue to use sentences in the form "the *G* is *F*" without meaning that the *G* is an *F* thing. Stallbaum cites *Philebus* 11b4, and *Republic* 505c6; cf. *Phaedo* 77a4. We should add that self-predicative sentences, of the form "the *F* is *F,*" need not be understood as making the *F* an *F thing.* See Nehamas' account of self-predication (1979). On the strength of 297a3, ff., which will allow no other interpretation, I take sentences of the form, "the *F* is *G*," as meaning: "*to be F* is to be *G.*" That is just another way of saying that *F* things are *G* because (logically) they are *F.* See pp. 153–5.

Aristotle apparently alludes to the question of 293c8 at *Topics* 102a6 and concedes that it is a matter of definition. (The passage at *Topics* 135a13 has no clear connection with the *Hippias.* There Aristotle says that the fine and the appropriate are the same, and that the appropriate cannot therefore be a property of fine. He is making a distinction between properties and definitions which was not used in early Platonic works.)

117 | 293e9, "we'd better not be deceived": Keuls suggests that here and at 294a7 Plato alludes to the theory of Gorgias that it is wiser in a way to be deceived by the pleasure of words (DK 82 B23; Keuls, 1978, p. 127, n. 3). That would fit with the connection we have already drawn between Hippias and Gorgias (p. 122, n. 14). Hippias' answers, like the tragedy Gorgias praises, are meant more to give pleasure than to be true.

Here the partners take over the inquiry themselves, omitting to mention the Questioner until they try a fresh approach (298a7). See note 153.

118 | 294a1, "be seen to be fine": here, in view of Hippias' answer at 294a5, and Socrates' talk about deceit, this expression would appear to be used to mean "be *thought* to be fine." But the argument works on any interpretation of this phrase, for, as Socrates argues at 294cd, not everything fine is *plainly* fine; and 294c3–4 depends for its plausibility on the objective reading: "both be fine and be plainly fine." On the two readings, see note 80.

119 | 294b2, "the projecting": a major crux in interpreting the *Hippias Major* vis-à-vis the *Phaedo.* The problem is that though the style of this formulation fits Socrates' approach to logical causes in the *Phaedo,* the specific example seems unfortunate in view of *Phaedo* 102bc: "for I don't suppose Simmias naturally projects (over Socrates) by this, by being Simmias, but by the largeness he happens to have." How could the projecting be the logical cause of largeness, if largeness is the logical cause of the projecting? The *Phaedo* doctrine does not exclude that possibility. [Nothing in the doctrine of logical causes excludes reciprocal causation (see p. 73 and note 148). Fine things are good because they are fine, and *vice versa.* In such a case, however, it is simply not useful to identify reciprocal logical causes, unless you do so to someone who already knows how to tell when *one* of the two causes is present.]

Which passage comes first? The matter has been of considerable interest to athetizers. But since the two are compatible, and since neither appears to echo the other, I do not see that we have any evidence bearing on the question. Capelle (1956: 182) and Moreau (1954: 191) think the *Hippias* passage must be understood in terms of the *Phaedo*'s theory of transcendent Forms (and from this argue against the former dialogue's authenticity). But in fact neither passage presupposes the transcendence of Forms (p. 163 and p. 166). Soreth (1953: 43) argues that the *Hippias Major* here represents an earlier stage in Plato's thought; that, indeed, *the projecting* is just the sort of cause the *Phaedo* rejects. Her conclusion would be welcome, but her argument is unconvincing (Cherniss, 1959: 100).

120 | 294c3–4, "the appropriate makes things both be fine and be seen to be fine": Hippias embraces two uses of "appropriate," and tries to make the appropriate a cause of two different things. This, probably, is one of the ways in which he looks at "the entireties of things" and avoids cutting things up with words (301b, see p. 48).

"Appropriate" has been used in two sorts of examples:

1. At 290d it is used of plain utensils that are useful for making soup.
2. At 294a it is used of clothes that make a man look better than he is.

By the first usage, being appropriate made the spoon actually *be* fine. By the second usage, having appropriate clothes makes you *be seen to be* fine. Socrates used the word in the first way, Hippias in the second. (The example at 290c8, ff., may be taken either way. Hippias may think the presence of stone in the eyes makes the statues look better; Socrates may think that stone is more useful than gold for making statues' eyes.)

"when it's present": Hippias still has in mind the physical presence of one thing to another, in this case, the presence of clothes on a body (294a). Cf. note 85.

121 | 294c8–d5, that fineness is a matter of strife and contention: Cf. *Euthyphro* 7c10–d5. The parallel is striking, but gives no clues as to which passage echoes which. Probably this was a commonplace among sophists.

Note that Socrates here shifts examples on Hippias. Hippias was thinking of the fineness of good looks (294a); here Socrates clearly has in mind the fineness of morally improving practices.

122 | 294e3, "but by itself it could not make things be seen to be and be, nor could anything else": the best I can make of a corrupt text, following Soreth (1953: 35; cf. Capelle, 1956: 184). Burnet's reading is obviously impossible. I keep *poiein* and drop the *to* before *auto*. The point of the sentence, given by the solitary *auto,* is that one thing cannot *by itself* be the logical cause of two different things. Since being fine and appearing fine do not always occur in conjunction, they must be different things.

123 | 294e10, "I think that's very strange": Hippias showed no signs of surprise at his earlier defeats; he did not even acknowledge them (see n. 112). Now he is shaken. The appropriate would indeed be a satisfactory definition for the fine if the fine were understood as the *visibly* fine. Whatever is visibly fine is plainly fine as well. A good-looking boy is manifestly fine. Hippias is here betrayed by the range of *kalon* (see p. 110). He misses a fine opportunity here to give a partial or Gorgianic definition (p. 117). He could say that the appropriate is what makes things fine when good looks are in question, and be prepared to give other accounts for other contexts.

[7. The Able and Useful | 295a1–296d3]

Socrates' second proposal is that the useful (*to chrēsimon*) is fine (295c1). This he proceeds to gloss as *the able* (*to dunaton*—see note 134). The proposal seems to come out of the blue. What connection could it have with the preceding argument? The first Socratic proposal failed because Hippias used "appropriate" of the way things and people look, so that the appropriate was a cause of being seen to be, and not of being, fine (294a5, 294e6). The proposal would not have failed for that reason if understood Socrates' way. Socrates has been using "appropriate" as a synonym for "useful." This is clear from the example at 290e. So the first Socratic proposal served to disambiguate "appropriate" by fixing it to Hippias' usage, while the second takes up what Socrates had intended by "the appropriate" in the first place. (On Socrates' interest in the useful, and his doctrine that the fine is useful for good, see below, p. 183).

THE ARGUMENT. Here Socrates comes against the problem of incompleteness, which has before now been in the background. As there are many uses for things, so there would appear to be many ways of being useful, not all of them fine. The fine may indeed be useful, but useful for what?

The argument depends on glossing "useful" as "able," and then on taking "able" in the weak sense in which it is convertible with "can." A person *can* do either good or evil; so we may speak of the ability to do either. But then, if the fine is the able, "fine" will not be a term of commendation, as at the outset we assumed it to be. The proposed definition does not fail to satisfy the principles of definition (p. 149); but it cannot be the definition of a word that is rightly used to praise things (286cd, see

p. 182). Here as usual Socrates assumes that what he seeks to define is not just useful but beneficial (cf. *Charmides* 161a). Hippias brings this to the surface at 296d4, whereupon Socrates considers it as a proposed definition.

124 | 295a4, "I'm sure if I went off . . .": Cf. 297e1. As at the beginning (p. 49), Hippias is more interested in shaking off an awkward question than in answering it.

125 | 295a7, "Ah": See p. 99.

126 | 295b3, ". . . look for it with me . . .": Cf. *Protagoras* 348c5, ff. An answer Hippias found on his own would not satisfy Socrates unless he had a chance to question Hippias about it (295b6).

127 | 295c2, "let this be fine for us: whatever is useful": On the form, see note 116.

Cf. *Gorgias* 474d–e. Some athetizers claim the *Hippias* here borrows imperfectly from the *Gorgias*. But the *Hippias* passage is an improvement: it has the unity Socrates requires of definitions. See note 130, p. 117, and note 152 (c).

Note that the definition makes of "fine" an expression that is incomplete. For *what* are fine things supposed to be useful? Thrasymachus' criticism at *Republic* 336d suggests that Socrates was known for proposing such apparently incomplete definitions (see p. 187).

128 | 295c4–6, "We say eyes are fine not when . . . they're unable to see, but whenever they *are able,* and are useful for seeing": The argument rests on an implausible assumption. "Whenever" translates *hoi an* and so introduces a sufficient condition for the fineness of eyes: whenever they are able to see, they are fine. (If true, that supports the proposed definition on the additional assumption that being able is necessary for being useful. Otherwise, we could not be sure that every useful eye was fine.) But merely being *able* to see does not make eyes *kaloi* as that word was usually used. Ability to see is only a *necessary* condition for fineness; this condition Socrates correctly states in the negative clause ("not when . . . they're unable . . ."). For Socrates' eccentric usage of the word "fine," see Xenophon, *Symposium* v.5, where he contends (without persuading the audience) that his bulging eyes are finer (because more useful) than Critobulus' young straight ones. Eyes are not a persuasive example for Socrates' case here.

129 | 295d1, "fine horse, rooster, or quail": These animals were used, and useful, in sport, the roosters and quails for fighting, the horse for speed.

130 | 295d6, the list of fine useful things: a similar list and the idea behind it occur also in *Gorgias* 474d. See Dodds (1959, *ad loc.*). Horneffer, Röllig, Tarrant, and most recently Thesleff (1976: 113) believe the *Hippias* author borrowed the material from the *Gorgias*. Grube (1926B: 144–6) agrees with them that the *Hippias* develops an idea from the *Gorgias,* but attributes both to Plato. We have no way of establishing the order of composition of these passages, but Dodds (1959: 250) gives good reasons for supposing that the *Gorgias* presupposes the *Hippias* argument. The idea that all fine things were useful, and called fine for that reason, was widely associated with the historical Socrates (see p. 183).

131 | 295d6–e2, "In each case we look at the nature it's got, its manufacture, its condition; then we call what is useful 'fine' in respect of *the way* it is useful, *what* it is useful for, and *when* it is useful; but anything useless in all those respects we call 'foul' ": Here Socrates recognizes various ways in which predications of "fine" must be completed. The three ways correspond roughly to the three answers Hippias gave in the first stage of the search. The girl was fine *as* a girl; gold is fine *for* parts of a statue; burying your parents is *sometimes* fine. Such things are said to be fine *with qualifications*. He does not say here what we know he believes (from Stage One): that none of these things is *strictly* fine. (See p. 48).

". . . anything useless in all those respects we call 'foul' ": This could mean either (1) useless in every way, for every purpose, and at every time; or (2) useless in all three of the respects mentioned (i.e., useless at some time, in some way, for some purpose). Symmetry with Socrates' account of "fine" requires the second reading.

132 | 295e5–6, "Then are we right to say now that the useful more than anything turns out to be fine?": *not* "turns out to be more fine than anything." "More than anything" (*pantos mȃllon*) governs "turns out to be," not "fine." Socrates is saying that the examples of 295d show that the useful—more than anything else—is what makes things fine. "The useful is fine" should be read, "useful things are fine insofar as they are useful." For the form of this sentence, see note 116 and p. 153.

133 | 295e7, "able": *dunatos*. The word means both "able" and "powerful." Similarly, *dunamis* (295e9) is both ability and power, depending on context. At 296a2 Hippias speaks of political ability.

134 | 295e7–9, "So what's able to accomplish a particular thing is useful for that for which it is able; and what's unable is useless": Socrates' argument requires him to establish that whatever is able in a given respect is useful in that respect. Then, since some things are able to do ill, some things will be useful for ill.

This assumption (that ability is sufficient for usefulness) would carry Socrates' argument, but it does not bear examination:

(i) "So" (*oukoûn*) represents the assumption as the conclusion of an inference. But no such inference has been warranted. The eye example at 295c4–5 presupposed correctly that ability is *necessary* for usefulness (see note 128); perhaps Socrates has mistaken a necessary for a sufficient condition.

(ii) "Able" has the sense "powerful" in political contexts (note 133); but powerful men are not necessarily useful even to themselves (cf. *Republic* 339c, ff.).

(iii) A person who can err is indeed *able* to err; but he is hardly useful for erring. "Useful," in English as in Greek, is reserved for things that can at least be thought to be beneficial.

Still, the worst we can say about Socrates' argument is that it is exaggerated. "Useful" is incomplete, and whether or not being useful is fine depends on how "useful" is completed in the context. If it is completed here with "for good," then Socrates has a new and more precise definition proposal: that the beneficial is fine.

135 | 296a5, "wisdom is the finest thing of all": a well-known Socratic theme. Cf. *Euthydemus* 281e. Here Socrates no doubt intends to play on the range of *sophia*, which extends from skill (part of ability) to philosophical wisdom.

136 | 296b1–2, "Why should you be frightened now? The discussion has gone really well for you this time": Not only has Socrates answered the question, but he has done so in a way that strongly recommends the profession of *sophia* ("wisdom"). Hippias speaks as if Socrates too were a sophist. On Hippias' lack of anxiety here, see p. 125. (The theme of quietness here picks up 295a4.)

137 | 296c1, "by ability": The construction is the dative associated with logical causation (cf. 287cd and p. 151).

138 | 296c5, "—and make mistakes unintentionally": Socrates is supposed to have believed that no one makes mistakes intentionally. Tarrant suggests that this and the line at 296b7 ("even when they do it unintentionally") were added to make the argument harmonize with Socratic doctrine (1928: *ad loc.*). She is probably right; but such an addition is no sign of inauthenticity.

[8. The Beneficial | 296d4–297d9]

Hippias makes a promising suggestion (as at 290d5–6), and by a simple qualification renders Socrates' last proposal highly plausible: the fine is what is able and useful to do good. In a word, the fine is the beneficial.

This account of the fine, though promptly and decisively rejected, is made to appear the best and most Socratic of all the bad answers. The best that can be said for several of the bad answers is that they lead naturally to saying that the fine is the beneficial. That account of the fine is recapitulated at 303e, as necessary medicine for the last failing answer. The same account is suggested, moreover, by three earlier discussions. The trouble with gold was that it is not always beneficial (290e); similar trouble plagued the appropriate (294e) and the able-and-useful (296cd).

Should we infer that this is therefore the right answer, the one Socrates himself believed? On this question, see p. 183, ff. Socrates probably believed that all and only fine things are beneficial, but not that being beneficial is what makes them fine. (Cf. *Euthyphro* 11a, where *being god-loved* is accepted as true of piety, but is rejected as a definition because it does not state the essence [*ousia*] of piety.)

Socrates would have been right to reject the proposed definition, and the *Hippias Major* clearly represents him doing so. The argument he gives is sound (see below) and transparent. No irony warns us to look for a fallacy. We may, however, draw an interesting contrast between this and the previous argument. Above, at 296d1–2, Socrates simply *denied* a proposed definition. Here we are told only that the definition is "not the finest . . . , but more laughable" than certain predecessors. Why does this typically Hippian antithesis stop short of denial? The answer is probably that Socrates considered the formula "the fine is *the* beneficial" to be *true* if taken as a biconditional, but not if taken as a definition. The expression is true, that is, but cannot be accepted as an answer to Socrates' question (see note 149). Such an answer would turn out to be circular on the deepest analysis, for it would define the fine as a productive cause of fine things. But that, of course, would be uninformative. Socrates does not yet know how to tell what sorts of things are fine.

THE ARGUMENT (296d4–297d9). The argument against the proposal is startlingly brief and ambiguously expressed. Each premise allows more interpretations than it is worth my while to record. I therefore offer here an interpretation that makes the argument work and fortunately also makes tolerably good sense of some very awkward Greek. I warn the reader that my account is speculative, and that its main support is the pragmatic principle of charity.

The argument is a *reductio ad absurdum*. It derives from the proposed definition, together with supporting premises, a conclusion that is unacceptable. It would fail if the conclusion were really acceptable, or if one of the supporting premises were false, or if the reasoning were invalid. Most commentators think the argument a failure. Guthrie calls it a "barefaced sophism" (1975: 186). Moreau (1941: 35–37) thinks the *Hippias* author leaves clues that this is a deliberate fallacy. But Socrates quite definitely rejects the definition. Hippias readily agrees, and makes no objection to Socrates' decisive summing up: "Then it doesn't turn out to be the finest account, as we thought a moment ago, that the beneficial—the useful and able for making some good—is fine. It's not that way at all, but if possible *it's more laughable than the first accounts . . .*" (297d). We should try to track down an interpretation that supports Socrates on that.

Here is an uninterpreted skeleton of the argument:

1. The fine is the beneficial (296e5).
2. The fine is a cause of the good (297a1).
3. A cause and a thing that it causes are different things. (Summary of 297a2–b1).

---

4. The fine is not good and . . .
5. . . . the good is not fine (297c3–4).

[The apparent fallacy is equivocation. Steps 4 and 5 (the conclusion) have the unacceptability Socrates wants if they mean: "the fine is not a good thing, and the good is not a fine thing." That would be a natural translation for 297c3–4, but it does not appear to be a logical consequence of Step 3. Step 3 correctly implies that if the fine is a cause of the good, then the fine and the good are *not identical*. Socrates apparently has confused two senses of "different" (*allo*): "not identical" for Step 3 and "lacking the quality of" for the suppressed argument leading from Step 3 to Steps 4 and 5. That is the fallacy diagnosed by Tarrant (1928: *ad loc.;* cf. Irwin, 1977: 323, n. 56).]

I shall develop the argument step by step.

Step 2 explicates the proposed definition: "the fine is a cause of the good." "Cause" here is not used not for "logical cause" (as at 299e4), but for "productive cause" (as at 297b5—see note 140). And the example at 297b4 (*phronēsis*) shows that Socrates intends "the fine" to range over fine things. Step 2 must therefore entail: 2a. *"Anything fine is a productive cause of something good."* But 2a does not give the full sense of Step 2, for Step 2 was supposed to state a definition, and 2a is not in the right form for that. Also, if 2a were substituted for Step 2, the conclusion would not be obtainable. The only satisfactory interpretation of Step 2 is: 2b "To be fine is to be a productive cause of something good." This states at least part of what it is to be fine. It is, in fact, a strict predication (p. 153 ff. and note 116). What it means is that any fine thing produces good *insofar* as it is fine.

Step 3 requires an interpretation along the same lines. It is established by the example at 297b9–c1: "the father is not a son and the son is not a father." This cannot mean that a father is not identical with *his* son; for that Socrates would have used a definite article with "son." Nor can it mean that no father is a son; that would be outrageously false. The absence of an article is a clue to the correct reading: it is not the case that to be a father is to be a son (i.e., being a son is no part of what it is to be a father).* That is a true example to illustrate Step 3. Step 3 (as I therefore propose to read it) says that being an effect is no part of being a cause (see note 142): 3a. "If to be *F* is to be a productive cause of something *G,* then it is not the case that to be *F* is to be *G.*"

Now, at the risk of causing confusion, I must introduce the notion of logical causation (p. 151). Sentences of the form "the *F* is *G*" entail that the *F* is a logical cause (but not necessarily *the* logical cause—see p. 262) of being *G.* So 2b entailed that being fine logically makes things producers of good;† and 3a entails that a logical cause of producing good cannot itself be good. Why? Socrates presents Step 3 as obvious, and Hippias accepts it easily. Its intuitive basis is simply the difference between cause and effect. But at a deeper level it depends on the rules of Socratic definition. If being a son actually were part of being a father, then being a father would *make you* (logically) both a father *and* a son; and *one* logical cause would be related to two different things, which is impossible. You cannot be different sorts of things in virtue of the same logical cause. (Cf. 294e with note 122 and *Phaedo* 101a7). Moreover, if being a son simply were what it is to be a father (as being good seems to be what it is to be fine—note 142), then a Step-2 style definition of *father* would be circular: to be a father would be to be the cause of a father (for then "father" could be substituted in intentional contexts for "son"). By the same token, you could not define the good as the cause of the good, or the fine as the cause of the fine.

Step 4 follows from 3a and the proposed definition: 4a. "It is not the case that to be fine is to be good." (For otherwise one logical cause would work in two ways: making things good and making things productive causes of good.)

Step 5 must be obtained separately, by a parallel argument that is easily supplied.

---

*This is consistent with the fact that every father is a son. A fatherless father (like the Judaic God) could turn up without forcing us to change the definition of what it is to be a father.

†The proposed definition makes the fine and the beneficial logical causes of each other. This reciprocity is no problem for Socrates. (See note 119.)

But why should Hippias and Socrates agree emphatically that these conclusions are not acceptable? What makes them unacceptable? They imply that being good is no part of being fine, and *vice versa*. But "fine" (*kalon*) is the most general term of commendation; being good must be at least part of being fine. Fineness and goodness are too intimately connected for the one to be defined as the cause of the other. Part of a satisfactory definition of the fine must be that being fine is *in itself* a good thing to be. But the proposed definition excluded that.

Hippias may or may not understand the argument. If he does, his commitment to "naturally continuous bodies of being" (301b6) would probably bar him from dividing the fine from the good. So he could not maintain the proposed definition by accepting Steps 4 and 5 (the conclusions Socrates intended to be unpalatable). If he is at all confused, he would understand Steps 4 and 5 in the most natural way: the fine is not a good thing and the good is not a fine thing. Understood in such a way, the conclusions would be clearly impossible; that they would not follow from the premises may have escaped Hippias' notice. Hippias is probably a victim here of his own weapon, a play on words, for the ambiguity of the conclusion allows the argument to appear at the same time plainly valid, and yielding a plainly false conclusion.

Though the *reductio* is sound, it depends on a hidden premise, Socrates' assumption that to be fine is to be good. This is so reasonable an assumption that we cannot blame Socrates for not stating it. Nor can we blame him for not stating the conclusion precisely. Socrates surely believed that fine things are beneficial (i.e., productive causes of good things —p. 183, ff.), and his argument allows him to maintain that belief. In a sense, "the fine is a cause of the good" is a true sentence—true, that is, if it is not taken as part of a definition of the fine. Socrates should have said that the proposal was true, but not a definition. (For the difference, see note 149.) He was wise, however, not to say such a thing to Hippias. For Hippias would not have allowed himself to recognize so subtle a difference.

139 | 296d8, "what our mind wanted to say": cf. 300c10. Grube cites *Symposium* 192c7 and *Republic* 365a6 as evidence that the language is Platonic (1926B: 138).

140 | 296d9, "for making some good": for producing some good. Cf. *Gorgias* 474d, with notes 127 and 152c. The Greek word translated "making" here is used differently for what I have called *logical* causation (e.g., at 290d2, see p. 151). The issue here is whether being *productive* of good can be the *logical* cause of the fine.

On the distinction between logical and productive causes, see p. 152. That Socrates has productive, but not efficient, causation in mind at 296d9, *etc.*, is clear from the examples at 297b: the causal relationship between father and son is productive, not logical. Moreover, if the causal relationship of 297a2–b1 (= Step 3) were logical, the premise would be unwarrantable. For, trivially, a thing can be its own logical cause: the fine is fine, and fine things are fine because they are fine (287c9).

We cannot know that Socrates or Plato was clear on the distinction. But here at least the argument does not stumble or equivocate on the various uses of "to make" and "cause."

141 | 296e9, "the maker is . . . the cause": See *Philebus* 26e7, "the maker and the cause would rightly be called one." The thought is obvious enough that neither passage need be taken as an echo of the other. The same goes for 297a6 with *Philebus* 27a8–9. But see note 152.

142 | 297a3, "I don't suppose the cause would be a cause of a cause": Most translators supply a definite article for the predicate: "I don't suppose the cause would be a cause of *the* cause" (understand: "a cause of itself"). But if Plato had meant that he would have said it. It would not, in any case, have any role in the argument. (But see note 143.)

A second possible reading is simply false—that a cause cannot be the cause of another cause. For surely many products do turn out to be causes of still further products.

The third possibility must be right: *to be* a (productive) cause is not to be a cause of a cause. For example, to be a father is not to be a father of a father, but to be a father of a child. Generally, "the *F* is *G*" in Plato means that the *F* is a logical cause of being *G* (p. 155). So the point is that being a productive cause does not make you the cause of something that is *itself* productive. Some sons, for good or ill, do not produce offspring; but their fathers are productive causes nonetheless.

On the omission of the article see note 116.

143 | 297a5–6, "the thing that comes to be [is] not *the* maker": Contrast 297a3 and 297c2 where the definite article is significantly omitted. The argument requires, however, that the thought be the same. So if 297a5–6 meant that the maker is not identical with his product, then the same sort of meaning should be read into the other passages. But then the argument would fail: Socrates could show only that each fine thing is nonidentical with the good thing it produces; but no awkward result follows from that for the intimacy of the fine with the good.

Accordingly, I propose (on grounds of charity) to read 297a5–6 as denying that it is the same thing *to be* the one that makes and *to be* the one that comes to be. This would naturally be said, as here, with the definite article in both positions.

144 | 297b2, "the good should come to be from the fine": Socrates concludes here, in effect, that no good thing comes to be unless a fine thing produces it. That, he conjectures, is why fine things are desirable. This is surprising, for we would suppose there can be several ways to produce the same result. Apparently Socrates conceives of productive causation biologically: there is only one way to produce a human being—from a father.

145 | 297b5, "their child—the good": The idea that the good is a child of something is supposed either to anticipate (so Friedländer, 1964: II, 111) or to be a reminiscence of (so Tarrant, 1928: *ad loc.*; and Thesleff, 1976: 109) the transcendental metaphysics of the *Republic,* where the sun is represented as a *child* of the good (506e). Cf. *Timaeus* 50d. But no connection of either kind is probable. The *Republic* casts the good as the father, not the son; and in any case the hypothesis illustrated in the *Hippias* with the father-son analogy is decisively rejected, unlike the famous theory illustrated in that manner in the *Republic.*

146 | 297b6, "is formally a kind of father": *en patros tinos ideai einai,* more literally, "is in the form of a kind of father." An unusual occurrence of the word usually translated "form." Similar usages occur at *Timaeus* 30c4 and in Speusippus, Fr. 40 (Lang). See Moreau, 1941: 34.

147 | 297c1, "the father is not a son, and the son is not a father": Understand as: "to be a father is not to be a son, and to be a son is not to be a father." See notes 143 and 144, and p. 72. The other possibilities are (1) "No father is identical with his son" (trivial and irrelevant); and (2) "no father is a son" (false).

148 | 297c4, "Then the fine is not good nor the good fine": To make the argument work we must understand this so that (a) it follows from the premises, and (b) it is obviously unacceptable (so that the argument will derive an absurdity from the proposal). The main alternative interpretations are: (1) "The fine is not identical with the good" (cf. alternative 1 in note 147). This would not follow from the examples unless further understood as "nothing fine is identical with its good product." But that would not be objectionable. (2) "Nothing fine is good." This would be objectionable, but does not follow from the examples, unless 297c1 is understood as making the false claim that no father is a son. (3) "To be fine is not to be good," i.e., the fine is not a logical cause of things' being good, and fine things are not made good *by being* fine. (a) This follows from the premises by Step 3 (p. 73). If being fine makes you productive of good, then it cannot also make you good, since being good and being productive of good are two different things. Similarly, being a father cannot make you both a son and a producer of a son. (b) The conclusion is objectionable to Socrates on interpretation (3) if Socrates does believe that the fine and the good are logical causes of each other (as appears to be the case, p. 188). If they are, then the fine and the good amount to the same thing, and the proposed definition is uninformative (through circularity).

149 | 297d6, "more laughable than the first accounts": For the general defects of the first accounts, see p. 48. Socrates' point here is that the present proposal has a more objectionable consequence than did the earlier ones. They merely made such things as fine girls fine when strictly they are not; but the present account would keep the fine from being good, thus undermining the point of Socrates' search (p. 182).

Note that the conclusion here is consistent with Socrates' holding that all and only fine things are beneficial (the biconditional thesis). The problem with the proposed definition was that it would, with the assumption unearthed in note 148, make the fine a logical cause of both being good and of being productive of good; but those, being different, require different logical causes. No such problem arises for the biconditional thesis: from "all fine things are beneficial" we are not entitled to infer that the fine is the logical cause (i.e., that being fine *makes* things beneficial).

150 | 297d8, "each one of those things mentioned earlier": This probably refers narrowly to Hippias' answers. "Each one" (*hekaston hen*) recalls Hippias' habit of mentioning one among many fine things each time he answered. The earlier proposals of stage two ("the appropriate," "the useful") may be subsumed by Socrates under the present account of the fine as the beneficial; each of them is taken by Socrates as an unsuccessful attempt to state this present proposal (296d8, cf. p. 67).

[9. Aesthetic Pleasure | 297d10–303d10]

Socrates' last failure, he says, has left him stymied. But he quickly produces an unexpected definition for the fine: it is what is pleasant through sight (as in the case of paintings) and through hearing (as in the case of music). Though Socrates draws no connection between this and the preceding definition, the one follows naturally from the failure of the other. The fine could not be what is productive of *good,* because the good really is what we are seeking to define. If the fine is to be explained in terms of what it produces, what it produces must be something we can describe in value-free terms. What more obvious tack than to make the utilitarianism suggested by the previous proposal explicit, and to say that the fine is what produces *pleasure?* That is defensible, of course, only if Socrates excludes the obviously foul forms of pleasure, like that of making love (299a). [Socrates' record elsewhere on pleasure suggests that he would not take the Questioner's radical hint at 298de, and define the fine simply as what produces pleasure (*Gorgias* 499c6–7 and *Phaedo* 68e). For a defense of the unusual position that Socrates *was* a hedonist, see Irwin, 1977, p. 103, ff.] So Socrates gives a list: the fine is pleasure through sight *and* pleasure through hearing.

Definitions in this multiple form had been given before, most famously by Gorgias (reported at *Meno* 71e, see p. 117). I shall call them *Gorgian* definitions. The idea behind them is that a term must be defined in different ways for different contexts. The courage of a woman would be one thing and defined in one way; the courage of a man would be defined in another. Gorgian definition makes no attempt to link the different usages of a word but treats it as simply homonymous in different contexts. Socrates now considers a pair of Gorgian definitions for the fine: in the case of paintings and other visible objects, it is what gives pleasure through sight; in the case of music and other audible things, it is what gives pleasure through hearing.

Socrates' argument against these definitions is long, complex, and unsatisfactory. A propounder of Gorgian definitions cannot be refuted except by begging the question against him, that is, by assuming that there is a single definition for the fine. But a propounder of Gorgian definitions assumes the contrary.

The argument's most interesting feature is its lengthy digression, in which Hippias is provoked for the first time to take a stand on a philosophical issue, and is demolished by Socrates.

Plato concludes the *Hippias Major* with a dramatic interchange in which Hippias advises Socrates to exchange philosophy for oratory, while Socrates ironically bewails his own ignorance and the abuse heaped on him (he claims) from all sides. We are left to ask what has been accomplished by pursuing Socrates' question to this bitter end.

THE ARGUMENT (297d10–303d10). At issue is the *unity* of definition (discussed in Chapter Six). We know that the fine is supposed to be the logical cause that makes *every* fine thing fine (287c9, cf. 288a10–11, and below, p. 156). Now the question is whether that logical cause is one and the same in every instance, or a composite of different causes for different sorts of instance. Aristotle takes on the same problem, using the same example, in the *Topics*. Though elements of the argument are probably borrowed from the *Hippias Major* (note 152), the result is more blatantly question-begging than is the *Hippias* argument. Aristotle's case against the proposed definition is that it leads to contradiction (*Topics* 146a21, ff.):

1. The fine is what is pleasant through sight or what is pleasant through hearing. (See note 154.)
2. The opposites of things that are the same are the same.
3. The opposite of "fine" is "not fine"; the opposite of "pleasant through hearing" is "not pleasant through hearing."
4. (From *1*) "Pleasant through hearing" is the same as "fine."
5. (From *3* and *4*) "Not pleasant through hearing" is the same as "not fine."
6. Whatever is pleasant through sight but not pleasant through hearing is fine (from *1*) and not fine (from *5*).

Aristotle's mistake is inferring Step *4* from the definition. The definition implies that being pleasant through hearing is one way of being fine, not *the* way of being fine. Step *4* should be revised to yield:

4a. "Pleasant through hearing or pleasant through sight" is the same as "fine."

From this we may harmlessly conclude:

5a. "Not pleasant through sight and not pleasant through hearing" is the same as "not fine."

Aristotle thinks Step *4* follows from the definition, presumably because he thinks that *any* definiens exhaustively defines its definiendum. But here we are given two definientes. The contradiction follows from the hypothesis that either exhaustively defines the definiendum. But what is at issue (as Aristotle is well aware) is whether two things taken separately can comprise a definition. In effect, Aristotle begs the question by assuming the unity of definition in inferring Step *4* from the definition.

Socrates' argument in the *Hippias Major* is more subtle and persuasive but ultimately begs the same question. He derives a relevant special case of the unity of definition from a general rule about "both" and "each," a rule established (wrongly, as it turns out) in the long excursus in which Hippias takes a stand. In setting out the skeleton of Socrates' argument, I observe these conventions: "pleasure through sight" becomes "pleasure^s" and "pleasure through hearing" becomes "pleasure^h."

1. To be fine is to be productive of pleasure^s (for visible objects) and to be productive of pleasure^h (for audible objects).
2. Whatever is not productive of pleasure^s or of pleasure^h is not fine (299c1–2, from *1,* on the assumption that it exhaustively defines the fine).

3. If both of any pair are *G,* then each of that pair is *G;* and if each of any pair is *G,* then both of that pair are *G* (where *G* ranges over a set of attributes including that of being fine). (This rule, hereafter BE—for "both" and "each"—is implied at 302b4 and stated firmly at 303c.)

4. Both and each of the pair (pleasure[s], pleasure[h]) are/is fine. (From *1* and *3,* e.g., at 302d1.)

5. The same logical cause makes both and each of the pair (pleasure[s], pleasure[h]) to be fine. (From *4* and the unity of definition.)

6. Being productive of pleasure through sight *and* hearing would make both *but not each* of the pair in question fine (obvious, at 302e).

7. Being productive of pleasure through sight and hearing is not what makes both kinds of pleasure fine. (From *5* and *6,* at 303d.)

Step *6* is misleading, since the definition proposed not one but two logical causes. The point stands nonetheless, for neither cause would make *both* and *each* of the pair fine. Step *5* is a special case of the principle of the unity of definition. It stands here not on its own, but as a purported consequence of the general rule governing "both" and "each" (BE). Hippias asserted the rule for any attribute whatever; but Socrates, in the excursus, narrowed its range to a list of attributes including that of being fine. We have to ask whether BE is true, and if not, whether Step *5* could be warranted independently (see note 170).

151 | 297e1, "a little while ago": 295a3, ff. Hippias tries again to put an end to Socrates' line of questioning.

152 | 297e6, "If whatever makes us be glad, not with all the pleasures, but just through hearing and sight—if we call *that* fine . . .": This seventh and last proposal has parallels in other texts:

a. Aristotle, *Topics* 146a21, ff. (see p. 78). Aristotle uses a simplified form of this argument to illustrate a point. Aristotle appears to be following the *Hippias* here; for if the *Hippias* author had read Aristotle, he would probably have been clearer in laying out the argument. In particular, he would have revised the refutandum to read ". . . through hearing *or* sight. . . ."

b. *Philebus* 51a, ff., distinguishes certain pleasures of sight and hearing, along with certain other pleasures, as pure; and it calls the sights and sounds it picks out "fine." The *Philebus'* distinction is more sophisticated and more clearly justified than the *Hippias'* crude division of visual and auditory pleasures from the rest. The most likely explanation for this is that the *Philebus* was written after the *Hippias,* which is possible even if a student of Plato wrote the *Hippias* (so Thesleff, 1976: 114). We cannot exclude, however, the unlikely possibility urged by other athetizers that the *Hippias* author crudely parodied the *Philebus* to point up Hippias' gullibility. Hippias has already been made to accept absurdities (note 6).

c. *Gorgias* 474d, ff. In an argument with Polus, Socrates takes the fine to be the pleasant or the beneficial. The argument makes no use of the account of the fine as the pleasant; in any case, the *Gorgias* account is not in the correct form to be a definition (note 127). The passages, therefore, have little in common and afford no clue on this score as to which echoes which (but see note 130).

153 | 298a5, "that tough man": The Questioner emerges again in the discussion. He has been ignored since 293e9, when Socrates and Hippias undertook to examine the Questioner's proposal on their own. The intervening argumentation has a certain unity (see note 150) and is technical in ways that would make the intrusion of the Questioner unbearably complex.

154 | 298a7, "the fine is what is pleasant through hearing and sight": Aristotle uses "or" where the *Hippias* uses "and," but the two come to the same. The present proposal is that being pleasant through sight is fine [for visible things] *and* being pleasant through hearing is fine [for audible things]. Aristotle's "or" makes the proposal look more like a definition; the *Hippias'* "and" emphasizes its disunity from the start.

155 | 298b5, "Those things might slip right past the man": Hippias, as we have noted, is more interested in evading the question than in finding an answer (p. 125). Cf. note 49.

156 | 298b9, ". . . when I'm not saying anything": Cf. 298d1. To say nothing is to speak false. The generic sophist pretends to say something but says nothing; that is Plato's complaint against him in the *Sophist,* and the origin of that dialogue's treatment of the problem of not-being (234c, 236d–237a).

157 | 298c1, "Sophroniscus' son": Socrates. By this time Hippias must know who the Questioner is (p. 108, see note 173). This personal Questioner is reminiscent of Socrates' *daimonion* (*Apology* 40a); but the Questioner, unlike the *daimonion,* has a great deal more to say than "no." Either, however, would prevent Socrates from declaring that he knew something he did not know.

158 | 298c4, "something else in the case of the laws": See note 91.

159 | 298d3, "in the case of laws and activities, those could easily be seen not to be outside the perception we have through hearing and sight": fine laws and the like could be fine in virtue of producing pleasures of sight and sound. (Stallbaum unnecessarily deleted the "not.")

160 | 298e8, "would you strip them of this word": This word apparently is "fine."

161 | 299b3, "our hypothesis": Cf. 302e12 and *Phaedo* 100a3, ff. Socrates' governing hypothesis, here as in the *Phaedo,* is that all fine things are fine by the fine. Here Socrates' hypothesis is the definition-proposal. For a different use of "hypothesis," see *Meno* 86e3.

162 | 299b6, "in view of what's been said": Nothing at all has been said to support this. Is Hippias lamely trying to parody Socrates' style?

163 | 299c2, "whatever is not pleasant in that way clearly would not be fine": does not follow unless the protasis is understood as, "to be pleasant through sight and hearing is *what it is to be* fine." Cf. my note 116, but observe that here the strict predication is supposed to be *exhaustive.* Only the present subject is said to be strictly fine. (See Nehamas, 1979).

164 | 299d2–6, "does one pleasant thing differ from another in *this:* in being pleasant?": Cf. *Philebus* 12d8–e2: "For how could pleasure be not most like pleasure?" On the parallel, see Thesleff, 1976: 114, and above, note 152(b).

165 | 299d9, "quality": *toiouton ti.* Plato has yet to invent the word usually translated "quality" (*poiotēs, Theaetetus* 182a8). The absence of that word here, where it would be useful, supports a relatively early date for the *Hippias Major* (p. 93).

166 | 299e1, "by looking at that": Cf. *Euthyphro* 6e4 and above, 295d6.

167 | 299e5, "if that were the cause": Here is the critical turn of this argument. Earlier proposals failed because none could state *a* logical cause of things' being fine. This proposal will fail because it cannot state *the* logical cause for that. See p. 156.

168 | 300a10, "that common thing": *to koinon touto.* Tarrant finds this objectionably vague (1928: *ad loc.*). Certainly, Socrates has not faced the ontological issues raised by this. See below, p. 166.

169 | 300b4, "if something is attributed to both": literally, "if both have suffered (*peponthasin*) something." *Pathos* and its verbal cognate are used loosely in the sense of "attribute" throughout this context. Note the pun at 301a2: suffer tribulation—have an attribute (*peponthōs-peponthoimen*).

170 | 300b6–302b6, Hippias takes a stand: probably the earliest treatment of the problem about how a whole can have different properties from its parts. Cf. *Theaetetus* 201d8, ff. (the "dream") for a discussion of a more sophisticated version of the problem. Aristotle is aware of the problem, and diagnoses it correctly as due to an ambiguity in words like "both" and "all" (*Politics* 1261b27–30—where his choice of examples suggests familiarity with this part of the *Hippias Major*).

So far Hippias has avoided open disagreement with Socrates. Now, sure of his ground and at the end of his patience, the worm turns. No longer caring to be insulated from him by the Questioner, Hippias takes a stand against Socrates himself. Hippias has said it is impossible for neither of a pair to have an attribute possessed by both (300b6–8). When Socrates said he thought maybe he saw some exceptions to that rule, Hippias replied that Socrates is "readily mis-seeing" (300c7–8). This, his first testy answer to Socrates' *propria persona*, implies that Socrates is perversely *trying* to see things wrong (so Grube, 1926B: 139). Now Hippias takes a firm stand on the issue, and challenges Socrates to find a counterexample (300d5–8). Socrates coyly holds his fire, giving Hippias plenty of time to dig himself into the position. Then Socrates makes it look ridiculous.

The issue is this: must each and both of any pair have exactly the same attributes? Hippias says they must. Socrates has counterexamples in mind: when he reveals them, finally, Hippias is forced to agree that though some attributes are shared by both and each of a pair, others are not (302b4). But Socrates and Hippias easily agree that being fine is one of those things that is shared by both and each (302d1), and that both and each are made fine (if they are fine) by the same logical cause.

Socrates and Hippias have divided attributes into two categories, according to the way they are supposed to be used with "both" and "each." On the one hand are *golden, sick, great, fine,* and so forth, which they believe are shared always between both and each of a pair. On the other are *one-in-number, odd-numbered, irrational-numbered,* and the like, which are not necessarily to be shared between both and each. This division of attributes, though not arbitrary, is not the right solution to Socrates' problem of "both" and "each." Socrates has not stopped to consider the various jobs to which "both" can be put. When "both" is used of two things severally, both of a pair will always have the attributes of each. (Hippias is using "both" that way; and "both" is naturally so used in the context of attributes from the shared list.) But when "both" is used of two things collectively, or in some combination or arrangement, we cannot be sure that both will have the attributes of each. (Again, in the context of numerical attributes, we tend to use "both" in this way, to collect or combine a pair of things.)

Hippias and Socrates are wrong about their categories.* Two men may each be weak, but both strong together (if they work together); yet *weak* and *strong* should be on the shared list. *Fine* is on the shared list, but

---

Pace Gadamer, who finds the categorial distinction useful (1980: 132, ff.).

the parts of a two-piece Henry Moore sculpture may each be ugly, and still be fine in combination. So attributes on the first list are not necessarily shared by both and each of a pair, depending on how "both" is understood. Again, on a certain interpretation of "both," even attributes on the second list must be shared by both and each of a pair. Hippias and Socrates are each one-in-number; it follows that they are both (severally) one-in-number. (Socrates must believe that "both" in numerical contexts carries with it the idea of addition or multiplication, but he is not explicit. For the question about addition and multiplication, see De Strycker, 1937 and 1941, with my note 187).

Socrates' general rule is incorrect; but the argument of this section depends on it (p. 80). If both of a pair are said to be fine, we cannot safely infer that each is fine as well. Let us return to the argument to see if it can be justified without that rule (BE, p. 80). Step 4 (that both and each of the two kinds of pleasure are/is fine) is acceptable. If pleasures are pleasant, it should follow that each and both (severally) of the two kinds of pleasure are fine, according to the proposed definition. Step 5 is another matter. Socrates wants to show that the two kinds of pleasure are fine (if they are fine) in virtue of having the same attribute, in virtue, that is, of one and the same logical cause. But that cannot be derived from the logic of "both" and "each." A fine day and a fine edge, to use an English example, are fine in virtue of very different logical causes. The question is whether in truth it is exactly one thing to be fine, and that cannot be settled in this way, by appealing to the logic of "both" and "each."

Socrates may be supposing that if *both* ways of being pleasant exhaustively define the fine, then *each* way of being pleasant should exhaustively define the fine as well, according to the rule BE. That supposition would explain Aristotle's illegitimate move (Step 4, p. 79), and could also stand behind Socrates' insistence that there be one logical cause, the same in each part of the definition and in the whole. Of course, the failure of BE would undermine that.

For his error Socrates has the authority of Hippias, who asserted BE without qualification (300b). Socrates may be using the fallacy deliberately to make a fool of Hippias. But neither he nor the author shows any sign that he is aware of the trouble.

In Socrates' defense, we may say that a word like *kalos* ought to mean the same thing every time it is used. Its use in the variety of contexts in which it is used does not seem to be an accident of historical linguistics. The word is used in each case for a reason, and it ought to be the same sort of reason. How are we to explain the apparent unity of *kalos*' meaning, when the word seems to scatter its meaning in different contexts? (See below, p. 110). Socrates' hypothesis is that what conects the various uses of *kalos* is a character or form, the *kalon* which occurs in every *kalon* thing and makes that thing *kalon*. That is fine for a working hypothesis. But Socrates would have to concede that the failure of his search for the fine casts doubt on his assumptions.

171 | 300d1, "since you're a man who's made the most money": Cf. 283b3.

172 | 301b2–301c3, Hippias' complaint: Cf. 304a4–304b6, and *Hippias Minor* 369b8–369c8. See Diès (1927, pp. 187–202) for a thorough discussion of the passage (in the context of a refutation of the madcap theory of Dupréel). The irony here is that it is Hippias who makes many out of one (see note 91, p. 125 and p. 174). What is it to look at the entireties of things? Hippias does not say. For some possibilities, see above, p. 48, p. 74, note 78, and note 120.

173 | 301b3, "the people you're used to talking with": Who are they? Hippias seems to have some experience of Socrates and his method, and no doubt knew Socrates' regular companions. But we do not know how far any of them aped Socrates' style. Most likely Hippias means Socrates' Questioner here by "the people." Either he still does not know the identity of the Questioner, or he is maintaining the fiction. At the end, this wears thin; in his final outburst against Socrates/the Questioner, he alternates between the second and third person (304ab). (Cf. Socrates' use of "we" at 301, presumably for himself and the Questioner: "What *we* had in mind.")

174 | 301b5, "cutting it up with words": In view of the parallels at 304a and *Hippias Minor* 369bc, Hippias' general complaint is that Socrates prefers scrappy question-and-answer to a dignified *agōn* of speech set beside speech. In the immediate context Hippias is complaining that Socrates cuts "each" off from "both." But Hippias must also be lamenting the fate of his fine girl and other answers. Socrates made fun of them by taking them out of (cutting them off from) the contexts in which they were fine (see p. 48). (Parallel language occurs at *Theaetetus* 154e2–3, of sophistic word-fights.)

175 | 301b7, "naturally continuous bodies of being": The word for "continuous" (*dianekē*) is not a Doric form, as claimed by those who wish to find Hippias' own words here (so Cherniss, 1973, p. 200, n. 3, against Tarrant *ad loc.,* 1928). This passage gives us no reason to attribute a metaphysical view to Hippias, as Diès rightly argues (1927, p. 200). "Being" is no more than a nominalization of the copula. "Body" does not appear to have the significance it has in *Sophist* 247bc. "Continuous" has to do with the persistence of predications through manipulations of "each" and "both." The continuity in question is presumably continuity of *speech:*

speeches are not to be broken up; predications are not to be interrupted by exchanges of "each" and "both."

On the translation, see Grube, 1926B: 147.

176 | 301b8, "some attribute or being": *pathos ē ousian.* Hippias treats these as equivalent, here indulging his taste for redundancy (cf. 301c2–3). Critics who believe Plato recognized Aristotle's technical distinction between *pathos* ("accident") and *ousia* ("essence" or "substance") find here a confusion that tells against Platonic authorship (cf. 300b7, 300e4). But the complaint, as Soreth observes, is anachronistic. (Soreth, 1953: 58, n. 3.) See note 81.

177 | 302a4–5, "or don't you consider *one* to be odd?": Cf. *Phaedo* 105b5–c8, with Gallop's note (1975: 211). *One* is not usually considered by the Greeks to be a number at all. But if not a number, how could it be odd?

178 | 302b6, "some are this way, and others are not this way": Socrates draws the wrong conclusion from his examples (see note 170).

Thus ends the long digression of 300b6–302b6. Socrates' argument against the final proposed definition depends indirectly on this point: "fine" is supposed to belong to those attributes that are distributed equally among both and each of a pair; but "pleasant through sight" can only belong to one of the pair in question.

The digression was an open dispute between Socrates and Hippias, in which the Questioner played no part. Now the main argument resumes, but, curiously, without the Questioner until 303d11.

179 | 302c7, "I thought it was by the being that adheres to both, if both are fine—it was by *that* they had to be fine, and not by what falls off one or the other": "both" here refers to both *both* and *each* (Soreth, 1953, p. 58, n. 3). Both pleasure-through-sight-and-hearing and each of pleasure-through-sight and pleasure-through-hearing must have the character (the "being") that makes fine things fine. For this use of "being," see note 181.

180 | 302d6, "Remember, we saw they were no less pleasures": 299d.

181 | 302e6, "Doesn't that attribute adhere in both?": Cf. note 174. What Socrates called a *being* at 302c6 (*ousia*) he now calls an *attribute* (*pathos*). Does this betray an unPlatonic confusion of essence with accident? The *Euthyphro* rejects a proposed definition on the grounds that it states not the *ousia* but a *pathos* of what was to be defined (11a). Here in the *Hippias Major* Socrates is clear that what he is looking for is an *ousia* (302c6) but that what he has found is merely a *pathos* (302e6). From the context, we may infer that Socrates is working with this distinction: a *pathos* is anything true of a subject; the *ousia* of something to be defined is simply what it is to be that something—its Socratic definition. *Ousiai* are according to this terminology a proper subset of *pathē*. If this is right, the *Hippias Major* is consistent in usage with the *Euthyphro* and does not display the unPlatonic confusion alleged by Tarrant (1920, p. 321). *Pathos* and *ousia* are readily conjoined above, where the point about "both" and "each" applies equally. See note 176.

182 | 302e13, "the hypothesis": Cf. note 161. The hypothesis is the proposal at 298a7.

183 | 303a3, "What's to stop us?": Cf. 296b1 and 298b5.

184 | 303a10, " 'each' itself and 'both' ": Some critics find here an allusion to the theory of transcendent Forms (e.g., Capelle, 1956: 190). But the "itself" here is not the "itself" that separates Forms in middle Platonic dialogues. It is emphatic and marks mention off from use. The point is that the predicates "both" and "each" themselves, unlike "fine," "just," and so forth, do not belong equally to both and each of every pair. Socrates takes no position here on the ontological status of such things as "both."

185 | 303c1, "the things I said I saw clearly": 300c9.

186 | 303b7, "When both of anything are even-numbered, each may be either odd- or possibly even-numbered": An even number may or may not be the sum of two even numbers.

187 | 303c1, "when each of them is inexpressible (*arrēta*), both together may be expressible, or possibly inexpressible": false on the face of it. *Arrēta* are irrationals, real numbers that cannot be expressed as *ratios* of integers. Plato probably knew at this time only of irrational *surds* (square roots of non-squares); but the sum of two surds is irrational. Heath (1921: 304) proposes that Socrates refers here not to the sum of irrationals but to the *apotome,* a rational straight line divided into irrational segments (Euclid XIII.6). Michel (1950: 504) supports that interpretation. De Strycker counters with the suggestion that Socrates refers to the *product* of an integer and a ratio of irrationals (1937, 1941). He contends that Heath's interpretation is anachronistic.

The evidence is not sufficient to determine an interpretation. Here as at 281c, Socrates may be enticing Hippias into agreement with a falsehood.

188 | 303c7, "That's *my* way, Socrates": See 300b6. This is what Hippias has maintained from the start.

189 | 303d11, "he'll say": He is the Questioner, here abruptly introduced after a long silence beginning at 300b6. See note 170, also note 47 and p. 107.

190 | 303d11–304e9, The last fresh start: How should an inconclusive discussion be brought to a close? Socrates will not discover the fine, and Hippias will not take the sort of initiative that would round out the dia-

logue. Plato solves the aesthetic problem neatly by bringing the argument
back to its most attractive failure, thereby achieving a sort of resolution.
(Cf. the similar ending of the *Euthyphro.*)

What is it, Socrates asks, that made us select two kinds of pleasure
as fine? Was it not that they were the most harmless and the best—in a
word, *beneficial?* Hippias agrees (303e10), and rightly so. Socrates probably did choose the pleasures of sight and hearing for the benefits they
confer. But now we are back in an old sticking-place: "beneficial" cannot
occur in the definition (pp. 71–74). Hippias tells Socrates he is wasting
his time, delicately turning to the third person to keep up the fiction of the
Questioner (304ab). Socrates brings the dialogue to its end with an un-
characteristically long speech. All he has learned, apparently, is that what's
fine is hard: the fine is hard to find.

191 | 303e4, "the most harmless pleasures": Cf. *Laws* 670d7. Tarrant
(1928, *ad loc.*) and Thesleff (1976, p. 107) both consider the expression
anomalous here.

192 | 304a4–304b6, Hippias' second complaint: Cf. 301b2–301c3
and *Hippias Minor* 369b8–369c8. For Hippias' advice to cultivate political
and forensic oratory, see 296a2–5. Moreau (1941, p. 23, n. 1) takes both
passages as echoes of the *Gorgias,* where Socrates is advised on several occasions to give up philosophy for rhetoric. But note that the power recommended at *Gorgias* 466b4, ff. is to be used to destroy people for one's own
profit; but the power Hippias urges on Socrates is for the defense of self
and friends (304b2–3). Cf. also *Gorgias* 486bc and 452de. The verbal
similarities between *Gorgias* 486c and *Hippias Major* 304b are striking,
but afford no clue as to which passage is the echo of which.

At 284a, Hippias accepts Socrates' claim on his behalf: he knows
better than anyone how to impart virtue to others. The present passage reveals what Hippias regards as the most important part of that virtue—the
ability to make an effective speech. But we have no reason to believe
Hippias would have distinguished that from moral virtue. (*Pace* Harrison,
1964, p. 189, n. 3). See notes 28 and 194.

193 | 304b2, "not the smallest but the greatest": Such antithesis was
apparently a hallmark of Hippias' rhetoric. Cf. 281c2–3.

194 | 304b4, "small talking": *smikrologia.* The word can be used of
any sort of stinginess or small-mindedness, but here the application is
clearly to language, with a pun on *logos.* Cf. Callicles' complaint at *Gorgias*
486c8 and 497b7. Plato's Socrates uses Hippias' words at *Republic* 486a4–
6, when he says that *smikrologia* (here, concern for what money can buy) is
contrary to the philosophical mind that seeks always the *whole.* But the
thought is too different for the *Hippias* passage to be a conscious echo of
the *Republic.*

195 | 304b6, "babbling nonsense": Cf. *Gorgias* 486c6–7.

196 | 304b8, "activities": What provoked Socrates to ask after the fine was Hippias' report of the speech he gave at Sparta, in which he had Nestor recommend certain fine activities to Achilles' son (286ab). Socrates is probably struck now by what Hippias implies. Would he really urge political rhetoric on a son of Achilles? We shall never find out what the speech actually did recommend: Hippias has been trapped in another absurdity. Though rhetoric is the core of what he has to teach, he does apparently believe he can teach *moral* virtue. Nothing less (certainly nothing usable only in a democracy) would have pleased the Spartans in the way Hippias claimed at 286ab.

197 | 304c4, "when I display it": Contrast Socrates' "displays" with those of sophists (note 15).

198 | 304d5–8, "he asks if I'm not ashamed that I dare discuss fine activities when I've been so plainly refuted . . .": implies the priority of definition. See p. 138.

199 | 304e7, "associating with both of you has done me good": What good has Hippias been to Socrates, except to be the occasion for an amusing and instructive display of Socrates' questioning?

200 | 304e8, "What's fine is hard": The scholiast attributes this to Solon. Plato uses it elsewhere (*Republic* 435c8 and 497d10, *Cratylus* 384b1). In this speech, by artful rhetoric, Socrates has made it appear that he and not Hippias was the victim of what passed between them. Yet Hippias professes rhetoric (note 192) and Socrates eschews it, ironically.

ESSAY

ONE
Date and Authenticity

If Plato wrote the *Hippias Major,* he most likely did so after the *Euthyphro* and before the *Phaedo.* The *Hippias Major* has the marks of a relatively early dialogue, but it foreshadows Plato's more metaphysical middle period and has rightly been called transitional (by Malcolm, 1968). My own account (p. 175) of the place of the *Hippias Major* in Plato's philosophical development agrees with this dating, as does the stylometric work of Brandwood, who places the *Hippias Major* after the *Euthyphro* and before the *Republic,* in a group with the *Gorgias, Lysis, Meno, Phaedo,* and *Symposium* (1976: xvii). The balance of evidence, as we shall see, favors attributing the *Hippias Major* to Plato. I would date it, accordingly, relatively early in Plato's career, about 390 B.C.[1]

If the *Hippias Major* was not by Plato's hand, then it was probably written late during Plato's lifetime by a student of the Academy. Both Aristotle and Xenophon, as we shall see, apparently knew of the work; and its style and vocabulary also place it in the fourth century. On this, most athetizers (scholars who reject authenticity) agree: Röllig (1900), Wilamowitz (1919: II, 327), Tarrant (1928: xvi), and most recently Thesleff (1976), who dates the work in the late 360s or early 350s B.C.

A few scholars have on insufficient grounds assigned a still later date to the *Hippias Major.* Pohlenz (1913: 123–8) fixes it in Aristotle's period; Gauss (1954: I.2, 207–8) detects in the dialogue the aroma of a "Hellenistic cookshop."

DRAMATIC DATE. Plato is elsewhere free with anachronism, so we may assign a dramatic date here only with caution. The conversation of the

93

Hippias Major takes place after Gorgias' famous visit to Athens in 427 B.C. (282b5), and apparently during a time of peace. It should, therefore, be set during the Peace of Nicias, or between 421 and 416 B.C. (so Taylor, 1926: 29).

AUTHENTICITY

Plato's authorship of the *Hippias Major* was not questioned in antiquity or in modern times until the work fell under the suspicion of nineteenth century scholars. Since then, most of those who have taken a stand one way or the other have done so on mainly subjective grounds. Athetizers think the *Hippias Major* a shoddy piece of writing and cannot believe Plato would have sunk so low. Defenders, finding it delightfully to their taste, cannot conceive of another author with such Platonic talent. Though I align myself firmly with the defenders on this point, I must concede that the subjective issue is not strongly germane. The question of authorship should be decided on the facts, whether or not they are to Plato's credit in the end; and the facts can neither establish nor deny Platonic authorship beyond doubt. What must be concluded from the arguments summarized below is that the *Hippias Major* should be provisionally accepted. It has as good a claim to Platonic authorship as do the *Ion* and *Euthyphro*. The historical tradition creates a presumption in its favor, and no consideration powerful enough to undermine that presumption has been brought forward. I shall therefore take the authenticity of the *Hippias Major* as a working hypothesis for this essay. The reader may judge whether the hypothesis bears sound fruit, whether, that is, the *Hippias Major* profits from being treated as a Platonic dialogue.

THE DISPUTE.[2] Schleiermacher started it. He was appalled by the rude levity of the *Hippias Major,* surprised by its lack of positive philosophical content, and suspicious of the presence in Plato's canon of two similar but unrelated attacks on Hippias. Though he brought the dialogue into doubt on these grounds, Schleiermacher nevertheless accepted it for its pleasantries in preference to the *Hippias Minor,* in which he found borrowings from the longer *Hippias* (1810: 341–46). His pupil, Ast, was not so generous. The first of the athetizers, Ast rejected the *Hippias Major* as un-Platonic in its satiric style, citing as well a number of specific errors and borrowings from Plato (1816: 457–62). Ast brought a great many Platonic works under suspicion with the *Hippias Major*. Most of these have now been cleared and a few have been firmly rejected by consensus, but the *Hippias Major* remains the object of vigorous dispute.[3] Although a consensus has not emerged, English-speaking scholars have tended to decide in the dialogue's favor, and many now treat the dialogue as genuine without comment.[4]

Historical Arguments. The *Hippias Major* was accepted by the canon of Thrasyllus, the greater part of which is genuine. Thrasyllus (d. A.D. 36) collected the works he believed to be Platonic and transmitted them in the tetralogies that have come down to us. Thrasyllus' authority in the matter of authenticity has been eagerly defended by George Grote, who argued that the canon was based on a Platonic tradition leading from Plato's heirs to the librarians of Alexandria (Grote, 1885: I, 264–300). Grote's argument cannot establish the authenticity of all the works Thrasyllus accepts. Scholarly consensus now rejects several of those works (the *Second Alcibiades,* for example), and has not been persuaded that the Platonic tradition has the sort of continuity Grote's argument requires (cf. Dillon, 1977). Still, its presence in the canon creates a presumption in favor of the *Hippias Major.* Thrasyllus had in the library at Alexandria better sources than we have on which to base his judgment; and most of his choices have stood the test of nineteenth-century German scholarship. Reasons must therefore be given before rejecting a work from the canon.

Though many reasons have come to the athetizers' hands, they do not severally or together undermine the presumption of authenticity:

1. Schleiermacher thought it unlikely that Plato would write two dialogues attacking the same figure. We have no other pair of genuine dialogues devoted to one interlocutor. If, as Geffcken alleges, Plato's pupils were in the habit of borrowing his titles for their work, then the longer *Hippias* could be the work of a student who took his title from Plato's shorter *Hippias* (our *Hippias Minor*). Indeed, that could be so; but Geffcken's argument establishes only that possibility (Geffcken, 1934: II, 182).

We know no reason, in fact, why Plato should not have written two dialogues about Hippias. As we shall see, Hippias represents the sort of sophist Plato found most objectionable (p. 115). And in any case, the two works are not redundant. The *Hippias Major* is more clearly an attack on Hippias, whereas the *Hippias Minor* treats a problem about *technē* that interested Plato in its own right.

One defender of authenticity, Apelt, has tried to connect the two dialogues; he understands the *Major* as solving a puzzle left over from the *Minor* (Apelt, 1907). His attempt has not been convincing to either side of the dispute (so Pohlenz, 1913, and Grube, 1926B: 143). The works need not be connected in that way for both to be genuine.

2. If Aristotle did not know of the *Hippias Major,* then the dialogue was probably written during or after Aristotle's career, and in any case

not by Plato. That Aristotle did not know the *Hippias Major* is supposed
to be shown by two texts. At *Metaphysics* 1025a6–13 he cites the *Hippias
Minor* as the *Hippias* only, thereby arousing the suspicion that he knew
of only the shorter work (Ueberweg, 1861: 175–6). And at *Topics* 146a21
he considers a definition like that of *Hippias Major* 298b, without naming
the work (Pohlenz, 1913: 126). In both cases, the suspicions are unfounded. Abbreviated titles like *Hippias* are frequently used by ancient
authors. Aristotle himself refers to the *Oedipus* of Sophocles at *Poetics*
1452a24; but we may not infer that he did not know of both of Sophocles'
plays about the Theban hero (Soreth, 1953: 2, n. 4; Hoerber, 1964: 144).
And the silence of the *Topics* about the *Hippias Major* is not surprising.
Aristotle's work is littered with allusions to dialogues of Plato in contexts
that he does not bother to furnish with citations of title or author.

3. Scholars have found a number of passages in Aristotle and one in
Xenophon that are reminiscent in theme and language of the *Hippias
Major.* Most take these parallels as evidence that Aristotle and Xenophon
did know the *Hippias Major,* a fact athetizers explain by dating the dialogue in Plato's lifetime. But we cannot definitely exclude the possibility
that the echo runs the other way, that the author of the *Hippias* is influenced
by Aristotle (as Pohlenz suggests, 1913).

The argument from parallels is inconclusive, but weakly supports
authenticity, and more strongly supports the consensus that the *Hippias
Major* was written in Plato's day. Aristotle appears to allude to *Hippias
Major* 297e3–303a11 at *Topics* 146a21–3, and to 293d6–294e10 at *Topics*
102a6 and 135a13. Also, his *Politics* 1261b29 may refer to 302a3–b3
(Shorey, 1953: 474). Xenophon alludes to 288c10–d5 at *Oeconomicus*
VIII, 19 (Chaintraine, 1947). I discuss the parallels in notes 75, 116, and
152(a) in the commentary above. Though I cannot say with Heidel that
the *Hippias Major* is "amply attested" (1896: 7), I conclude that the
most likely account of each parallel makes the *Hippias Major* the source.
And if Aristotle and Xenophon saw fit to echo the *Hippias Major,* that is
likely to be because it was Plato's work, not the exercise of a student.

If Aristotle had cited the *Hippias Major* by title as Plato's work, we
could be certain of its authorship. But we are so fortunate for only a
handful of the dialogues we accept as Platonic, as can be seen from the
evidence listed in summary form by Bonitz (1870: s.v. Plato, p. 598). The
Ion and *Euthyphro* are not attested at all; while the *Lysis, Laches, Charmides,* and *Protagoras* are supported only by allusions that cite neither
title nor author, as is the case for the *Hippias Major* (if I am taking the
parallels the right way). In short, the Aristotelian evidence for accepting
the *Hippias Major* is as good as what we have for many Platonic dialogues,

and better than what we have for some. The balance of the evidence on this score therefore favors Platonic authorship.

The Argument from Style. The style of the *Hippias Major* is out of harmony with the athetizers' conception of Plato. In literary tone and vocabulary the dialogue is more sharply comic than they consider appropriate for Plato. Such inappropriateness has been their main reason for clearing the *Hippias Major* from the canon of authentic works, but the athetizers' argument depends too much on taste to be compelling. Scholars of Plato's style who rely more soberly on the counting of distinctive devices and usages (stylometry) have no difficulty accepting the *Hippias Major* as Platonic (Brandwood, 1976: xvii; cf. Soreth, 1953: 4): so far as stylometry is concerned, the dialogue does not carry the distinctive marks of another author's hand.

The literary objections have to do with the characters of the piece. Some complain that Hippias is mercilessly ridiculed (Schleiermacher, 1810: 344) and inconsistently characterized (Horneffer, 1895: 17–18). Hippias, they say, is too stupid to understand Socrates' quest for definitions yet intelligent enough to make first-rate suggestions (as at 290d5 and 296d4). Thesleff objects that "the stupidity of Hippias is exaggerated beyond what Plato can be fairly credited with even in his wilder moods" (1976: 106). Wilamowitz finds the characterization of Socrates un-Platonic; it has "keine sokratische Ethos, und es fehlt der platonische Witz und die platonische Charis" (1919: 328). All the athetizers are upset by the use in the dialogue of an anonymous Questioner who turns out to be Socrates' *alter ego*. This, they say, is a poor device, and without parallel in Plato's genuine work.

The athetizers are wrong about Hippias. He is not represented in the dialogue as a stupid man, but as one who is clever in a misguided, non-philosophical way. So I argue in Chapter Four. The portrait of Hippias is consistent, I think, and not unworthy of Plato.

The characterization of Socrates in the *Hippias Major* is a strong point in its favor. The pseudo-Platonic Socrates we meet in dialogues that are universally rejected is a very different character, a sweet and fatherly old man (cf. Tarrant, 1938). But the Socrates of the *Hippias Major* is sharp, ironic, and not without a streak of cruelty (below, p. 119). He is the Socrates Plato presented in the *Apology,* the man who fascinated a generation of Athenians and goaded them to the point of irritation at which they committed judicial murder. Only Plato, so far as we know, represented Socrates in that manner.

As for the Questioner, subjective judgment must prevail. Guthrie finds this entertaining device a convincing touch, and so do I (Guthrie, 1975: 176). It has loose parallels in the personified Laws of the *Crito*

(50a, ff.), the many hedonists of the *Protagoras* (353ab, ff.), and the daimonion and god of the *Apology* (40a4, 33c5). It serves, moreover, the useful function of enabling Socrates to attack Hippias indirectly, when Hippias apparently would not face a direct attack (below, p. 107). But the value of the device does not concern us. Such considerations depend on the scholar's taste in the matter of what is worthy of Plato, and that, as I argued at the outset, is irrelevant. (See note 47.)

One literary objection deserves to be taken seriously. The rhetorical style of parts of the *Hippias Major* is strikingly unusual. There are more puns on *kalon* than we would expect from Plato, even though we know him to be a pun-loving writer (Ast, 1816: 459; see my note 46). There is also frequent parody of the high style of Hippias (p. 132), which matches Plato's parody in the *Protagoras* (337c, ff.), and is characterized by a toying with the sounds and rhythms of words. Socrates occasionally picks up the style (as at 281c2–3), and he may mean to make fun of Hippias by his excessive punning on *kalon*. These puns must remain, however, a slight embarrassment for defenders of authenticity.

More serious embarrassments threaten from lexical considerations. The vocabulary of the *Hippias Major* includes words Plato does not use elsewhere, or at least does not use as the *Hippias Major* uses them. Some of them can be explained by the unusual comic intensity of the work, or by its frequent parody of Hippias. Some of the words that have been questioned require no explanation at all, for they belong in the fourth century, and therefore we cannot know that they would never occur in Plato's works. Still, the athetizers have established the lexical oddity of the *Hippias Major*. Tarrant lists questionable expressions exhaustively (1928: lxxviii–lxxx); Thesleff discusses the ones he considers important (1976: 106–7). Some of these expressions Thesleff dates in the mid-fourth century, too late for early Platonic authorship; but the currency of colloquial expressions cannot be fixed so precisely in the absence of firm evidence. The expressions challenged by Tarrant are defended by Grube (1926B, 1929) to the satisfaction of most scholars.

The most peculiar expressions of the *Hippias Major* have to be explained in the same way, whether the dialogue was written by Plato or not. They are expressions that do not belong in prose, and in the *Hippias Major* must therefore either be quoted from poetry or used in burlesque imitation of a high poetic style (as would be appropriate in parodying Hippias). Athetizers and defenders of the dialogue adopt such explanations equally; what divides them is the question of whether such quotation or burlesque imitation is Platonic or worthy of Plato. I must again decline to consider what is or is not worthy of Plato; but Grube is surely right to say that toying with high poetic language is appropriate to the dialogue's comic treatment of Hippias (1926B).

Here is a judicious selection of the most questionable expressions (others are mentioned in notes 59, 77, 88, 103, 109, 139, 146, and 181):

1. eudoxōs (287e5). No other instance of this word used as an adverb is cited by LSJ. Socrates adds it most likely in parody of Hippias' fondness for adverbs (cf. 301c2), as Grube suggests (1926B: 139). Thesleff proposes to read *eudoxōs* as an allusion to the astronomer Eudoxus of Cnidus, who appeared on the Platonic scene about 367 B.C. (1976: 111–112); but this, in the absence of any connection between the context and Eudoxus, is wholly implausible.

2. surphetos (288d4). Plato uses the word collectively of the mob at *Gorgias* 489c and *Theaetetus* 152c; elsewhere it is never used of a single person before Roman times (Thesleff, 1976: 106). This usage is as puzzling to athetizers as it is to defenders; for no one would date the *Hippias Major* in Roman times. Thesleff must be right that Socrates is here quoting some malaproprian insult from comedy. If so, the expression does not tell either way on the issue of authenticity.

3. mermeros (290e4). Wilamowitz thought this an unmistakable stigma (1919: 325n1); the athetizers have mostly agreed. It is not Platonic because it belongs in epic poetry, not prose (Thesleff, 1976: 107, citing LSJ). As such, it most likely finds its way into the *Hippias Major* by way of imitation or quotation (so Friedländer, 1964: II, 298, n. 1). Either way, it does not affect the authenticity dispute.

4. ā mē mega lege (295a7). The particle *ā* does not occur in prose, and must be another poeticism.

5. dianekē (301b7). Another poetic expression, as Tarrant notes (1928, *ad loc.*). Thesleff suggests that it belongs to a quotation from comedy (1976: 113). That is possible, and consistent with any account of the work's authorship (below, p. 100). On the passage, see note 175.

The most that can be concluded from the lexical argument is this: the *Hippias Major* uses poetic and bombastic language playfully in parody of Hippias, possibly by quoting comic authors of Plato's period. In this the dialogue stands out from Plato's unquestionable works. It is only another aspect of the unusually marked comedic element in the *Hippias Major* and is not sufficient to undermine the presumption of Platonic authorship.

Though none of the arguments from style by itself undermines the presumption of authenticity, such arguments may add up to a persuasive case (so Thesleff, 1976). Two inconclusive arguments against the authenticity of a work are often stronger than one. But that principle does not apply to the case at hand. There are indeed several suspiciously unusual features of the *Hippias Major:* its comic treatment of Hippias, its frequent punning, and its burlesque vocabulary. If these were independent peculiarities of the piece, they would together justify a substantial suspicion against authenticity. But they are not independent; they are all aspects of the same central oddity of the *Hippias Major*—that it holds the person of Socrates' interlocutor up to uniquely sharp ridicule. Here, then, is only one argument from style against authenticity, rather than a set of different mutually supporting ones. The argument is inconclusive because Socrates' unusual ridicule of Hippias can be explained (below, p. 131). Moreover, the athetizers' assumption that Plato would eschew such ridicule is not well supported.

The Influence of the Stage. The athetizers' main unstated complaint against the *Hippias Major* is that it shows too much influence of theatrical comedy: Hippias is too much like the stupid braggart of the comic stage, and Socrates too much like the nasty creature who deflates the braggart (cf. Aristophanes' *Acharnians* 572, ff.). Odd expressions, moreover, keep cropping up in the dialogue, usages that are most plausibly explained as borrowings from comic writers (above, p. 99). Other comic elements include the threatened beating (292a; cf. Aristophanes' *Clouds* 1297–1345), and the humorous treatment of Hippias' earning power (esp. 283b; cf. Webster, 1970: 53).

Our question is whether Plato could have written under the influence of theatrical comedy. The dating of the *Hippias Major* relative to its comic models is at issue, and so is Plato's notorious attitude toward the comic stage. We meet no serious problem about dates. The *Hippias Major* was probably written about 390 (above, p. 93). By then a great deal of comedy, now mostly lost, had been written, and so-called Middle Comedy had begun to evolve. One possible source for the language of the *Hippias Major,* Anaxandrides (suggested by Thesleff, 1976: 113), began his career about that time. And most of the more obvious comic devices of the *Hippias Major* would already have been familiar from Aristophanes' earlier works.

The *Acharnians* (425 B.C.), for example, contains scenes that have much in common with the *Hippias.* Lamachus, the braggart soldier, comes to aid a faction of the chorus in a brawl (572, ff.). Dikaiopolis mocks him relentlessly, mainly through a vulgar parody of Lamachus' lines (as at 1097, ff.). Though Lamachus objects (as at 1117), his patience in bearing this treatment is remarkable. He is, after all, armed with a spear to his opponent's phallus; but he never uses it. Like Lamachus, Hippias comes boastfully to the aid of someone in distress, and, like Lamachus, he is faced by an ironical adversary who apes his style and diverts the dialogue from lofty to vulgar subjects (as at 288cd). Unlike Lamachus, Hippias actually excoriates his adversary in the end (301bc and 304ab); but for the most part he patiently bears Socrates' wit (see my notes 4, 35, and 41; also p. 119).

For all this, however, the *Hippias Major* is not as a whole in the genre of Aristophanic comedy. It ends on a note of genuine regret. Socrates' ignorance is no joke. It is painful to him (below, p. 138, ff.). And in the long central part of the *Hippias Major* philosophy holds our interest more than comedy. There, Socrates' conception of definition is elaborated, and the beginnings of an account of the fine are revealed (see below, Chapters Six and Eight). Though the author of the *Hippias Major* was clearly influenced by comedy in vocabulary, characterization, and dramatic style, he was not overwhelmed by his theatrical models.

We know no reason why Plato could not have been that author. Elsewhere in his earlier dialogues he does not scruple to write in a comic vein, though not so marked a one as surfaces in the *Hippias Major*. Ion and Euthyphro are mocked in the dialogues that bear their names, and the *Protagoras* is teeming with parody.[5] Plato knows that a pretense to wisdom is laughable, and apparently sees no harm in our laughing at such a pretender if he is not a friend (*Philebus* 49a–e; cf. Webster, 1970: 57). The earlier Platonic dialogues are mainly devoted to exposing pretenders of this sort; so we should not be surprised to find those works laced with comedy. True, Plato objects to comedy in the *Republic,* mainly because he does not want his citizens acting like buffoons (395c–e). He fears that laughing at comic performances will undermine the restraints a person's reason sets up against the temptation to buffoonery (606c). But these concerns do not appear to have affected him outside the *Republic.* We have seen that he was not above ridiculing pretense to wisdom. And in the *Laws* he permits comedy in his state under two restrictions: it is to be performed by slaves or aliens (816e), and it must never be turned to the ridicule of citizens (935e). The *Hippias Major* was not staged, and does not ridicule the citizen of an ideal state. Plato would never have made any complaints about such a work, so far as we know; even if he had, he might still have been its author. Rousseau, the most ferocious enemy of theater in the history of philosophy, was also a playwright. In short, we know nothing whatever to support athetizing the *Hippias Major* for showing the influence of comic theater.

The Argument from Content. Athetizers have disagreed as to whether the doctrines of the *Hippias Major* are Platonic. A minority, led by Tarrant (1928), think the dialogue is actually an attack on Plato's metaphysics. Most athetizers, however, seem to follow Moreau (1941) in taking the philosophical point of the work to be thoroughly Platonic. Their objection is that it is too Platonic, too dependent on developments in Plato's theory that could not have occurred at the time Plato wrote the dialogues of search (such as the *Hippias Major* appears to be). In Chapter Seven, I argue that the *Hippias Major* is Platonic in the right degree and fits neatly into the story of Plato's development; it belongs to the transition toward his mature thinking about Forms.

Some athetizers cite errors or incongruous statements of Socrates as evidence that the work is un-Platonic. Pohlenz, for example, finds it strange that Anaxagoras is classed with the ancient wise men (281c); and it is certainly odd that those men are said to have avoided affairs of state. All this strangeness I take as part of the humor of the passage. Plato's Socrates is not immune from uttering absurdities in any case, so the point is irrelevant.[6]

More serious is the charge that the dialogue lacks a philosophical structure, and that the definition-proposals considered bear no relation to one another (Gauss, 1954: 207–8). This charge I have met in the Commentary where I show that the proposals form an orderly sequence (p. 46).

As for doctrine, the *Hippias Major* is like many Platonic works: some of the relevant doctrines known from other dialogues show up in it; others do not. Athetizers fault the *Hippias Major* on both points: the Platonic doctrines that occur were borrowed by the author; the absence of others, they say, shows his distance from Plato.

The absences from the *Hippias Major* are not surprising. Like other early dialogues the *Hippias Major* lacks the enthusiasm of the *Phaedrus* and *Symposium* for the fine. It also omits to use Socrates' conception of inner beauty, adumbrated in the *Charmides* (154de); and it pays no explicit attention to what Socrates elsewhere takes to be especially fine— virtue. These latter ideas would not have furthered the inquiry or had any obvious place in the discussion. Still, they are compatible with the *Hippias Major*. I appeal to them below, when I try to construct speculatively a Socratic conception of the fine, using all available evidence (p. 181).

The alleged depredations of the *Hippias Major*'s author on genuine Platonic works are too numerous to discuss here. Each has its place in the Commentary. I list them below in an Appendix with appropriate references. In each case a passage from the *Hippias Major* has a Platonic parallel elsewhere. If any of these established a relatively late date for the *Hippias Major*—say, after the *Phaedo* or *Symposium*—then the athetizers would have won the day. But no relative dating is *established* by this method. We can say, however, that the most likely place for the *Hippias Major* is after the *Euthyphro* and before the *Phaedo, Republic, Theaetetus, Sophist,* and *Philebus*. Its standing with respect to the *Gorgias, Meno,* and *Hippias Minor* is too close to call. See below, pp. 175–9, and the notes cited in the appendix to this chapter (p. 104).

The argument from content is the weakest of the three. It affords no reason whatever for doubting authenticity.

CONCLUSION. Much of what I have said in defense of authenticity has yet to be supported. The remainder of this Essay completes my argument, by justifying the comic style of the *Hippias Major,* and by explaining the work's philosophical significance. Anticipating these results, I shall state here the conclusion toward which all these arguments lead: there is an historical presumption in favor of authenticity, a presumption which none of the athetizing arguments, even in combination with the others, is able to undermine. Readers of Plato should, therefore, accept the dialogue provisionally as authentic.

APPENDIX: PLATONIC PARALLELS

These have been cited by athetizers as evidence for depredations by the *Hippias*-author on Plato's works. Some are not true parallels; many cannot be counted as evidence on either side of the dispute.

HIPPIAS MAJOR	PARALLEL	DISCUSSED IN NOTE
287c8	*Phaedo* 100d7	55
289d1	*Phaedo* 74b8–9	83
289d4	*Phaedo* 100d4–6	85
290b2	*Republic* 420cd	90
290e9	*Republic* 372c1–2	98
292e2	*Symposium* 210e–11b	106
294b2	*Phaedo* 102bc	119
294c8–d5	*Euthyphro* 7c10–d5	121
295c2, ff.	*Gorgias* 474d–e	127
295d6	*Gorgias* 474d	130
296a2–5	*Gorgias* 466b4	192
296e9	*Philebus* 26e7	141
297a6	*Philebus* 27a8–9	"
297b5	*Republic* 506e	145
297e6	*Philebus* 51a, ff.	152
"	*Gorgias* 474d, ff.	"
299d2–6	*Philebus* 12d8–e2	164
301b4	*Theaetetus* 154e2–3	174
301b5	*Hippias Minor* 369bc	173
301b7	*Sophist* 247bc	175
304a4–b6	*Gorgias* 452de, 466b4, 486c, and 497b7	192
304b4	*Republic* 486a4–6	194

NOTES TO CHAPTER ONE

1. Absolute dating of Plato's works is highly speculative. The earlier dialogues are usually located after the death of Socrates (399 B.C.) and before Plato's first trip to Sicily (387 B.C.). The *Hippias Major* should come late in this period, before the *Phaedo,* which is dated by Hackforth about 387 B.C. (1952: 7). The *Symposium,* which also appears to postdate the *Hippias Major,* is fixed by a reference to Mantinea to a period after 385 B.C. (Dover, 1980: 10). For a summary discussion of the place of the *Hippias Major* relative to other Platonic works, see below, p. 175, ff.

2. The history of the dispute is well told by the defender Soreth (1953: 1–4) and by her reviewer Gigon (1955: 15). The leading recent attacks are by Tarrant (1920, 1927, 1928, 1938) and Thesleff (1976); the most thorough modern defenses are Grube's (1926B and 1929) and Soreth's (1953). See also Friedländer (1964: II, 316, n. 1), Hoerber (1964: 143), and Malcolm (1968: 189), for references to the literature.

3. Ast was followed by a distinguished train of athetizers: Ueberweg (1861), Zeller-Nestle (1922: II.1, 481), Wilamowitz (1919: II, 328), Pohlenz (1913), Joseph Moreau (1941), and Gauss (1954: I.2, 207–8), to name a few. These have been opposed by a no less distinguished army of defenders: Apelt (1907), Grube (1926B and 1929), Dodds (1959: 7, n. 2), and Guthrie (1975: 175–6), for example.

4. Kahn, following Thesleff (1976), is the leading exception (1981).

5. *Protagoras* 314c, ff., pokes fun at leading sophists; and 337a–338a parodies the style of Prodicus and Hippias.

6. A famous example of Socrates' uttering absurdities with a straight face is in his interpretation of Simonides (*Protagoras* 342–47). There, as in the *Hippias,* he probably has a serious end in view (see Taylor, 1976, *ad loc.*).

TWO
Plot, Humor, and Subject

Socrates greets Hippias and interrogates him first about his profession (he is the sort of teacher and public speaker known as a sophist), then about whatever it is that makes fine things fine. Although he has done nothing to provoke this, Hippias answers patiently and politely (at least until very near the end). He makes it clear he cannot take Socrates' question about fineness seriously (286e5, ff.) and apparently hopes to dismiss Socrates' question with a pleasantry. When he says, for example, "a fine girl is a fine thing," as if *that* answered the question, Socrates is no doubt supposed to chuckle, nudge Hippias in the ribs, and change the subject. But Socrates pursues Hippias relentlessly; he will not allow anything the sophist says to stand. And although Socrates himself makes no progress, and Hippias makes the best suggestions (290d5, 296d4), Socrates smears him with ridicule for his inability to answer the question. In the end, Hippias ventures to criticize Socrates' methods, with justified asperity. Socrates pretends in his reply that *he* is the insulted party, and so the dialogue closes.

Though they may find Socrates offensive, readers tend to side with him against Hippias. He is obviously the winner, and Hippias' defeat is ignominious. Moreover, because Hippias is presented as a proud man, self-important, and given to rhetorically inflated magisterial utterances, we are amused and delighted by his downfall. The dialogue is low comedy, a verbal equivalent of the slapstick in which someone seeks out and (without provocation) deflates a pompous clown. The attacker in this sort of comedy is mean (but we seem to like him anyway); and his victim unbelievably patient (we laugh at him nonetheless). (For Plato's comic models, see p. 100).

106

What distinguishes the *Hippias Major* within this genre is its length. Hippias is discomfited again and again, and each time in very much the same way. Repeating a comic effect is fatal to comedy; after a certain point it bores the audience. Certainly, we have little cause for laughter in the great middle stretch of the *Hippias Major*. The work is long for a Socratic dialogue, and stands out in another way as well: usually in a dialogue of search, Socrates' interlocutor makes a series of interestingly *different* mistakes, progressing from one level of misunderstanding to another. But here Hippias tries the same sort of tactic on Socrates more than once; and Socrates, when it comes time for him to make suggestions, tries a series of approaches all of which are at about the same level of unsophistication.

This peculiar structure of the *Hippias Major* must be explained mainly with reference to its philosophical theme. But something of its oddness is no doubt derived from the presence of a trained sophist, who has a specific technique for dealing with questions (see p. 127, ff.). The other dialogues of search for definitions pit Socrates against amateurs, who are malleable if not sympathetic. Some of them (like Euthyphro at 6e10) actually learn from the process to give progressively more satisfactory answers. All of them are at least trying to play Socrates' game. Hippias, on the other hand, disarms questions by pointing ridicule at the questioner (p. 134, n. 5). He does this with Socrates' questions not only because it is his habit as a public speaker, but also presumably because he has seen Socrates in action before. He knows how dangerous it is to answer Socrates' questions, how everyone who tries is ignominiously defeated. Hippias tries not to be drawn into direct conflict with Socrates. But Socrates is accustomed to being taken seriously; deprived of a philosophical opponent, he turns his sharp irony against the person of Hippias.

Such a confrontation would not ordinarily be long enough to develop any dramatic interest. One character belabors another with insulting questions; the other displays his technique for making a questioner look ridiculous. Neither one would put up with such treatment for very long, were it not for the device of the Questioner. When the time comes for Socrates to ask his unanswerable question he does not do so directly. Instead he relates how someone rudely questioned him about the fine when he was so bold as to praise parts of speeches as fine or to criticize others as foul (286cd). He then takes the part of this anonymous questioner (287a), asking as he would ask and refuting as he would refute, keeping up the act to the end except when the argument is technical (293e–298a) and when Hippias wishes to confront Socrates (300b6, ff.).

The Questioner is a wonderfully convenient buffer between the two antagonists. His absence from the scene allows the conflict to persist behind a shared fiction of agreement. For Hippias, as we shall see, it is vital to keep up at least an appearance of agreement with those around him (p. 125). If someone opposes him, he needs a sympathetic audience to whose laughter he can appeal. So the real opponent, Socrates, erects an imaginary antagonist, and draws Hippias out by playing the sympathetic audience (see 292c4).

The device has been criticized on a number of grounds (see note 47). The most potent complaint is that Hippias' acceptance of the Questioner is incredible. Nowhere does he show he sees through the thin disguise to Socrates himself. Yet Socrates provides a give-away at 298b11 (by identifying the Questioner as Sophroniscus' son), and Hippias still does not react (cf. 304d and 290e2). (The scholiast, striving for dramatic credibility, rejects the whole passage at 298b.) It is impossible to read the dialogue and believe that Hippias did not recognize the Questioner. Either the dialogue is bady contrived, or Hippias does, from the very start, understand what Socrates is doing. He must have recognized the Questioner: we know from their greetings and the interchange at 301b, ff., that Hippias was familiar with Socrates and his methods. He must have known that it was Socrates who asked such questions, and Socrates who characteristically used such vulgar examples. If he does not let on that he knows, surely that is because the device is in his interest. It gives him an opportunity to attack Socrates while remaining on ostensibly friendly terms. If for no other reason, the device of the Questioner is justified as well because it makes the humorous conflict of the *Hippias Major* possible. Neither Hippias nor Socrates would have tolerated the naked antagonism that would arise if the Questioner were unmasked. (See note 60.)

HUMOR

The *Hippias Major* is the most forthrightly comic of all the works attributed to Plato. Nowhere else is a companion of Socrates made to look so vain and foolish. Some scholars think the humor here is overdone. Schleiermacher, for example, wrote: "the personal ridicule indisputably appears here under a far coarser form than everywhere else . . . and it would, exaggerated as it is, have certainly destroyed its own effect.

"This manner, or rather absence of anything deserving the name, scarcely reconcilable as it is with the propriety and polish of Plato, may perhaps excite a suspicion in the minds of many as to the genuineness of the dialogue. . . . " (1810: 344).

The ridicule is certainly without parallel in Plato. Worse, it appears internally inconsistent. Hippias is shown making some intelligent suggestions (290d5, for example, and 296d3–4), without, apparently, ever grasping the nature of Socrates' question. The evidence of his magnificent success, an astonishing pile of money, should prove that he was nobody's fool. Yet, according to Schleiermacher, the dialogue exhibits Hippias "as guilty of such an unheard of degree of stupidity, as not to be even in a condition to understand a question about how a word is to be explained" (1810: 344). If all this were right, the portrait of Hippias here would be impossible, say the critics, even in comedy.

Hippias is being ridiculed, of course, not portrayed. But the ridicule (if Schleiermacher is right) is unbelievable, and inappropriate besides. What had Hippias, who after all was no Callicles, done to deserve an attack so viciously mendacious? To Grote this is "misplaced and unbecoming," and if it were not for his low opinion of Plato he might have been driven to athetize it on these grounds (1872: VII, 64). Stallbaum was shocked, and concluded that the *Hippias Major* must belong to Plato's juvenilia (1857: IV, 191).

The humor of the *Hippias Major* raises two questions for the dialogue's interpretation: (1) Is its portrait of Hippias incredible? And (2) is its ridicule inappropriate? The second question depends on the first, and the first reduces simply to this: Is Hippias represented in the dialogue as unbelievably stupid? To answer that question we must free ourselves from anachronistic prejudices. Schleiermacher thought it an "unheard of degree of stupidity" in Hippias not to understand Socrates' request for a definition. But no one made such requests before Socrates, if we may believe Aristotle (*Metaphysics* 987b3–4), and the questions here are put in terms of an inchoate theory of forms which no one (except, arguably, Plato) understood. Modern Platonic scholars cannot agree among themselves about what Socrates was looking for; so we have no business criticizing Hippias for missing the point.

In fact, I shall argue, Hippias understands Socrates' point as well as anybody Socrates meets. He gives the answers he does not out of stupidity but because he is trying to dodge the question. And that is quite a clever thing to do. *Really* trying to answer Socrates is a mug's game: you always lose. If that is right, the case for Hippias' stupidity is much weakened. We shall have to look more closely at how each character is drawn in the dialogue. Before any of that, we must examine its subject.

SUBJECT

Philosophically the dialogue is an analytical inquiry into what it is to be *kalos* ("fine"). Though the discussion never answers Socrates' question, it illuminates the logic of the term and at the same time illustrates the general character of Socratic inquiry.

Most translators render *kalos* as "beautiful," and they are partly right. Like beauty, *to kalon* is something splendid and exciting; and in women or boys it is the loveliness that excites carnal desire. But the use of *kalos* for that quality is embraced by its use as a quite general term of commendation in Greek. "Noble," "admirable," and "fine" are better translations, and of these "fine" is best of all in virtue of its great range. Different sorts of things are commended as *kala* for different sorts of qualities: boys for their sex appeal, horses for their speed, fighting cocks for their spunk, families for their lineage, acts of war for their courage, speeches for their truth, and so on. Our "beautiful" translates *kalos* in only a few of its many uses, and is wholly inappropriate for the word as Socrates uses it. Whatever the context, Socrates uses *kalos* seriously to commend people and things for one quality only, their utility with respect to the good (p. 184). The aesthetic use of the word (i.e., the use of *kalos* to commend something on its looks: translate, "visibly fine") is eschewed by Socrates in the *Hippias Major* and elsewhere (most famously in Xenophon, *Symposium v*). He considers aesthetic definitions of *kalos* in the *Hippias Major* only to reject them, and that in one case *because* it is aesthetic (293e9–294e9, and the argument that culminates in 303d7–8, with the implication of 303e).[1]

The *Hippias Major* is therefore not a treatise in aesthetics, and beauty is not its subject. The dialogue is concerned with commendation itself, and the logic of commendation. In fact, *kalos* is used in the *Hippias Major* as a synonym for *agathos* ("good"), as becomes clear at 297c (note 148 and p. 188).

What seems to interest our author is precisely the wonderful versatility of the word in commendation. It can be said of almost anything, provided it is good for something: a goddess or a chamber pot, a sacred statue or a monkey, a bright idea, a good-sounding speech, or Hippias' homemade shoes. Words like *kalos* are disconcerting because along with their vast range comes an apparent indeterminacy of meaning. There are many different ways of being fine, different ways for different purposes, and different ways for different sorts of things. The same thing may be fine considered in one way, but not at all fine in another. We have fine chamber pots and fine china; but even though a fine chamber pot is china, and even though it is fine (if it holds enough and will not break), it is not fine china. Fine china is delicate, lustrous, and not very useful; whereas a fine chamberpot is heavy, commodious, and utilitarian. The meaning of "fine" taken by itself seems indeterminate because "fine" is a *logical attributive*. Logical attributives demand to be used in attributive position with nouns that (intuitively) complete their meaning. The adjective "big" is a classic example. Unless we know who Jeremy is, we do not know what to make of the sentence "Jeremy is big." But if we know that he is a frog, we understand the sentence as "Jeremy is a big frog," and we know how big *that* is. The indeterminacy of logical attributives is particularly upsetting for terms of commendation. We may know which qualities would make a person a fine man, and which would make him a fine president; but knowing *that* is not knowing which qualities are simply *fine*—which qualities we would want our children to have no matter what (cf. Woodruff, 1978B). So the same word, "fine," seems *logically* to demand treatment as an attributive; but *morally* we want it to stand alone, stripped of the nouns that would skew its meaning in unpredictable ways.[2]

The sophists, including Hippias, apparently responded to the logical demand, as is proper for those whose concern was with correct and careful speech (p. 115). Socrates took the other route. Because he wanted to know how to live, and not merely to speak, as he ought, he insisted on isolating words like "fine" from the qualifications that ordinarily determine their meanings (p. 153). Whereas the sophists were satisfied to catalogue the various ways of being fine or good or useful or brave, Socrates and Plato sought to tie each such word by definition to a single *eidos* ("form" or "character") which would explain all its proper uses. Socrates hoped it could be done; Plato virtually invented metaphysics to insure that it *was* done; but the sophists (so far as we can tell) did not think it was possible.

That is the philosophical battleground on which the comic struggle of the *Hippias Major* is waged. Hippias, relying on the common sense of ordinary usage, does not even entertain the possibility of giving *kalos* a unitary definition. But Socrates belabors him for not knowing what it is.

NOTES TO CHAPTER TWO

1. On the range of *kalos* see Dover (1974: 69) and Adkins (1960, esp. p. 193). On Plato's use of the word, see Dodds' interesting note on *Gorgias* 474c, ff. (1959: 250). He calls attention to a decline in the use of works of representative art as examples of things that are *kala*.

2. In almost every attempt to define a virtue, Socrates establishes early that the virtue is fine (*Charmides* 159c, *Laches* 192c, and Xenophon's *Memorabilia* IV.vi). In the *Euthyphro* the point is made indirectly: piety is something that is in itself lovable (loved because it is pious—10d). And the fine, of course, is fundamentally what makes things lovable. Cf. *Meno* 87d.

It would appear then that Socrates wants to define the fine because it is what his other objects of search have in common. In all his discussions of the fine, I suggest (as an hypothesis) that Socrates' prime example of a fine thing is virtue itself (p. 186). The *Hippias Major* has virtue as its underlying theme: that is what Hippias' fine speeches are supposed to teach (note 28), and that, presumably, is the goal of the fine customs, laws, and activities that recur as examples (286b, 295d, 298b).

THREE
Milieu

The *Hippias Major* is one of a set of dialogues that oppose Socrates to various figures known as *sophists:* the *Protagoras, Gorgias, Euthydemus, Republic I,* and of course the *Hippias Minor.* The opposition between Socratic philosophy and sophistry is indeed one of Plato's major themes (*Apology* 19de, for example, and *Sophist* 231a). He harps on it loudly, probably to drown out the many voices of his own day that called Socrates —and Plato too, for that matter—a sophist (DK 79). The word "sophist," before Plato went to work on it, had both general and specific uses without pejorative undertones (Guthrie, 1969: 33). Plato seems to think his contemporaries are overlooking an enormous difference between true philosophers and sophists. To bring that difference to light he repeatedly attacks sophists individually and as a class; and though he treats Protagoras and Gorgias with a measure of respect, his comments on sophists as a class are unreservedly hostile.

Since Plato is our main source for the sophists, his verdict on them has been until recently the verdict of history. But that was challenged by George Grote, who vindicated the sophists in a stirring and influential chapter of his *History.*[1] In our own day scholars must take the sophists seriously. The best of them were, even as Plato represented them, men of good character, thoughtful, and even original. We have to ask, then, what Plato found so deeply offensive in their work. It was not, apparently, that he thought them stupid or morally corrupt; it was that they did what Plato thought only philosophers should do—without being philosophers. He was right, I think, on the second point: serious thinkers they may have been, but the sophists were not serious about ontology or epistemology, and their interest in ethics was fundamentally different from Socrates'. They were teachers and, perhaps, reformers; but Socrates thought teaching and reform must wait on the knowledge that would show itself in an ability to give definitions and withstand Socratic questioning. Such knowledge was not on any sophist's program. The sophists knew how to get things done; Socrates knew how to show that they did not know what *ought* to be got done.

THE OLDER SOPHISTS

Understanding the sophists is no easy matter. Our chief witness, Plato, is hostile and may bend the facts not only to suit his brief, but also to fulfil his literary intentions. Defenders of the sophists are therefore tempted to reconstruct them as magnificent philosophers from the meager evidence Plato affords.[2] More modest interpreters are still tempted, following Plato, to suppose that there was just one sort of thing that the sophists were. Both temptations must be resisted. The sophists were probably not as exciting as anti-Platonists would like them to be; but they were varied and original thinkers, each of whom must be considered independently. In this Section, I shall therefore recall briefly what Plato said generically about sophists before I set down certain facts about the leading figures, concentrating on what relates to Hippias.

THE GENERIC SOPHIST. The typical sophist, as Plato represents him, was an itinerant who professed to teach virtue for a whopping fee. This teaching he did not actually know how to do; he was therefore an impostor. Such a man was popularly supposed to be a corrupter of youth,[3] but that is not Plato's brief against him (*Republic* 493ad). The sophist does not know enough to originate corruption of that kind; he simply feeds his clientele what it wants (cf. *Gorgias* 463a). Because his clientele has varied interests and is spread across many cities, the sophist must be a man of many shapes and many devices, a man who adapts himself to his social context easily.[4] Plato thinks the sophist really *is* polymorphous; that is why he eludes definition and crops up under many different divisions (*Sophist* 218d, 223c, 231c, 240c). A true philosopher, by contrast, would take on various appearances only to the ignorant; for he would have the real integrity of a god (*Sophist* 216c). The knowledge a philosopher wants would be unified by definitions of unitary Forms, and these in turn would be ordered in some way by the Good. But what the sophist claims to know is multifarious and universal. His, therefore, must be a spurious sort of knowledge (*Sophist* 232e): he says he knows more than could possibly be known in the way experts know things (cf. *Republic* 598cd). He is an impostor, and what he teaches is a shadow of what ought to be taught.[5] The chief difference between the sophist and the philosopher lies, I think, in the Platonic theme of the contrast between *many* and *one* (cf. p. 151). Not only does the sophist work in many places and profess knowledge of many subjects, he also gives many answers to one question: when asked about the fine (since he does not know the unitary form of the fine) he will answer that *many* things are fine, or perhaps give you the answer he thinks you want, different answers on different occasions.[6] What Plato requires to be a single reference point for judgment—the good or the fine—the sophist believes to be multiple, or at least complex. It follows (for Plato) that the sophist cannot know what he is talking about, since there is no one form to which all his judgments are referred.

The generic sophist, then, is objectionable because he is the simulacrum of a philosopher. Plato knows he is not a philosopher because of the many shapes he takes and the many complex answers he gives to simple questions. This objection, vehement against unnamed sophists, is muted in Plato's dialogues with the leading older sophists, Protagoras and Gorgias. Though these men satisfy much of what he says about sophists in general, they do not appear to be really persuasive examples of the bad genus, for they strike us through Plato's text as men of character who command a certain respect.[7] The clown-like couple of sophists in the *Euthydemus* are even more useless examples. Since no one could mistake *them* for philosophers, the charge that they are impostors would carry little conviction. The only sophist Plato represents as a thoroughly convincing example of his objectionable genus is Hippias. Hippias, who belonged to the first generation of sophists after Protagoras and Gorgias, was as versatile and shallow as the generic sophist was supposed to be. That, at least, is the way he was if Plato's portrait of him is true. What we know of Hippias I shall set out in the next Chapter. Here I shall merely venture the hypothesis that the *Hippias Major* devotes itself to ridiculing Hippias' versatile accomplishments, showy style, and flexible arguments mainly because Hippias is just the sort of example Plato needs to show what is wrong generally with sophists. But Hippias was not the only member of this class; and because he followed in famous footsteps, I shall need to say something about the leading older sophists, Protagoras and Gorgias.

PROTAGORAS.[8] Protagoras (c. 490–c. 420 B.C.) was perhaps the first sophist, and very likely the first to take fees (*Protagoras* 349a). His income from teaching was apparently enormous (*Meno* 91d). What he undertook to teach was the sort of virtue desired by ambitious men (*Protagoras* 318e5, ff.). This is a practical virtue, and therefore far removed from the goal of Kantian ethics; but it is not, for all that, a merely amoral technique for holding political power. (See note 20.) Protagoras apparently held theories bearing on ethics and epistemology, but we do not know enough about them to say with assurance what they were. The famous *homo-mensura* fragment ("man is the measure . . . ," DK 80B1) seems to have come to Plato with virtually no theoretical underpinning; that is probably why Plato needed to supply a "secret" doctrine to make sense of the quotation (*Theaetetus* 152d, ff.). We have no evidence in his case to set against Plato's generic charge that the sophists were not real philosophers: no clear sign of a developed ontology or epistemology has survived. Protagoras was concerned chiefly with practical matters, with rhetoric, politics, and the law.

One point of difference between Protagoras and Socrates is important for our purposes. Drawing perhaps on the contextual richness of language, Protagoras seems to have thought that there really are many ways for things to be good or beneficial, different ways for different contexts, and that the good is therefore, "many-colored and of all sorts" (*poikilon* and *pantodapon*), as he is made to say in the *Protagoras* (334b6–7). His speech there provokes a strong reaction from Socrates, who threatens to walk out on the discussion if it is to be carried out in such long (and, I presume, distastefully complex) speeches. Here, as in the dispute over the unity of virtue (329c, *etc.*), Socrates and Protagoras clash over the sort of one-many issue mentioned above: what Protagoras thinks he knows is a complex good; what Socrates wants to know (and probably thinks Protagoras does not know) would be the one good itself.

GORGIAS.[9] Contemporary with Protagoras, but much more long-lived, Gorgias was most famous as a teacher of rhetoric. Unlike Protagoras, he professed to teach not virtue (*Meno* 95c), but merely the power of persuasive speech.[10] His *Peri Physeos* (444–441 B.C.) is a series of attacks on Parmenidean positions, leading to a result that is either nihilist or skeptical. He apparently believed there is nothing on which knowledge can be based, and that we must therefore make do with unfounded opinion (cf. DK 82B11, 11). Whether this was a truly philosophical essay or a parody of one is in dispute.[11] I am inclined to take it as a serious argument for not doing what philosophers after Parmenides generally did—developing theories to ground knowledge in intelligible being (or beings).

Here we are concerned mainly with two contributions of Gorgias: his style and his approach to definition. His style was enormously influential and widely imitated—most grossly (if we are to believe the implication of Plato's parody) by Hippias.[12] It was characterized by rhyme and balanced antithesis, and by the use of inflated euphemisms (DK 82A32, B5a, and

A1a). He would give extemporaneous speeches on topics selected by his audience (82A1a), and, presumably, would offer to take questions.[13] He communicated his art to students not by technical training, but by example, giving them speeches and exchanges to learn by heart (Aristotle, *De Sophisticis Elenchis,* 183b38, ff.). That Gorgias could have great influence through this method testifies to the effectiveness of his style.

Definition is the substantial issue on which Plato (and Aristotle, following Plato) understand Gorgias and Socrates to be in disagreement, specifically, the definition of virtue (*Meno* 71e, Aristotle, *Politics* 1260a21–28). Gorgias (they said) thought there were different ways of being virtuous for different sorts of people. Socrates thought there must be one general definition of virtue. Gorgias, in effect, would give a list of *partial* definitions: e.g., courage for a man is doing this; but courage for a woman is doing the other; and each of these is a part of courage. Of course, no partial definition is really a definition at all. It cannot say what the various alleged ways of being courageous have in common. If Gorgias is content with partial definitions, that is probably because he does not believe there is any common being underlying the various uses of "virtue." And that is what he should believe, if he is serious in the *Peri Physeos;* for there he denies that there is any being whatever.[14] Here the one-many issue surfaces most importantly between Socrates and a sophist, for the unity of definition is essential to Socrates' purpose (p. 156). On this point too we shall see Hippias follows Gorgias; he is prepared to identify a number of fine things instead of a single form (note 91).

SOCRATES

Of the historical Socrates (c. 469–399) we know too little that is reliable, and too much that must have been distorted by the imagination of his brilliant pupils, the prejudice of his enemies, or the devices of the comic stage.[15] I shall therefore confine myself in these pages to treating Socrates as a literary character in Plato's earlier dialogues. Much the same character appears under the name "Socrates" wherever he is opposed to sophists (the *Protagoras, Gorgias, Republic I, Euthydemus,* and the two *Hippias* dialogues), wherever he searches vainly for definitions (*Laches, Charmides, Euthyphro* and *Lysis*), and in the *Apology* and *Crito.* Elsewhere, Plato makes of Socrates a different sort of character, one that need not concern us here (p. 175). Where Xenophon's account of Socrates agrees with Plato's, I shall call attention to that fact. Otherwise, the Socrates of this book is merely the role in the dialogues I have listed above.

SOCRATES AND THE SOPHISTS. Unlike the generic sophist, Socrates kept to one place, his own city, even at the cost of his life (*Crito* 52b). He did not take money for teaching, and, indeed, proclaimed that he did not know enough to be a teacher at all (*Apology* 19d–20c). But a teacher he most assuredly was, and of the very subject professed by the sophists—moral virtue. And just as Protagoras would apparently accept the moral authority of the city he addressed (*Theaetetus* 167c), Socrates accepted the authority of the man he questioned—at least for the premises of his arguments. He did not, of course, tell people what virtue was. But he tested for knowledge of the matter those who ought to know (*Apology* 21b, ff.), possibly hoping that those who failed the test—and everyone failed—would be spurred to overcome their ignorance (*Sophist* 230bc, but see p. 137). Others he exhorted directly to take up the pursuit of wisdom (*Euthydemus* 278d, ff.; cf. *Apology* 29d–e). In either case, Socrates spoke to change the direction of a person's conscious interests, unlike the sophists who spoke to communicate by example a way of speaking.

Plato uses Socrates as the example to set against the nonphilosophical sophists. But, curiously, he does not represent Socrates as a successful Platonic philosopher either. Socrates shares with the sophists a disregard for science and ontology. From the first he is distracted like the sophists by a driving interest in practical virtue; from the second he is barred by the same thing, and perhaps also by his ignorance (p. 141). Socrates was not a Platonic ontologist; but he asked questions that pointed the way to ontology (p. 168, ff.), and that, more than anything, sets him apart from the sophists. Their work led nowhere beyond itself. They were satisfied if their customers were satisfied (*Republic* 493a–d, cf. *Gorgias* 463a, ff.; cf. notes 136 and 155). But Socrates' chief lesson was the self-induced dissatisfaction (304e) that has become the hallmark and mainspring of serious philosophy.[16]

DOCTRINES. Dissatisfied as he was, Socrates was committed to a substantial body of doctrine.[17] Here I shall discuss only what pertains to the *Hippias Major;* and even that I shall only mention here, for the remainder of the Essay is mainly a discussion of Socratic philosophy. Socrates' quest for definitions employs general principles, which I discuss in Chapter Six. He also exhibits in the *Hippias Major* and elsewhere definite views about the nature of the fine (Chapter Eight). His political beliefs show up twice in the *Hippias Major* and must be given their due (notes 27 and 104). Socrates' main doctrinal differences with Hippias in the *Hippias Major* are on the following points, all discussed in detail elsewhere in the Essay:

1. The acceptability of proposed examples of the fine (p. 111, n. 2, and note 122).
2. The unity of definition (note 91 and p. 156).
3. The insufficiency of the self-predication requirement (p. 169).

Socrates does not patiently explain these points to Hippias nor attempt to persaude him. Instead, he treats him, through the Questioner, with contempt.

CHARACTERIZATION. Socrates is of course the most striking character in the piece. He is, from the very first line, derisively ironic about Hippias. Yet Hippias has done nothing to deserve this, so far as we can tell. Socrates simply approaches him, and without provocation launches into a thinly disguised attack on Hippias' profession. Hippias' worst sin at this point is merely his self-importance. There may be some condescension in his politeness, but politeness it is: he avoids showing that he understands Socrates' remarks as an attack on himself, even when Socrates delivers the naked insult at 286a: ". . . they (the Spartans) use you the way the children use old ladies, to tell stories for pleasure."

Yet Hippias *does* understand the insult, as his reply proves; he is eager to show that there is more than entertainment value in the tales he tells at Sparta. Why does Hippias put up with this treatment? Perhaps as a public speaker he had trained himself to bear with nasty hecklers like Socrates. Whatever the explanation, Socrates is taking advantage of Hippias, playing him along, getting in all the insults he can, and (and this is really foul) pretending that *he* is the one being insulted! Everything Hippias says is true, at least "in a sense," as we would now say, and much of it quite intelligent. But Socrates perversely finds a way of making each of Hippias' offerings look silly. And what could be more rude, considering that Hippias is merely trying to show Socrates how to squelch his own heckler? Hippias is trying to help, and Socrates is not the least bit grateful. In the last section of the dialogue he actually entices Hippias into making absurd claims (note 170).

Socrates comes off badly in the dialogue. He is ironical and insulting. He punishes Hippias for no apparent crimes, and takes advantage of whatever it is that makes Hippias stand up to such treatment. He is not much better in the other Socratic dialogues—the ones everyone accepts as Plato's. Even in the *Apology* we see his arrogance and irony, contempt for his prosecutors and the jury as well.

So the portrait of Socrates in the *Hippias Major* has an undeniably Platonic ring to it. Others who wrote favorably of Socrates made him a pleasant figure, an often fatherly old man. That is how we find him in Xenophon, and that is how we find him in clearly pseudo-Platonic dialogues. Only Plato (so far as we know) had the courage and the devotion to present Socrates as he must have been, repellent and endlessly fascinating.[18]

What is different about Socrates in the *Hippias Major* is the gratuitous cruelty of his attack on Hippias. It is not an attack on a false or immoral doctrine, but an assault on a *personality*. That is what makes it uniquely comic among the works attributed to Plato. Hippias is no Callicles; yet even Callicles for all his wickedness meets with more respect. Hippias is a man of ordinary and quite harmless ideas, with enough vanity and pomposity about him to make us laugh when he falls. But why should *he* of all people fall? What is there about *his personality* that makes it a fit object of ridicule? Unless we can answer that question satisfactorily, we will have to agree with Grote that the comedy of the *Hippias Major* is "misplaced and unbecoming" (1872: VII, 64). And then, unless we share Grote's sour judgment of Plato, we shall have to make room for Schleiermacher's suspicious (1810: 344, see p. 108, above). We need to look at exactly how Hippias is introduced to us, and to which features of his personality the author calls our attention.

NOTES TO CHAPTER THREE

1. For a brief history of scholarly opinions about the sophists, see Guthrie, 1969: 10, ff. Grote's defense of the sophists is Chapter LXVII of his *History of Greece*.

2. An extreme example of such reconstruction is Dupréel's thesis that Plato was in fact an imitator of the sophists (1948:9). On this see Cherniss' review (1952).

3. *Republic* 492a–c, *Meno* 91c. Consider also the care Socrates takes in the *Apology* to distinguish himself from the sophists, and cf. *Protagoras* 317b and *Phaedrus* 257d.

4. *Euthydemus* 288bc, cf. 271c–272b, 297c, and *Timaeus* 19e.

5. *Gorgias* 463d2: "rhetoric is an image of the political art"; *Sophist* 234c and *passim; Laws* 908d.

6. *Republic* 493c1: "all these things"; cf. 476a and 479a. The generic sophist is most likely meant to be among the lovers of sights and sounds (476b).

7. Socrates' respect for Protagoras shows through the irony at *Protagoras* 309c10 and 361e4, and in the contrast between the way he treats Protagoras and the way he deals with Hippias. See also Guthrie,

1969: 265. Plato is similarly much more gentle with Gorgias than with Polus and Callicles. Such men, I think, could not have been convincingly treated otherwise.

8. For bibilography on Protagoras see Classen (1976); for a translation of the evidence, see Sprague (1972). Guthrie's general account of him is the most useful available in English (1969).

9. Gorgias' place among the sophists has been disputed (see Harrison, 1964); but his place here as a precursor of Hippias is secure.

For bibliography on Gorgias see Classen (1976); for translations of the relevant texts, see Sprague (1972), and for a general account, Guthrie (1969).

10. See Harrison, 1964: 188. Gorgias did apparently use the word *aretē* for the ability he taught (implication of *Meno* 71e and 73c9; cf. inscription *b* of DK 82A8, and *Apology* 19e, ff.). Gorgias taught what other sophists taught; and if he scrupled sometimes to call it virtue, that was probably due either to his skeptical turn, or to his related denial that there is a single *aretē* for all contexts (so Guthrie, 1969: 272, n. 1). On Hippias' aim, see note 49.

Gorgias' speaking aimed at the likely and the persuasive, rather than the truth or being (see Guthrie, 1969: 273).

11. The *Peri Physeōs* survives in two paraphrases: Sextus *Adv. Math.* VII 65 (= DK 82B3) and *Pseudo-Aristotle,* "On Gorgias" (in *Melissus, Xenophanes, and Gorgias*). Of these, the Sextus paraphrase is widely, but wrongly, held to be more authoritative. Its language and structure belong to Sextus himself.

Robinson describes the *Peri Physeōs* as "the work of a clever mimic" (1974: 60). Kerferd has argued for taking it as serious philosophy (1955). Newiger makes the case against Sextus and gives an impressive interpretation of pseudo-Aristotle, taking the *Peri Physeōs* as a serious and influential work (1973; reviews by Guthrie and Mejer, 1975 and 1976).

12. Isocrates, Thucydides, and Agathon all are supposed to have come under Gorgias' influence (DK 82A1 and A16).

Hippias and Gorgias are not linked by ancient authors; and this is surprising, for, as we shall see (p. 125), the style Plato parodies as Hippias' is heavily Gorgianic. (But see *Phaedrus* 267b for a difference between them.)

Hippias may have studied the Gorgian style in Sicily (282de), or when Gorgias was in Elis (DK 82B10). He dressed like Gorgias (DK 82A9), and married his daughter to Gorgias' most famous pupil, Isocrates (DK 86A3). He was versatile in much the way Gorgias was (p. 130, cf. DK 82A26), and in various other ways is linked with Gorgias (see notes 49, 74, 104, 105, and 117).

13. As he does briefly in the *Gorgias,* Hippias made a practice of answering questions about speeches he had made (below, p. 125). For the display speeches sophists made, see Commentary note 15.

14. See this Chapter's notes 10 and 11. Socrates asks for an *ousia* ("being" or "essence"—*Meno* 72b1). But that is the sort of question the *Peri Physeōs* would urge us to avoid, on the interpretation I have suggested.

15. On the Socratic question I am inclined to the consensus most recently defended by Guthrie (1969: 323–377) and Lacey (1971), though I would not make my discussion here depend on so slender a foundation. The consensus is that we are to learn of Socrates' philosophy mostly from the writings of Plato, but not from those dialogues in which Socrates is made to state the theory of transcendent Forms, on which Guthrie follows Aristotle (*Metaphysics M* 1086b2–8). If this is right, our knowledge of Socrates as a philosopher must be carefully and speculatively culled from Plato's admittedly imaginative and original earlier dialogues, with support from some other authorities, mainly Aristotle. The *Hippias Major* may be accepted into the canon of Platonic works that are evidence in this way for Socrates, if its main argument is disentangled from the many hints of the theory of Forms (see Chapter Seven).

16. Guthrie, 1969: 442.

17. For elaborate discussions of Socrates' philosophy, see Guthrie (1969) and Santas (1979).

18. For a balanced treatment of Socrates' character and contribution to philosophy, see Gregory Vlastos, "The Paradox of Socrates" (1971: 1–21).

FOUR
Characterization of Hippias

Scarcely anything is known about Hippias as an historical figure if we discount Plato's testimony and imitation. Plato is notoriously unreliable as an historian of philosophy; his literary and philosophical interests were often at odds with historical accuracy, and in the case of Hippias he appears to have been unusually hostile to his subject. So we cannot derive from Plato an altogether satisfactory account of Hippias as speaker and thinker. Certain facts emerge nonetheless, facts Plato would have had no reason to misrepresent. And from the nature of Plato's attack on Hippias, we can draw speculative conclusions about Hippias' technique as a sophist, his thought, his rhetorical style, and even his personal character.

THE HISTORICAL HIPPIAS[1]

Like Gorgias (who may have been his model)[2] Hippias combined a career as diplomat with a lucrative business as a teacher and public speaker. He would give paid demonstration speeches on subjects chosen by his audience, and afterwards deal with their questions. Probably like Gorgias, he expected his paying students to learn public speaking from his example (above, p. 117). At this trade he was a great financial success, at least by his own report (282de). He was a master besides of a great many practical and theoretical disciplines. He appeared at Olympia in clothes and shoes of his own making; he wrote tragedies and dithyrambs; he could deliver pleasant speeches on literary subjects; and he could furnish them with character-building anecdotes. He was an expert on mnemonics, speech rhythms and harmonies, astronomy, and mathematics (in which he is supposed to have made an important contribution).[3] He was able to make virtually any subject his own, owing to his mnemonic powers, and could find something in his vast repertoire to suit any audience.

All we know of his moral theory was that he recognized the dichotomy between law (*nomos*) and nature, which was just then becoming fashionable, and strongly upheld the latter, rejecting *nomos* as artificial, fluctuating, and tyrannical. But the moral views he defended (presumably as being natural) were, so far as we know, inoffensively conventional.[4]

In speaking he adopted elements of the high rhetorical style of Gorgias, no doubt applying his own analysis of speech to the production of euphony. (See pp. 210–12.) Plato unkindly represents him as a speaker more interested in the sound of what he said than in the sense. We may be certain that Hippias was devoted to euphony, and that he was more a maker of speeches than a dialectician. The sort of contest he was accustomed to winning (*Hippias Minor* 363a8) was a contest of speeches to be compared by an audience, not the lonelier battle of question-and-answer at which Socrates and the Eleatic sophists were adept. This we can infer from his challenge to Socrates to make his own speech, so the hearers may judge which is better (*Hippias Minor* 369c6). Though he boasts of his ability to handle questions (363d3), he clearly had little experience of dialectic as Socrates practiced it; hence his anger at Socrates' style (*Hippias Major* 302a). The questions he was used to answering must have been directly related to a speech he had just made. Answering them was apparently part of his trade as a public speaker (286e8). From his performance as Plato represents it we may suppose that his intention in answering questions was mainly to silence the questioner. An answer that "slips past" him is good enough, whether or not it is true (298b5). Hippias conspicuously lacks the philosopher's obsessive fear that he may have said something wrong (296b1). His goal in answering appears to be to shame the questioner by making him seem ridiculous to the audience.[5] He would say something obviously true, punning, perhaps, on the question, and pretend to think the questioner had not known *that* (as at 289e). It is this technique of shutting people up (known to every public speaker) that Hippias is represented teaching to an ungrateful Socrates in the *Hippias Major*. There the technique fails miserably, partly because Hippias has no audience to laugh with him at the Questioner, and partly because the Questioner is so stubbornly philosophical as to be immune to such tactics. All *he* seems to care about is philosophy, a subject in which Hippias neither professes nor betrays the slightest interest. Alone among Socrates' interlocutors in dialogues of search, Hippias cares nothing for the subject or the method of Socratic inquiry. No wonder he and Socrates are talking at cross purposes. One is trying to engage in philosophy, the other to display a popular rhetorical defence. Here we must remind ourselves, out of respect for the rest of the world, that not caring for philosophy is no sign of stupidity. Socrates seems to count it against Hippias that he is no philosopher. But why should he? Hippias' talents, like those of other sophists, are of another sort altogether. Certainly, neither Plato nor any other ancient authority attributed a developed philosophical position to Hippias.[6]

Nevertheless, Hippias had opinions on philosophical themes, and we may speculate as to what they were:

1. What is said in a speech (the "being" or "truth" that it asserts) must be taken as a whole, and not divided into sentences. A sentence, *a fortiori,* must not be broken up, but understood together with the appropriate qualifications. This means, among other things, that we should understand the sentence "Helen is fine," for example, not in isolation but as equivalent to "Helen is a fine girl." (See p. 48, and contrast pp. 153–6.)

2. When conventional differences are put aside, we are all in natural agreement with one another. So the purpose of debate is not so much to win an argument as it is to end it, and to do so by uncovering hidden areas of agreement. That is the import of Hippias' speech at *Protagoras* 337c ff., and is suggested by his behavior with Socrates in the *Hippias Major*. Hippias appears to agree with Socrates as a matter of principle, even when (as at 284e1) we know he held an opposite position (cf. 282a, 285b, and 292b5 with my notes *ad loc.*). Elsewhere, when demonstration speeches are given, he compliments a colleague's speech, and, without suggesting a debate, agreeably asks to exhibit his speech as well (*Protagoras* 347a). His philosophy of agreement may help explain his reluctance to take umbrage at Socrates' insults. Professional diplomat that he is, Hippias seems to have made a virtual science of being agreeable. Socrates takes advantage of that, like the bully he is.

3. Hippias believed in human progress through invention, as we may infer from 281d, ff. (on which see note 4). That may have been why he, too, tried always to make progress. Like an artist who prizes originality, Hippias tried to say something new on each occasion (Xenophon, *Memorabilia,* IV.iv. 6).

RHETORICAL MANNERISMS

Certain striking mannerisms occur frequently in Hippias' speech and in Socrates' speech when he is mocking Hippias. The most common of these is rhyme, achieved often by the simple repetition of words or word components. When he is making a strong point, Hippias likes to pile up words redundantly, often linking them with rhyme. He seems devoted to clumsy and ostentatious antithesis, also accompanied by rhyme. These mannerisms are especially prominent in the early pages of the *Hippias Major,* as we would expect (for that is given over to a study of Hippias' accomplishments), but they occur throughout the dialogue. They show up also in the speech Plato gives Hippias in the *Protagoras* (on which see Adam's note *ad loc.,* 337c7–338b1). I have listed examples from both dialogues, on p. 132.[7]

Plato himself is given to using similar devices. If the *Hippias Major* is an imitation of Plato's style, then the mannerisms could have been inserted to make fun not of Hippias, but of Plato. That appears unlikely. Plato's use of rhyme and repetition is much less clumsy, and usually serves a logical point. The *Hippias Major* contains examples of *that* sort of repetition as well, in passages given over to logical analysis (see the list on p. 133). So even if the *Hippias Major* is a forgery, it represents mannerisms I have cited as distinctively Hippian. That conclusion is supported by the occurrence of those devices in the appropriate part of the *Protagoras.* We know Plato frequently parodied or imitated the style of Socrates and his contemporaries: Socrates everywhere, Protagoras in the *Protagoras* at 320c8, ff., Prodicus at 337a2 of the same dialogue, Agathon in the *Symposium,* and possibly Lysias in the *Phaedrus.* That the mannerisms are absent from the *Hippias Minor* is no great objection to my thesis. Hippias there speaks little and has little to do with the subject of discussion. In the *Hippias Major,* by contrast, the personality of the sophist, as well as the character of his work, is a major source of interest, and is connected with the main philosophical subject (see p. 130).

Hippias' mannerisms (if we are right that they are Hippias') are for the most part unnecessary, inappropriate, and just plain silly. Words of no obvious importance are selected for emphasis through alliteration or repetition ("most," 281b1–2, "before," 282b5–6); totally unnecessary phrases are added to create an antithesis ("not to be despised, but," 281c2–3); and words of roughly the same meaning are fatuously strung together with "and"s and rhyme to create an effect ("unreasonably and unobservantly and foolishly and uncomprehendingly," 301c2–3). Hippias was apparently an expert at creating effects with the sounds and rhythms of words (285d). As Plato represented him he was not concerned with the precise meaning of what he said, but cared most about effects on the audience, effects he could apparently achieve by attending mostly to the sound of his speech. That of course is why Socrates frequently compliments the aesthetic qualities of Hippias' answers (e.g., at 282b1, 287b4, and 300c5) and by implication contrasts those with the philosophical merits of the positions

Hippias takes. And that is why, at the beginning, Socrates' urgent interest in the fine grows out of a question about Hippias' speeches. Are they in the final analysis fine because they sound good? When is a speech really fine? Because he is the kind of speaker he is, Hippias is ideally suited to be the interlocutor—and more than the interlocutor, the test case—in Socrates' attempt to clear up the nature of evaluation.

PLATO'S HIPPIAS

On a careless first reading of the *Hippias Major* one naturally concludes that Hippias is represented there as stupid, vain, and rude.[8] But that conclusion depends on the assumption that Socrates was right and good. Once Socrates' performance in the dialogue is more carefully evaluated, Hippias' personality looks better than it did. He is in fact rather clever in his own way; he is self-confident, not vain; and far from being rude he is a prodigy of patience and self-restraint. True, Socrates makes a fool of him; but that, as we shall see, is a far cry from simply being a fool. The features of Hippias' personality to which the author calls our particular attention are his versatility and superficiality; those are no doubt the character traits Socrates most abhorred. It is because of them that Socrates' treatment of Hippias is so remarkably savage.

Our main task is to assess the intelligence of Hippias; that is the point on which athetizers find the dialogue's characterization incompetent. How could it be, they ask, that Hippias is bright enough to make the very best suggestions (at 290d5 and 296e3–4), yet too stupid to understand the question? Until recently, all commentators agreed on Hippias' stupidity. Horneffer first noticed the discrepancy, and others followed his example.[9] Now two scholars have defended Hippias' intelligence on the main point. Previous commentators had thought that when Hippias gave his first answer ("a fine girl is a fine thing"—287e4) he was confusing a universal with a particular (Tarrant, 1928, *ad loc.,* for example). The text does not show that, runs the counterargument. Hippias offers "a fine girl" (understood as "*being* a fine girl") as a serious definition of the fine.[10] If Hippias is doing that, the received evaluation of his intelligence is grossly mistaken. (See note 63.)

Now that we have discussed the plot, comic genre, and philosophical subject of the dialogue, we are in a good position to determine how Hippias is characterized and how well his characterization fits with other elements of the whole. Certain of Hippias' questionable features are required for the comic technique. His pride and self-confidence, for example, are necessities of the dialogue's comic genre whether or not they are historically or morally justified. Hippias is quite sure he can handle Socrates' questions and is genuinely puzzled when he fails. All that, of course, is what makes his failures funny. In fact, Hippias' self-confidence was probably justified by his great success. He is not represented in the dialogue as a *vain* man (*pace* Tarrant) but as a seasoned professional who is quite frank about his success (cf. *Ion* 530c, ff.). A truly vain man would not have suffered five minutes of Socrates' banter. But Hippias is certainly capable of pomposity, and this too contributes to the comic effect.

Hippias' patience in putting up with Socrates is another necessity of the comic technique (again, cf. *Ion,* 523c). The victim in slapstick must come back for more punishment. Owing to what I have called his philosophy of agreement, Hippias is historically well suited to the role. He avoids confrontation with Socrates when he is insulted and mocked in the first round. Later, Socrates makes it easier to avoid confrontation by supplying the convenient fiction of a Third Party—the Questioner—who, because he is absent, may freely scold Hippias, and be scolded in return.

Another necessity of the comic plot is that Hippias not be a fool. There is a crucial difference between *being* a fool, and *being made* a fool. Socrates could not make a fool of Hippias, if Hippias were making a fool of himself. Hippias is not like the sort of clown who falls on his face as he enters the ring; he is like the soberly dressed clown who is thrown on his face by someone else. Comedy of this type depends on the fact that the character to be ridiculed is not by himself ridiculous. Otherwise, his mere entry would suffice.

Hippias is not characterized in the dialogue as stupid. True, he is defeated by Socrates, and he fails to show that he understands Socrates' insults. But everyone, after all, gets to be defeated by Socrates; no one really understands the logic of his questions (Hippias has the rare good sense not even to try); and Hippias demonstrably does realize that he is under attack. An agreeable nature and a philosophy of agreement keep his anger in check for the greater part of the dialogue.

HIPPIAS' FAILURE TO REACT. The most blatant Socratic irony washes off him; he seems to understand it as praise. Despite an early hint (the bizarre claim that Pittacus and Bias did not engage in affairs of state, 281c), Hippias shows no sign that he recognizes the irony of Socrates' demonstration that archaic wise men were inferior in wisdom to those of Hippias' generation. "They were so simple," says Socrates, "they didn't realize the great value of money" (282d1–3). Hippias does not react. Later he accepts the incredible conclusion that Sparta's treatment of him is illegal (285b5), even though it stems from a premise he surely did not believe: that a statute is not a law if it fails to do good. "I grant that," says Hippias. "You've said your say in my behalf, I think, and there's no need for me to oppose it" (285b3–4). Most commentators think Hippias is blinded by his own stupid vanity, and so takes whatever Socrates says as praise. He is, on this view, simply incapable of recognizing Socrates' irony.

That cannot be right. No one could be so stupid; and Hippias certainly is not. Look how he responds to the unmistakable insult at 286a2, the line in which Socrates compares him, in effect, to an old lady: Hippias is aware of the criticism, and he responds to it (286a3 ff.). But first he says "yes." Hippias has made a diplomatic practice of agreeing with Socrates. That is certainly the best thing he could do in the circumstances, even if it did not accord with his philosophy of agreement. What, after all, is the appropriate response to Socrates' irony, short of physical violence? It is not wise to show that you are hurt; the best thing is to put a brave face on the absurd conclusion he pushes toward you, to accept it, poker-faced, as Hippias does, and pretend it is a serious contribution from Socrates. That is what he does at 285b, where his agreement ("I grant that") is clearly a concession, and the tone of the sentence suggests he has *chosen* to regard Socrates' argument as favorable to himself. There is no better defense against Socrates.

Understood this way, the opening scene of the dialogue shows Socrates savagely, but with great delicacy and precision, exposing the absurdities to which Hippias could be drawn, exploiting the latter's philosophy of agreement (above, p. 125), and ruthlessly exercising his own power of irony.

HIPPIAS' FAILURE TO ANSWER. Hippias disregards Socrates' question. Though he says he understands the difference between *the fine* (to kalon) and *a fine thing* (kalon), he proceeds immediately to treat them as the same (287e). And though he agrees with Socrates that the fine is what fine things are fine *by* (287d1) he never attempts to say what that is. No one (save perhaps a besotted lover) could be so foolish as to think that a fine girl is what makes all fine things fine. Hippias clearly does not think that; he ignores a rhetorical question from Socrates on that very point (288a). He is not trying to answer the Questioner, he is trying to shut him up. Knowing, from his experience of Socrates (cf. 301b), that no answer he gave would satisfy Socrates' conditions, he gives an answer which, though not addressed to the question, nevertheless is supposed to be incontrovertible, and witty besides: "A fine girl is a fine thing." When Socrates makes a hash of that, Hippias, without admitting defeat, tries the same sort of tactic again and again. Surely this is a joke on Hippias' vaunted versatility. Hippias is limited to dealing with Socrates rhetorically. He is not a philosopher.

In all this Hippias is not represented as being stupid. Rather, he is represented as being defeated by Socrates, and at a game he chooses not to play. Socrates does indeed make a fool of Hippias; but that, as we have seen, is a far cry from simply being a fool.

I turn now to the important traits Hippias does exhibit in the *Hippias Major:* versatility and superficiality.

HIPPIAS' VERSATILITY. The focus of the first section of the dialogue is entirely Hippias' versatility. He is a public servant and makes money for himself as well. He commands so many different subjects, Socrates pretends he cannot even remember all of them. Hippias is quite ready to master a new subject for a new audience. At Olympia he would let his hearers choose the topic for his speech. He could be all things to all people. He would agree with virtually anything to avoid a quarrel.

In his amazing flexibility he is personally a model for the logical behavior of the word *kalos*. Neither one stands for anything by itself; both depend on their contexts for what they are. As Hippias is a mathematician in Athens, but an antiquarian in Sparta, so fineness could be *gold* for jewelry but *figwood* for cooking spoons. Thus the long opening of the dialogue has the effect of calling our attention to ways in which Hippias is a living metaphor for its philosophical subject.

That Plato distrusted personal versatility of the kind Hippias displayed is well known. Socrates probably held the same view, and for similar reasons.[11]

HIPPIAS' SUPERFICIALITY. Socrates calls our attention to another way in which Hippias is personally connected with his subject. Hippias is *kalos;* he is dressed *kalōs;* and, most important of all, he speaks *kalōs*. Socrates readily accords Hippias this measure of praise; and he does so, I think, with less than his usual irony. Hippias probably is dressed well; and his speech, as we have seen, is full of pleasant sounds, if nothing else. (See above, p. 125, ff.).

Hippias here is more interested in making nice sounds, and in achieving a specious agreement with Socrates, than he is in saying anything true or important. To say he is superficial is an unkind way of saying he is not a philosopher, and that he is more concerned with what Plato would call appearances than with reality.

The word *kalos* is often used of the superficial aspects of things; and Socrates in the *Hippias Major* seems much concerned with the danger that his term of commendation degenerate to that level entirely. He argues more than once that *kalos* not be given a merely aesthetic sense—"fine in appearance," "fine looking," or "fine sounding."[12]

In both his versatility and his superficiality, Hippias is an illustration of tendencies in the word *kalos* that Socrates wants to overcome. He wants to reduce its apparent versatility to a single referential meaning; and he wants that meaning to be genuinely rather than superficially commendatory. Not only is Hippias well chosen to be Socrates' interlocutor on this subject, but he is an appropriate target for Socrates' personal attack. For Hippias personally represents what is in Socrates' eyes the corruption of the word *kalos:* its facile and superficial use in ordinary language.

WHY HIPPIAS?

Why is Hippias made the target of an attack unparalleled in Plato's work? If we cannot answer that question satisfactorily, we will have to agree with critics of the dialogue that the attack is inappropriate.[13]

There are five good reasons for Socrates (or Plato through Socrates) to attack Hippias. The *first* and most obvious is that Hippias does represent certain ideas that were common among sophists, which Socrates considers highly dangerous: the radical idea that modern wise men are wiser than the ancients (281d) and the pretentious idea that virtue is taught by men such as Hippias (284a). The *second* reason for attacking Hippias is one we have already given: Hippias has character traits to which Socrates must have objected strongly, and which are exhibited by the word *kalos* in ordinary usage (p. 110). Of course, Hippias was not unique for either of these reasons; his ideas were common and so was his personality. Why then did Plato select him for such sharp treatment? The answer is most likely that Hippias came closest to personifying the type Plato abhorred as the generic sophist (above, p. 114). And not being rude or morally corrupt or a teacher of demonstrably false doctrines, he displayed no extraneous evils to confuse the issue. What is most dangerous about persons like Hippias is their being pretentious and versatile. In Hippias, these qualities may be in sharp focus; for we find little else in the man as Plato represents him.

Third, it is both fitting and Platonic that Hippias be attacked with laughter. He was a pretender to knowledge, and such pretense is ridiculous (*Philebus* 49a–c). Hippias and Gorgias used laughter themselves (note 5, 134), but in a different manner: to disarm serious opposition. Plato here illustrates its proper use, in exploding pretensions.

Fourth, Socrates has no recourse but to ridicule Hippias' personality. He cannot attack the positions Hippias takes, because Hippias takes no positions of his own. Whatever Socrates says (up to the breaking point at 300b), Hippias will agree, even when consistency demands he dig in his heels (as at 287e2, when he agrees there is no difference, but proceeds as if there were one, or at 284e, where he accedes to a most un-Hippian view of law). In agreeing so lightly, Hippias breaks the first rule of dialectic as Socrates practices it, that a participant say only what he personally believes. For that reason Hippias cannot be defeated in the ordinary way. Since he cannot defeat Hippias' positions, Socrates can do nothing against Hippias but attack his personal style. And though positions may be refuted by sober argument, a style is most convincingly defeated by ridicule. That is why the *Hippias Major* is a comedy, and that is why Hippias personally is its object.

Fifth, and most important, Hippias was probably a genuinely amusing figure, unlike Callicles and Thrasymachus on the one hand, who were simply scary (cf. *Philebus* 49bc), and Gorgias and Protagoras on the other, who must have worn an impressive air of authority. Hippias the polymath, massively self-confident in his homemade clothes, long-suffering and agreeable, endlessly adaptable, and given to sonorously inflated rhetoric; Hippias, who was probably all those things as a matter of historical fact, was a natural target for ridicule, a very funny man. Although the ridicule of Hippias here exceeds any to be found in Plato's other work, I believe it accords with what Schleiermacher called "the propriety and polish of Plato." The characterization of Hippias is consistent, and the attack on his personality is properly motivated in a dramatic sense.[14] We see why Socrates does it, and—even as modern readers—we laugh. That, more than anything, proves the comedy a success.

APPENDIX: MANNERISMS OF HIPPIAS' RHETORIC

1. Rhyme and repetition:

πλεῖστα . . . πλείστων [281B1–2]
προτέρους [282A5–6]
–κείμενος [286A6]
παμ– . . . παγ– [286B3–4]
λογ– . . . λεγ– [286B3–4, 286A8, 300C3]
ὀνόματα ὀνομάζειν [288D2]

κεκεραμευμένη ... κεραμέως [288D7]
—μοῦντος [282E1]
—βούμενος [282A6–7]
εἴπω [291B7]
ἐκφύγω φεύγων [292A6]

Compare these examples from the speech in the *Protagoras:*

συμ– ... συμ– ... συμ– [337E2–3]
—έστεροι [338A4]
Ἑλλήνων ... Ἑλλάδος [337D5–6]

Contrast these more Platonic repetitions, which bolster a logical point:

ποιεῖν οἱ ποιοῦντες ἃ ποιοῦσιν [296C2–3]
αἴτιον αἰτίου αἴτιον [297A8]

2. Redundancy (Often Accompanied by Rhyme):

ἐκμεμαθηκέναι τε καὶ ἐκμεμελετηκέναι [285E1–2]
ἀλογίστως καὶ ἀσκέπτως καὶ εὐήθως καὶ ἀδιανοήτως [301C2–3]
πάθος ἢ οὐσίαν [301B8]
κνήσματά ... περιτμήματα [304A5]
εὖ καὶ καλῶς [304A7]
λήρους καὶ φλυαρίας [304B5]

Compare these examples from the *Protagoras:*

μεγαλοπρεπέστεροι καὶ εὐσχημονεστεροι [338A4]
ποιήσετε καὶ πείθεσθε [338A7]
ῥαβδοῦχον καὶ ἐπιστάτην καὶ πρύτανιν [338A8]

3. Ostentatious antithesis (sometimes with rhyme):

281C2–3, 282A6–8 (Note how Socrates calls attention to this at
282B1–2), 284b8–c1, 298C6–7, 304B2.

Compare *Protagoras* 337d1   φύσει, οὐ νόμῳ
                    and 337d3–e2   σοφωτάτους ... φαυλοτάτους

NOTES TO CHAPTER FOUR

1. What we know of Hippias is conveniently summarized by Guthrie (1971: III, 280–285). The sources are translated by David Gallop in Sprague (1972: 94–105, a translation of DK 86). Untersteiner's study of Hippias (1954: 272–303) makes him out to be a far more interesting figure; but Untersteiner arrives at his portrait on slender grounds. More sober accounts are given by Björnbo (1913: in R.E. VIII, s.v. Hippias), Schmid und Stählin (1940), Nestle (1942), H. Gomperz (1912) and T. Gomperz (1896).

2. See p. 121, n. 12 above, and p. 116 on Gorgias. In some ways, particularly in the wide scope of his knowledge, Hippias may also have modeled himself on Democritus (so Keuls, 1978: 127).

3. He is credited with the discovery of the quadratrix by the majority of scholars, following the evidence of Proclus (DK 86 B21). But the Hippias associated with that discovery need not have been our Hippias, and the discovery in any case would not prove him a great mathematician (so Cherniss, 1952: 203–04, n. 11).

4. That he makes Nestor the mouthpiece for his moral views in the speech he gives at Sparta makes it more than likely that the views were morally orthodox, as Grote argues (1872: VIII, 63–4): "amidst so much unfriendly handling, not only we find no imputation against Hippias of having preached a low or corrupt morality, but Plato inserts that which furnishes good, though indirect, proof of the contrary." He did, however, uphold natural morality against the "tyranny" of *nomos* ("law" or "convention," see note 32). On that point, the evidence of Plato (*Protagoras* 337d) and Xenophon (*Memorabilia* IV.iv. 14 and 24) is in agreement. (See Johann, 1973.)

5. He says that his object is to draw laughter onto the opposition, at *Hippias Major* 288b1–3 and 288d1, 290a1, 291e8–292a1. Examples of lines clearly intended to provoke shaming laughter are: 288d1–3, 291d10, and 292b7. Hippias' method here may have its origin in the techniques of Gorgias, who said that the seriousness of opposing speakers should be destroyed with laughter (Aristotle, *Rhetoric* III.18, 1419b3=DK82B12). Notice, however, that the exchange between Hippias and Socrates beginning at 300b6 is on a more serious level.

6. Socrates' reference to Hippias' "continuous theory of being" (301e) is probably ironic; if not it is opaque, for we do not know what the theory was (note 175). Certainly that reference is not evidence that Hippias had thought much about the matter.

7. These devices belong to the high style of rhetoric developed by Gorgias. Their Gorgian character has escaped most commentators; but see Shorey (1922: 262). On Gorgias, see above, p. 116.

8. The chief representative of this reading is Tarrant (1928: xxviii, ff.). Hippias is supposed to be stupid because he repeatedly misunderstands Socrates' questions, and does not penetrate the thin disguise of the Questioner. He is conceited, because of his boasts (284a3–4); and rude in virtue of his strong language (as at 293a2). Tarrant does not observe that the boast she cites is put into Hippias' mouth by Socrates (284a1–2), and that the piece of rudeness by which she associates Hippias with Thrasymachus is entirely Socrates' doing (the "old lady" insult at 286a1–2, cf. *Republic* 350e2). On 293a2 see note 109.

9. Horneffer (1896: 17), Horn (1964: 79, ff.), Gauss (1952: 1.2, 208).

10. Nehamas (1975: 299, ff.), followed by Irwin (1977B: 8, n. 1). Cf. Irwin 1977A: 42, 294, n. 5.

11. For Plato's view, see *Republic* 422a; the rejection of versatility is one of the guiding principles of Plato's political philosophy. For Socrates' attitude, see *Ion* 541e (the comparison of Ion to Proteus). One of the things that disturbed Socrates about poets and their interpreters was the claim of poetry to authority on an impossibly wide variety of subjects. On this feature of the generic sophist, see above, p. 114.

12. 293e9–294e9 and the argument that culminates in 303d7–8 (with the implication of 303e).

13. Grote's suggestion that there was an historical enmity between Socrates and Hippias has scant support from the evidence (Grote, 1888: II, 34). Dümmler's theory that the true target of the dialogue is not Hippias but Antisthenes and Isocrates is highly unlikely (Dümmler, 1889: 52 ff.). There is little in either style or content to connect the Hippias of this dialogue with either of those figures.

14. Whether the attack is justified also by the historical facts about Hippias is another, more difficult, matter. Plato's representation of Hippias is plausible and as likely as any of Plato's portraits to be accurate. But in the absence of a second major source on Hippias, we cannot reach a verdict on Plato's accuracy.

FIVE
Socrates' Question

"What is the fine?" asks Socrates through the Questioner (286d). At first his question seems only a pretext for exploding Hippias' pretensions; but later the dialogue's theme shifts from Hippias' amusing failure to Socrates' own search for an answer (293de). Socrates pursues the definition of the fine in the serious manner of one who wants to succeed. In the end, when his failure is clear, he concedes it with regret, hoping to make the best of a bad situation (304c; cf. *Euthyphro* 15e). Here the mask of irony slips to reveal a searching philosopher intent on his goal, in striking contrast to the public speaker who cares mainly to appeal to the tastes of his audience, and thinks he knows enough for that. Socrates does not think he knows yet what the fine is, and he has commanding reasons for seeking that knowledge.[1]

INDEPENDENCE OF THE QUESTION

Though the question arises first as a trap for Hippias, it must have an independent claim on Socrates' attention. Otherwise, we could neither explain his persistence in pursuing it, nor the character of the arguments he uses in the process. Socrates pursues the question because he wants to know its answer (304e2–3), and also because, above all, he does not want to let himself be content with a bad answer (298bc; cf. *Apology* 21d).

He does not argue as he would if his sole interest were in either exposing or educating Hippias. If all he wanted was to expose Hippias' pliability, a few bad arguments would have sufficed—bad so that Hippias'

136

agreement to them would be foolish, and few because such a demonstration would not need to be repeated. But the arguments Socrates uses are neither few nor as bad as some commentators would have them.[2] The arguments between 293e and 297d show up failures for which Socrates himself is chiefly responsible. These arguments are not the sort of obvious fallacy Socrates might use to make a joke of Hippias' pliability. As I argue in the Commentary, they are good enough to bring plausible Socratic attempts at definition to a dead end, and must therefore be part of Socrates' own unsuccessful inquiry into the nature of the fine.

If, on the other hand, Socrates hoped to further Hippias' education, he should be sadly disappointed. Generally, Socrates fails in the dialogues of search to reduce his partners to the proper state of modesty envisaged at *Sophist* 230bc. Nicias, at the end of the *Laches,* is modestly prepared to learn, but that is no change for him; he was so at the start (188ab). Many of Socrates' partners respond to refutation by attacking him or his way of questioning—Laches, for example, Anytus, Callicles, and of course, Hippias.[3] Charmides' response is violent, though positive (176cd); Euthyphro in the end is evasive, and so is Protagoras. Since none of these characters shows any sign of improvement under Socrates' purgative treatment, charity forbids our taking their improvement to be part of his goal.

In any case the pedagogical method described at *Sophist* 230cd is not applied in the *Hippias Major.* The *Sophist* proposes to refute ignorant persons in order to purge them of their conceit of wisdom, and so to prepare them for positive learning. But Socrates has no positive lesson in reserve for Hippias, so far as we can tell. His arguments, moreover, have a different thrust from those mentioned in the *Sophist.* Purgative arguments of the type envisaged there elicit and point up contradictions in an ignorant person's thought, with a view to changing his attitudes and preparing him to correct his ignorance. The conclusion of such an argument is that the person's beliefs are inconsistent, from which it follows that at least one of his beliefs is false. But exactly *which* belief is false the argument alone cannot say and does not need to say in order to accomplish its goal. The purpose of purgative argument is not to show that a given view is false, but that a given believer is confused. By contrast, Socrates' definition-testing arguments in the *Hippias* are supposed to disqualify certain proposed definitions. The main point of difference is this: the premises of a merely purgative argument would all be on the same footing, having no more authority than comes to them from being believed by Socrates' adversary; whereas definition-testing arguments depend on key premises supplied by Socrates himself—privileged doctrines against which proposed definitions are measured. These doctrines, which I discuss below (p. 149, ff.), govern the form and content a definition must have to be acceptable. Proposed definitions that fail to satisfy these doctrines fail to answer Socrates' question. On that matter Socrates is an authority; the question, after all, was framed by Socrates. Usually he completes an argument against a definition-proposal by reminding his partner of the original question or of the privileged doctrines that explicate that question (288a, 289cd, and 292cd; cf. *Euthyphro* 8ab). He rarely calls attention in such contexts to a contradiction (as he should in a purgative argument). A purgative argument, then, need assume nothing but the rules of logic and prove only that some confused arguer is trying to hold a contradiction. Socrates' definition-testing arguments, on the other hand, assume conditions necessary for successful definition, and prove that certain proposals fail to satisfy them.[4]

I have shown that some of Socrates' arguments in the *Hippias Major* serve primarily not to discredit Hippias or to further his education, but to test definitions of the fine. Socrates appears to be directly interested in the inquiry, and anxious with a philosopher's fear that he might take a false step (296a8, cf. 298b). The arguments serve to save Socrates and Hippias (to say nothing of us the readers) from the false conceit of wisdom; but they also illustrate the principles of Socratic definition. And by showing what the fine is *not,* the arguments illuminate the fine (below, p. 182). Socrates cares about knowing what the fine is, because he considers such knowledge necessary for knowing what things are fine (p. 138).

But if this is his goal, why does he question such characters as Hippias, from whom he should not expect good answers? Though they pretend to wisdom, and he to respect for their wisdom, he cannot honestly hope to learn from them as he says he does.[5] Hippias was discredited early in the dialogue as a thinker who could neither help nor be helped by Socrates. Why then does Plato weave together a genuine Socratic inquiry with a spoof on Hippias? The answer must lie in our author's complex purpose. He seems to have wanted to contrast Hippias' pliable rhetoric against Socrates' earnest and self-critical search; and to do this he had both to show up Hippias and to present Socrates seriously at work. The inquiry into fineness is important to Socrates. That is because he thinks great issues hang on it, and because he does not think he knows the answer. Each of these points is controversial and calls for special discussion.

PRIORITY OF DEFINITION

Socrates' ignorance is a disappointment to him (304ce, cf. *Euthyphro* 15e). That is because he thinks he must know what the fine is before he will know what sorts of things are fine (286c8–d2, 304d8–e2), and before he will be able to discuss fine things without crippling embarrassment (304d5–8). In such a condition, he asks himself, does he think his life worth living? Certainly he is missing something wonderful, if he is right about what knowledge of definitions will do for a person. One who knew what the fine is could justifiably set up as teacher of fine things, for unlike Hippias he would be able to prove his qualifications to the Spartans. Better than that and more tantalizing (though not said in the *Hippias Major*), the sort of knowledge Socrates lacks—knowledge of what the fine virtues are—is both necessary (cf. *Charmides* 158e) and sufficient for having those virtues (cf. the implication of *Euthyphro* 16a).

Knowing what the fine is is knowing its Socratic definition. Socrates puts so much stress on the priority of knowing definitions that a fallacy along that line is named after him. The "Socratic" fallacy is supposing that a person cannot use a word correctly unless he can define it.[6] That is a fallacy, but Socrates does not commit it. It is a fallacy because (1) it entails the falsehood that in working towards definitions you cannot employ examples of correct usage; and (2) it contradicts experience: you *can* use words correctly without being able to pass Socrates' test for knowing definitions. Socrates, if we are to believe him, knows few definitions; but he clearly uses words correctly, even ones he wants to define.

To understand Socrates' disappointment, we need to be clear about what he makes definition prior *to*. Here is what he says:

> Just now someone got me badly stuck when I was finding fault with parts of some speeches for being foul, and praising other parts as fine. He questioned me this way, really insultingly: "Socrates, how do *you* know what sorts of things (*hopoia*) are fine and foul? Look, would you be able to say what the fine is?" (286c5–d2)

> So when I go home to my own place and he hears me saying those things, he asks if I'm not ashamed that I dare discuss fine activities when I've been so plainly refuted about the fine, and it's clear I don't even know at all what *that* is itself! "Look," he'll say. "How will you know whose speech—or any other action—is finely presented or not, when you are ignorant of the fine? And when you're in a state like that, do you think it's any better for you to live than die?" (304d4–e3)

If Socrates meant that knowing the definition of the fine is prior to knowing only what *sorts* of things are fine, his doctrine would be innocuous. It would say merely that one does not know of what sort a thing must be to be fine until he knows what it is to be fine. That is a tautology. But what

Socrates wants later is stronger; the question of the second passage implies that he will not know whether a speech or action is finely done until he knows what the fine is. That is why Socrates' ignorance is so serious a matter. The aim of his life is fine action and speech; but he appears not to know what actions or speeches are fine. What saves him (though he never says so) is the body of tested opinion he has on the subject. That, I will suggest (p. 145), is good enough to guide choices for his own life. Only knowledge, however, would qualify him to "discuss fine activities" for the training of others—as Hippias is known to do (286b1 with 304d6), and as Socrates would like to be able to do (*Apology* 20c).

Knowing the definition of the fine is prior to knowing of anything that it is fine; such is the burden of the two passages. Notice that what Socrates makes dependent on definition is not opinion but knowledge. Knowledge here is more than the ability to speak of fine things without contradiction; that ability could come from what I shall call *tested opinion,* which lacks a foundation in definition, but nevertheless is sturdy enough to withstand the sort of purgative questioning discussed above.[7] Knowledge would carry you further, being based on a definition; it would establish your authority as a judge of fineness, an authority to which opinion, however well tested, could not entitle you.

Notice also that Socrates does not make definition prior to correct usage, as this is narrowly understood. Correct usage requires that "fine" be used as a term of commendation, that it be employed within a certain range, and that it enjoy certain entailment relations with "good," "beneficial," and other such words. All this, we shall see (p. 144), one can observe and even know without knowing the definition of the fine. Socrates does not say or imply that a person cannot use "fine" correctly (in the ways I have listed) without knowing what the fine is. There are two more important things Socrates does not say in the *Hippias Major:*

1. He does not say that you cannot know what properties the fine has until you know its definition. A principle like that would embarrass the arguments that depend on taking the fine to be beneficial (296cd) and good (297c). Though he appears to apply similar principles elsewhere to other *definienda* (*Meno* 71a, 100b; *Republic I* 354b), Socrates is not committed to the general rule that you cannot know what properties the *F* has until you know its definition (Santas, 1979: 126).

2. Socrates does not say that for *any* attribute, *G*-ness, he cannot know what things are *G* until he knows the definition of the *G*. If he did, he would have made it impossible to know of anything that it is fine. For if the fine turned out to be the *G*, he would need to know what things are *G* before he could know what things are fine, and for that he would need a definition of the *G*. But the *G* will turn out to be something else, the *H*, and he could not know what things are *H,* not until he mastered yet another definition. There is no noncircular way to end this regress. (See Santas, 1979: 311, n. 24.) But nothing Socrates says commits him to the general position from which the trouble follows. Socrates seems to assume that one definition will be enough, that once he has defined the fine he will have satisfactorily demonstrated his qualifications as a judge. The Questioner is not looking for an ultimate foundation for judgments of fineness in the modern epistemological sense. Such searches inevitably lose themselves in regress.[8] He is looking for evidence that Socrates, or Hippias, knows what he is talking about. One definition could suffice for that.

All Socrates implies in the *Hippias Major* is that no one can satisfy the Socratic questioner of his authority to judge fineness unless he knows what the fine is. Since Socrates is the one who controls the elenchus we had better believe him. He is saying he will not accept a use of "fine" as justified unless its user can give a satisfactory account of what the fine is. This is, apparently, to set superhuman standards of justification, but we should not be surprised that Socrates does so. For Socrates does not count on finding the knowledge he seeks among human beings, not after his many failures (cf. *Apology* 23a). Such standards for knowledge are hard to live with, but they do not constitute a fallacy.

That Socrates does not commit the "Socratic" fallacy should now be clear. The fallacy was supposing that a person must know definitions if he is to use words correctly (in the narrow sense illustrated above). But Socrates supposes that one must know the definition of the fine in order to establish his authority to make judgments on what is fine.

This superhuman standard is appropriate for Socrates' concerns. Since the fine is good and the good fine (297c), when Socrates asks after the fine he is seeking nothing less than the knowledge of good and evil, the foundation of justifiable praise and blame. A person who knew this would indeed be superhuman; he could take to himself the governance of other people's affairs and the guidance of other people's children. For this sort of role Socrates may reasonably expect candidates to meet the highest standards. Socrates has a conception of definition so strong that knowing definitions would qualify a person for that role. No wonder he does not think he knows the definition. The role of teacher and arranger of other people's lives is not for him.

THE BOUNDS OF IGNORANCE

Socrates asks, "What is the fine?" and says he does not know the answer. He can say this sincerely even though he has firm views about fine things, and even though he acts as if he had a measure of knowledge about the fine itself.

The general issue of whether Plato's Socrates thinks he knew the answers to his own questions will never be resolved. Certainly Socrates is never satisfied in a dialogue of search with a definition for which he is searching (never, at least, before the *Republic*). That does not appear to be because he thinks *a priori* that he cannot be satisfied; rather, he talks as if the right answer simply has not yet turned up. But though he never acknowledges a successful definition in a dialogue that searches for definitions (except by way of example), he does introduce definitions of critical terms in other contexts. (For a list, see Santas, 1979: 100.) The issue is whether those definitions are meant to satisfy the unsatisfied quests of other dialogues. The *Laches'* quest for courage could be answered by *Protagoras* 360d, and the *Hippias Major's* for the fine by *Gorgias* 474d. But the *Protagoras'* definition of courage is soundly refuted in the *Laches* (Woodruff, 1976) and the *Gorgias'* two definitions of the fine are severally refuted in the *Hippias Major* (296d–297d and 297d, ff.). Such accounts as we find in the *Protagoras* and *Gorgias,* though possibly true of their subjects, cannot have been intended as the sort of definitions wanted in the dialogues of search. Knowing them would not establish moral expertise. It is one thing to speak truly about fineness—by saying, for example, that it is good for people. It is another to show that you know what the fine *is*. We need a way of distinguishing the definitions Socrates says he does not know from the many things he does appear to know, if we are to understand his profession of ignorance.

In the *Hippias Major* he is shown seeking the nature of the fine and failing to hunt it down. We are accustomed to Socrates' failures, and accustomed to treating them with suspicion. Socrates loves to report his ignorance; he does so with an ambiguous pride. It could be the sincere self-congratulation of a man wise enough to see his shortcomings; or it could be an attitude assumed ironically, to needle his floundering opponents. In the case of the fine, Socrates' claim to ignorance is particularly hard to credit. How could he not know what *to kalon* is? The word is always on his lips. He appeals to it at critical stages in his arguments, where he uses a definite conception of the fine, a conception so unusual as to make a deep impression on both Plato and Xenophon. Unlike his contemporaries, who use *"kalon"* in different ways in different contexts, and most passionately of the loveliness that excites desire, Socrates keeps mainly to a utilitarian usage (see p. 183). He must have a reason for that. But what could it be, if he does not think he knows what the fine is? We shall have to decide how far to believe Socrates in this. The case is central to our understanding of all his ignorance claims. Socrates appears to have adequate knowledge of the definitions of some things (speed, for example—*Laches* 192ab). What he does not know—what he begs other people to tell him—are the definitions of the fine itself and things antecedently known to be fine, principally, the virtues. (See p. 111, n. 2). If Socrates knew what the fine was, he would probably be able to answer all his other questions as well. The fine is at the core of Socrates' alleged ignorance.

What Socrates chiefly does not know is the definition of the fine. Knowing that, as we have seen, is necessary for knowing what things are fine. But Socrates does confidently ascribe fineness to things and generally seems to know a great deal about the fine. To dampen the suspicion that Socrates knows more about the fine than he is letting on, we shall have to identify clearly what Socrates *can* do without knowing the nature of the fine. Knowing a definition is a different matter from (i) having opinions and (ii) knowing what you have to know to look for a definition. I do not suggest Socrates made these distinctions explicitly; but I am certain he used them, and I propose we use them to define the scope of Socrates' ignorance.

OPINION. Before the *Meno* and *Gorgias,* Socrates does not distinguish between knowledge and opinion; but we must not conclude that in the early dialogues of search he allows no middle ground between knowledge of definitions and total ignorance (*pace* Beversluis, 1974: 333). He does not talk about that middle ground, but he quite plainly and self-consciously lives in it. Without knowledge of definitions, you are ignorant, insofar as you do not know enough to set up shop as a teacher. But you may know enough to live a good nonteacherly life, nonetheless; and indeed Socrates believes he has done just that (*Apology* 30a5–7, 33ab; cf. 39b). You will live better or worse depending on the quality of your opinions. A well-tested and consistent body of opinion enables you to make good choices for your own life, and furnishes sufficient warrant for that, even to the death. It is, after all, opinion that keeps Socrates in prison awaiting execution, an opinion with no more authority than it earned by serving Socrates well throughout his life in practice and argument (*Crito* 49ab; cf. *Gorgias* 509a4–b5). Knowledge would be preferable of course, but opinion has many sound uses.

Socrates allows opinions to stand in his arguments if they have the assent of both parties. But the conclusion of an argument is no stronger than its premises; so if Socrates' premises depend on opinion, then his conclusions have the same uncertain basis. Nevertheless, Socrates seems quite certain that he has disqualified all the definitions proposed in the *Hippias Major*. How could this be?

ANTECEDENT KNOWLEDGE. Fortunately, the arguments Socrates uses against definitions have a more dependable basis than mere opinion and the agreement of partners. I shall say that the doctrines privileged by this more dependable basis are known by *antecedent knowledge*. Now Socrates does not call these doctrines "knowledge"; indeed, he pays no attention to the problem of their status in his arguments—not until the Platonic doctrine of recollection surfaces in the *Meno* (80e). Such privileged doctrine lies somewhere between opinion and the knowledge that could be derived from definitions. It is best understood as Socrates' understanding of what his question means, and not as mysterious knowledge about the undiscovered object of Socrates' search.

Socrates' problem, unstated before the *Meno,* is this: until he knows what the fine is, how can he pursue it? How will he know what to look for, or be sure, once he has found it, that he *has* found it? The search for a definition presupposes antecedent knowledge of the subject. But knowledge of the subject should await the outcome of the search, or so it would seem.

Socrates successfully negotiates this problem in the early dialogues of search without calling notice to it. In the *Euthyphro* he distinguishes between what piety *is* and what it *is like*. Socrates does not know, and wants to know, what piety *is;* but he tells Euthyphro, and so seems to know in advance, what piety *is like:* piety is the same in all instances, and quite the opposite of impiety (5cd). Though Euthyphro readily agrees to these premises, their use in the argument does not depend on his agreement. If he balked, we may infer from Socrates' practice elsewhere that Euthyphro would be quickly shamed into agreement. Unlike mere opinions, which derive their standing in the argument from the partners' agreement, such premises are forced on Socrates' interlocutors as conditions of participating in the search. Everyone must agree, for example, that the fine is such as to be the same in every instance. When Socrates encounters someone who overlooks such a principle, he treats him with derision as failing to understand the nature of the search (as at 292ce), or presses the principle on him with dubious examples (as at *Meno* 72a, ff.; see p. 157, below).

The reason Socrates' partners have to agree to such privileged doctrines is that otherwise they would not be partners in Socrates' inquiry at all. To be party to Socrates' inquiry, you have to be looking for the same thing he is. The inquiry is defined by the conditions that must be satisfied for it to be successful. Socrates might be wrong to undertake a certain inquiry, but he cannot be wrong in stating the conditions that define an inquiry he has undertaken. If he can give satisfactory reasons for taking up a search, then he need do no more to justify his antecedent account of its quarry. A farmer, for example, might believe that a dog has killed his chickens, and therefore propose to seek out the dog who ate the chickens.

He knows what the dog must be like (in order to be the killer of chickens) and he can reasonably set about screening and rejecting candidates even if the presupposition of his search turns out to be false. Even if his chickens had been taken by a clever thief, the farmer's search would still be for a dog of a certain sort, and (though he would be mistaken in seeking it) he could truly say that the dog *he sought* was of a certain sort. No one who joined him in the hunt could reasonably ask, "How do you know the dog we want ate the chickens?"

I shall say that what Socrates knows antecedently about the definition he wants comprises its *guiding properties*. One of these is a general property Socrates expects of any definition: that it state a logical cause which is self-predicating and the same in all instances. That I discuss below in Chapter Six. Other guiding properties belong particularly to the hoped-for definition of the fine. He expects the definition of the fine to make it both beneficial and good (below, p. 183). If the fine were otherwise, he would have no interest in knowing what it is. What is in question is Socrates' authority to praise morally improving speeches (and, indirectly, Hippias' qualifications to teach young Spartans). If the fine were neither good nor beneficial, then knowledge of the fine would not be to the point. Socrates' question, therefore, calls for an answer that makes the fine both beneficial and good. Answers that do otherwise must be rejected—and for good reason. For Socrates to accept an account of the fine that made it of indifferent value would be like our chicken farmer's declaring himself satisfied with the capture of a toothless lap-dog. Elsewhere, Socrates hopes to define each virtue as something fine and rejects definitions of virtues that do not make them fine (e.g., at *Charmides* 159c). Socrates' searches are always for definitions of things that are fine and good and beneficial. Why else would he urgently want to know what they are?

Of all these guiding properties Socrates can be certain without compromising his ignorance of the definition of the fine. That is because knowing a Socratic definition is different from knowing its guiding properties. When you have said that the fine must be defined as a logical cause, self-predicating, the same in all instances, and moreover as being good and beneficial, you have still not said what that definition *is,* not, at least, to the Questioner's satisfaction. The knowledge Socrates wishes he has—the knowledge Hippias *ought* to have, to do what he does—goes beyond this. It is, I suggested earlier, the very knowledge of good and evil.

Socrates' question commands his attention in its own right, independently of the use he can make of it to explode Hippias. It is a question to which, so far as we can tell, he honestly does not know the answer. And it is a question he thinks one must answer *first,* before embarking on the wonderful career of a Hippias or Protagoras. Socrates, without an answer, must daily face the paralyzing inquisition of his own Questioner. And that, like most fine things, is hard.

APPENDIX: SOCRATES' USE OF EXAMPLES

By the priority of definition, Socrates cannot know of anything that it is fine until he knows the definition of the fine. It should follow that he cannot depend on examples in his search for the definition (Santas, 1979: 116). But he does use examples. How can this be explained?

The examples Socrates actually uses do not threaten either his disclaimer of knowledge or the priority of definition. They fall into three classes: some things are said to be fine and introduced as examples; other things are cited as counterexamples and said to be foul; still other things, proferred as examples by Hippias, are shown to be neither fine nor foul. Let us see how Socrates uses each sort of example.

Examples Proferred. Socrates says that a fine pot or mare or lyre is fine, but only dialectically, *en route* to the conclusion that none of these things is really fine after all (288b–289d; see p. 153). He depends on examples of things *he* believes to be fine for one purpose only: to establish the range of the fine. "Fine" is a term of commendation usable in most areas of life; so a definition of the fine should be suitable for the evaluation of all sorts of things. Socrates can refute the proposed definition of pleasure as what is pleasant to sight and hearing by mentioning the example of a fine law (not a particular law that is fine, just *a* fine law). He can do this without asserting of anything in particular that it is fine (*Hippias Major* 298b). Such examples are innocuous reminders to his hearers of the different sorts of things that can be fine. The range of the fine should be considered among its guiding properties, and Socrates' ignorance is safe on this score.

Counterexamples. These are more difficult. Socrates reminds his interlocutors that it is not fine to bury your parents if they are immortal (*Hippias Major* 292e); that quickness in cithara-playing is finer than quietness (*Charmides* 159c); and that wise endurance is fine, but foolish endurance foul (*Laches* 192c, ff.). The partners agree and so must abandon definitions they had proposed. Their agreement is sufficient for that. But for Socrates it will not do. Socrates, remember, concludes from the argument of *Hippias* 292e that *he* does not yet know what the fine is. Yet Socrates' conclusion can be no better than his premises, and such premises cannot be known *until* he knows what the fine is. So it would appear that Socrates does not know that he does not know what the fine is.

I think, however, that Socrates' arguments can be saved, on the assumption that knowledge of what the fine is guarantees the knowledge of what things are fine (i.e., that knowledge of the definition is sufficient, as well as necessary, for knowledgeable judgments). Then, if you knew what the fine were, you would not assent to any countervailing examples. Once given the definition, you would know exactly which things were fine and which foul; but if you could entertain examples excluded by the definition, you would not be in that condition. Socrates' mere assent to the counterexamples proves that the proposed definition does not convey the knowledge he wants; for that would sweep all before it. He need not know that the counterexamples are true; and, indeed, he never claims to have that knowledge.

Examples Rejected. In the *Hippias Major,* Socrates undertakes to show Hippias that his examples of fineness (which he offers in lieu of definitions) are no more fine than foul, and so are neither (above, pp. 48–9). Hippias' fine girl, his gold, his good life including the burial of parents, all these turn out to be not strictly fine. The premise in each case is that for a thing to be strictly fine, it cannot be foul in any way—not in any comparison, or use, or instance. This curiously restrictive premise we shall discuss below (pp. 153-56). For now, it is enough to point out that it states one of the guiding properties of the fine. Once Hippias admits (as he does readily) that an example is in some way foul, he must therefore retract it as an example of fineness. On this also Socrates can insist without compromising his ignorance.

NOTES TO CHAPTER FIVE

1. How can we be sure the mask of Socrates' irony slips at all? Any attempt to find the serious core of Socrates is bound to be speculative; this Chapter and its successors are no exceptions. For a discussion of irony and other obstacles Plato leaves lying for rash interpreters, see Tigerstedt (1969 and 1977).

2. The argument at 296e–297d, for example, is widely misinterpreted as a howling fallacy. See p. 72 above.

3. *Laches* 197d, *Meno* 94e, *Gorgias* 485a, ff., and *Hippias Major* 304ab.

4. Vlastos, in his influential introduction to the *Protagoras,* offers a different account of Socrates' arguments: their purpose is "to increase one's insight into the logical relations between propositions and thus one's ability to estimate how the truth claims of one proposition are affected by those

of others" (1956: xxx). This is precisely what purgative arguments achieve *en route* to their goal of instilling modesty. But arguments used to reject definitions must be more ambitious.

Irwin makes a good case that Socrates uses argument constructively, in support of positive doctrine (1977A: 36, ff. and 68, ff.). That may be; but in the *Hippias* we find only definition-testing arguments. If positive conclusions may be drawn from them, that is a happy accident.

5. *Hippias Major* 286de; cf. *Euthyphro* 5ab and 15a, *Charmides* 166cd, and *Protagoras* 348ce.

6. Geach, 1966; cf. replies by Santas (1972 and 1979: 311, n. 26) and Irwin (1977A: 40–41, 63, 294, n. 4). See also the elegant treatment by Burnyeat, 1977.

7. Socrates' most cherished moral views seem to have no better basis than this tested opinion. See *Gorgias* 509a4–7. On the usefulness of opinion, see *Meno* 97b, ff. On the unstated dependence of Socrates on opinion in the *Hippias Major,* see, p. 143, ff. On the supposed priority of definition to opinion, see Santas, 1979: 115–126, for a view like mine, but put in different terms.

8. See the treatment of this problem in Williams, 1977: 60, ff.

SIX
Principles of Definition

The *Hippias Major* belongs to those dialogues in which Socrates asks for definitions[1] and is never satisfied with the answers proposed. In the *Laches* he asks after Courage, in the *Euthyphro,* Piety; in the *Charmides,* Soundness of Mind; and in Book I of the *Republic,* Justice. Because none of these searches is successful, we cannot be sure what a Socratic definition would look like. (Plato, however, must have been on the right track in defining Justice as he does in *Republic IV.*) A Socratic definition is not the sort of thing that makes up dictionaries. Dictionary definitions are definitions of *words* (like "justice"), and they are based on usage. Socratic definitions are of *forms* (like Justice), and not of the words that stand for them (Santas, 1979: 106–108). A Socratic definition would be based not on word-usage, but on the truth about the subject of definition. It has, however, this connection with meaning: once found, a Socratic definition would give to the word for what was to be defined an *ideal* meaning, the meaning the word would have in discourse informed by a true theory about the way things are. Socratic definition accordingly invites metaphysical speculation as to what is the real nature of the things words signify. Plato eventually accepted the invitation, and developed a metaphysical theory of Forms in the *Phaedo* and *Republic.* Socrates himself is unlikely to have gone so far. (See Chapter Seven.)

What conditions does Socrates expect a definition to meet? Because Socrates does not discuss definition abstractly in any of the relevant dialogues, we must infer his principles from his practice in testing proposed definitions. For this the *Hippias Major* is particularly interesting. There Socrates rejects seven proposals, for reasons that can be discussed under three headings. Socrates is apparently looking for something that

149

1. *explains* the fineness of fine things in such a way as to *justify* his praise for them (286cd);
2. *is* fine (292e2); and
3. *occurs in every fine thing* (289d).

What these requirements mean, and why Socrates requires them, are the main questions of this Chapter. I begin with a summary interpretation of each, and a comment on their logical connections with one another.

1. The explanation requirement. Whatever the fine turns out to be, it must be something I shall call the *logical cause* of fineness: it is what *makes* all fine things fine (290d2). A logical cause is the ground for explanations of a certain sort. The presence of the fine in something will explain that thing's being fine (if it is fine). A person who knows what the fine is will be able to satisfy a Socratic Questioner that he knows what sorts of things are fine and is entitled to praise them. The other two requirements state conditions necessary for being a logical cause.

2. The self-predication requirement. What makes things fine must be strictly fine itself; that is, it must in no way or circumstance be foul. If the life that includes burying parents were fine "always and for everyone" (292e), then it would stand a chance of being *the* fine; but, as it happens, some instances of that life would be foul, because some people's parents should never be buried.

3. The unity requirement. What makes things fine must make *every* fine thing fine. A logical cause must not only always bring fineness with it, if it is to be *the* fine, but it must also be found wherever there is fineness. This means that the fine must be *one* and the same in every case of fineness. The test is applied at 303d, ff. and mentioned at 288a9–10 (cf. 289d) and 298b–d.

The requirements of self-predication and unity are independently necessary, but not sufficient, for the explanation requirement. That they are necessary will emerge in the detailed discussion of each. That self-predication and unity are independent is easily shown by the following examples. Defining *man* as *animal* would satisfy the unity requirement, for every man is an animal, but would fail the self-predication test, since animal is in no sense man. Again, defining *the fine* as *pleasure through sight* would satisfy self-predication if such pleasure is fine (as Socrates is prepared to concede); but it would fail the unity requirement if, as is the case, pleasure through hearing alone is also fine.

That self-predication and unity are neither severally nor jointly sufficient for the explanation requirement is also to be shown by example. For suppose that the beneficial is fine and occurs in every fine thing, as Socrates appears to believe (below, p. 183). It could still fail to be the logical cause of fineness. If you try to say that something is fine because it is beneficial, the Questioner will ask how you know it is beneficial. If you then say it is beneficial in virtue of its fine products, he will ask how you know the products are fine, and if you say the *products* are beneficial too you will be on your way into an unsatisfactory regress. The explanation requirement is not so helpful as the others, since we do not know exactly what *would* satisfy the Questioner. We can say, however, that it adds to the others the condition that definitions not be circular. If *x* is to be the fine, the *x* should be something we can identify without already knowing what the fine is (cf. *Meno* 79cd).

Why should Socrates lay down these conditions? The answer has to do with the purpose he expects the definition of the fine to serve. When Socrates praised a speech as fine, he was interrupted by the Questioner, who asked him to show his knowledge of the subject. Socrates was required to say what the fine is in order to establish his authority to give praise. What he now accepts as the definition of the fine should be such as to satisfy the Questioner of his qualifications to recommend this or that activity as fine. For that the fine itself must be of a certain sort: it must be a logical cause, one and self-predicating. If it were otherwise, the authority Socrates would like to have would not be possible for anyone. Suppose someone wants to establish himself as a reliable and expert guide to snark hunting. We need to know nothing about snarks to be sure that his claim will be bogus unless snarks have a nature, the same in all snarks, which does not occur outside of snarks, and on the basis of which an expert can predict and explain their behavior. Otherwise, snarks will comprise too indefinite a subject for expert knowledge. Something like that is what happens to poetry, according to the argument of the *Ion* (and cf. *Gorgias* 463a–c), but must not befall the fine if anyone is to be a teacher of fine things. Socrates' general conditions for definition are in fact conditions a *definiendum* must satisfy to be an object of authoritative knowledge. To say that Socrates wants definitions is misleading in a modern context. What he primarily wants is a certain sort of knowledge, which is to be conveyed by the Socratic definition of the fine.

EXPLANATION AND LOGICAL CAUSES

An expert on fine things must know what it is that makes them fine, so he can explain their fineness to those who doubt it, and predict the fineness of things unseen. What makes fine things fine is a logical cause. Socrates emphasizes the causal role of the fine in the *Hippias Major,* using a variety of language:

The dative: "that *by which* fine things are fine." 287cd, 298d2, 294b1, 300b5, 302c2, 302e9. (Cf. *Euthyphro* 6d11, *Phaedo* 100d7, and my note on 287c2.)

"What *makes* fine things fine." 290d2, 294a1, 294b1 (where it is equivalent to the dative construction), 294d7, 300a9, 302d1.

"The *cause* (*aition*) of its being fine." 299e4. (Cf. *Phaedo* 100b, ff.)

"That *because of* which . . . " (*dia*). 288a10, 299d8, 302d4. (Cf. *Meno* 72c8, *Protagoras* 360c1–2).

"*Because* (*hoti*) they are _____ they are fine." 302c1, d3. Cf. use of "if . . . then . . . " at 288a9.

In using such language about what is to be defined, the *Hippias Major* is more insistent than other early dialogues of search. But they too treat their objects as *causes*. The theory common to the early dialogues and the autobiographical part of the *Phaedo* (96a6–102a1)² boils down to this: *F* things are *F* because *the F* (a form or character) is present in them. The dialogues of search seek to identify for various different *F*'s (mainly virtues) what it is that plays that causal role.

What sort of cause does Socrates expect the fine to be? He uses distinctions he does not make explicit. We must therefore identify the various sorts of things Socrates calls "causes." 1. Causes like the fine are had by, or occur in, other things, and impart their natures to those other things. Such causes I shall call "*logical* causes."³ 2. The causality of *productive* causes is of a more familiar stamp. A father is the productive cause of his child. This sort of causal connection (unlike logical causality) occurs between things of the same ontological level (like two men), and actually excludes the effect of logical causes. As a logical cause, the fine makes things fine; as a productive cause, a father makes offspring but he does not make them fathers. 3. The causal connection that occurs between something and that out of which it came to be is still another matter. This Plato distinguishes from logical causation at *Phaedo* 103ab. Such causes and what come out of them have mutually contrary characters. When a plant grows, something bigger comes from something smaller, for example. But the *logical* cause of being bigger is not something smaller; it is the big itself. 4. Plato also seeks to distinguish logical causes from the sorts of causes Anaxagoras posited (*Phaedo* 96a–102a). The passage is extraordinarily difficult, and not enough is known of Anaxagoras' theory for a satisfactory interpretation (*pace* Teloh, 1976). But it appears that an Anaxagorean cause is a constituent of the body on which it operates; it is not a character, but it has the character it imparts (or tries to impart) to other things. A logical cause, by contrast, need not be a bodily constituent of things, and it does not *have* the character of which it is the logical cause. Though

the fine *is* fine, we should not say that it *has* fineness (below, p. 154).
5. Socrates seems to have yet another sort of causality in mind at *Lysis*
217c–e, where he considers the bad as a cause that may or may not make
bad the bodies in which it occurs. Logical causes always impart their
characters wherever they are.

We must not suppose Socrates thinks logical causes actually *act* on
the things that have them. So far as we know, nothing is lost of what Socrates intends if "the *G* is what makes fine things fine" is paraphrased "fine
things are fine because they are *G*." Socrates asks for the logical cause of
fineness in much the same way an apprentice might ask an expert what it
is that makes antiques valuable, so that knowing in general what to look
for he may set a proper value on each piece he sees. Socrates is interested
also in defending himself; he expects that if the *G* is the logical cause of
fineness, he will be able to justify saying that certain things are fine by
showing that they are *G*. Though trivially the logical cause of fineness is
the fine itself, that is not the cause Socrates wants when he asks what the
fine is. He needs a noncircular and informative answer he can use to silence
a Questioner who interrupts Socrates' praise of fine things by asking, "How
do you know such things are fine?" The cause Socrates wants is nothing
less than the ground of appropriate praise. This turns out to be something
that is both self-predicating and one, as we shall see.

SELF-PREDICATION AS STRICT PREDICATION

When you define the fine, you must say it is something that is itself
fine. That is the uninterpreted burden of the self-predication requirement,
and a consequence of taking the fine to be a logical cause. The causes
Socrates accepts in the "autobiography" of the *Phaedo* are all said to *be*
what they make other things to be. Hot fire makes things hot, living soul
makes things living, and the fine—being fine—makes things fine.[4]

All three answers of Hippias fail the test. Neither a fine girl, nor gold,
nor the life that includes burying your parents, is fine in the way the fine
is supposed to be fine. Since Socrates can use the test with people who
are not initiated into Platonic ontology (cf. *Republic* 479a), he must not
mean anything esoteric by "the fine is fine." My hypothesis for explaining
such self-predications is that they are instances of a strict use of "to be"
in predication, a use recognized as primary by Socrates and his contemporaries.

STRICT PREDICATION. Socrates understands sentences like "the fine is
fine" to mean that the fine is *strictly* fine; fine, that is, regardless of how

the sentence is qualified.[5] Socrates shows that many fine things—the girl, gold, the life Hippias praises—are at best fine under certain restrictive qualifications. They fail, therefore, to be strictly fine, and for that reason cannot be the same as *the* fine.

A strict predication is never restrictively qualified. Sentences that require restrictive qualification are accordingly not strict predications. For example, "the finest girl is foul compared to gods" (289b6) is restrictively qualified, because only by such a comparison is the girl foul. She cannot be said to be strictly foul for that reason. Suitably qualified in each case, the finest girl is both fine and foul, but strictly she is no more fine than foul, and fails to be either. In strict predication the subject-predicate core of the sentence is complete semantically, and keeps its truth-value regardless of what happens in the rest of the sentence or in the general context. You can therefore safely drop the qualifications from such sentences: if justice is good for men *strictly,* then it is good without qualification as well. (And that is right, according to Socrates; there is no one for whom justice is bad.)

Strange fallacies result from taking sentences to be strict predications when they are not, a fact exploited by the sophists of Plato's *Euthydemus* (at 392c, for example) and diagnosed by Aristotle (*De Sophisticis Elenchis* XXV). If you take it as *strictly* true that Socrates is ignorant of some things but not ignorant of others, you will have the odd result that he both is, and is not, plain ignorant. Such results are to be avoided. Socrates avoids the difficulty by accepting as strictly true only sentences that are safe in all contexts. That is why if he finds any context in which the girl is foul, he cannot allow that she is strictly fine.

Plato later tries to reserve the verb "to be" for strict predications, and uses "to become" and "to have a share in" for sentences that are restrictively qualified. The finest girl, for example, has a part of fineness (the part that goes with girls); and Socrates has that part of ignorance that belongs with the subjects he does not know (cf. *Sophist* 257cd). But the fine itself *is* fine. As there is no way in which it is foul, we need not assign it a mere part of the fine. It is fine strictly. Plato's later contrast, then, is between *being* fine and *having a part of* the fine. This he develops, I think, to mark technically the strict sort of predication Socrates finds in Greek usage and requires in the dialogues of search.

Strict predication occurs frequently in ordinary contexts:

a. The fire *in the stove* is hot.
b. Socrates is a human being *in Athens*.

In each case, the italicized phrase is nonrestrictive and can be dropped without affecting the sentence's truth. Fire is hot wherever it is, and Socrates is human no matter what. The qualifying phrases (though interesting and informative) are not glued to the subjects by strict predication.

That fire is strictly hot makes it a logical cause for heat (and indeed Socrates treats it so—*Phaedo* 105c).[6] Wherever there is fire, there is heat. Similarly, gold could be what made things fine, if, that is, it were itself strictly fine. But gold, we know, is not fine without qualification. In the form of a spoon stirring soup, it is a disaster (290e–291c). So gold is not strictly fine, and not being a sure sign of fineness, it cannot be a logical cause of the fine.

SELF-PREDICATION. What does it mean to say that the fine is strictly fine? Socrates paraphrases strict predication in another context, but one that illuminates the logic of self-predication: "When I ask whether the pleasure itself is good, then, I mean whether things are good insofar as they are pleasant" (*Protagoras* 351e1–3). Substituting "the fine itself" for "the pleasure itself" and "fine" for "good," we would have: "By saying that the fine itself is fine, I mean that things are fine insofar as they are fine." As a requirement of definition, this means that if the G is the fine, things are fine insofar as they are G. If the appropriate were the fine, then things would be fine insofar as they were appropriate. That is a requirement we would expect, and it is probably all Socrates wants from self-predication. Socrates wants his definition to give him, among other things, a test for fineness. He wants assurance that whatever he finds to satisfy the definition will have its share of fineness.

The proposed paraphrase is supported from within the *Hippias Major,* where a similar move is required to make an argument work. A premise for a Socratic induction is: "the father is not a son, and the son is not a father" (297b9–c1). This is true and relevant to the argument only on one interpretation: it is not the case that people are sons insofar as they are fathers, or that they are fathers insofar as they are sons (see note 147). I conclude that in early Plato, whenever "the G" appears to have a general reference, "the G is F" should be understood, "things are F insofar as they are G."

To this paraphrase we should add the following principle: nothing *strictly* fine is in any way foul; so anything that is in any way foul fails to be strictly fine, and so fails to be *the* fine. That is the principle applied, for example, at 289c. The fine is not foul under any qualification (cf. 291d2). Otherwise, it could not be trusted to make things fine, but being in part fine and in part foul, it would bring both qualities with it as a logical cause. But the fine must be a dependable cause, and make things *only* fine, if it is to be what the expert on fineness knows.

When Socrates requires that the fine be identified with something that *is fine,* he means that the candidate must be fine, in every context, and never ever foul. For the appropriate, for example, this means that things must be fine insofar as they are appropriate, and not foul. That is the essence of the self-predication requirement. (I review other recent accounts of self-predication in an Appendix to this Chapter, and I consider the ontological presuppositions of such predication on p. 172.)

UNITY AND GENERALITY

Not everything that is strictly fine is *the* fine; that is the point on which Hippias is mistaken at 287d (p. 169). Courage is strictly fine, virtue is strictly fine, perhaps even visual pleasure is strictly fine, but none of these is the fine itself. That is because the fine itself is *the one* logical cause set over every case of fineness. Not every logical cause is a one over so many. The number three, for example, is *a* logical cause of being odd, because it is the nature of three to be odd. But oddness itself is *the* logical cause; it is set over every case of oddness (*Phaedo* 104a).

Socrates assumes that there is one supreme logical cause for fineness —that there is one character, the same in every case, which makes all fine things fine (288a, 289d, 300a10, 303d, ff.). The assumption is implausible on the face of it. There seem to be many different ways of being fine. One set of characteristics makes a monkey fine, another does the job for a goddess, still another for a law and another for a burglar. And even a man is made fine-looking by different things at different stages in his life, as Aristotle observed (*Rhetoric* 1361b7, ff.). Why should Socrates assume without argument that this sort of pluralist account of the fine is wrong? In the final analysis, there simply may be no common character for the many different sorts of things that are fine. That, at any rate, is what Hippias as a follower of Gorgias is likely to have believed (p. 117 cf. note 91).

Socrates generally assumes without argument that the subjects he wishes to define are one and not a Gorgianic many: *Euthyphro* 5d, 6d; *Meno* 72a, 72c, 75a; and *Laches* 191d. The *Hippias Major* is unique in attempting to supply an argument against Gorgianic definitions (p. 77, ff.); elsewhere, he does the work by expostulation and example, as in the *Meno.* But the argument of the *Hippias Major,* as we have seen, begs the question.

Why does Socrates hold that each of the things he seeks to define is a unity? He cannot have been led to this by the naive principle that each word must have one meaning. He knows that is not always the case (*Euthy-*

demus 277e3, ff.). Nor can he have been convinced by the example he uses in the *Meno* (72ab): bees have one essence. But why should the various virtues be like bees? They might just as well be like the different parts of a bee, which do not have one essence (cf. *Protagoras* 329d, and Woodruff, 1976).

The answer is that Socrates holds the unity requirement because he knows no other way to satisfy his purpose in definition. He does not have available the Aristotelian conception of focal meaning, or the Wittgensteinian tool of family resemblance, either one of which could have gathered together various ways of being fine.[7] Instead, he has to choose between extreme accounts of the matter: he can either list different ways of being fine without connecting them (in the tradition of Gorgias), or he can insist on there being simply one way of being fine. We cannot wonder that he chose as he did. If Gorgias' approach were right, knowledge of the fine could not be given by a definition or even by a finite list of partial definitions. There could always be a further unknown way of being fine, *the* way for an unforeseen context. Still worse, in a given context one could never be sure that he had judged correctly. A Gorgianic sophist may know what is fine in war and what is fine in peace, but he cannot know which of those conditions is *simply* fine, and so he cannot be sure what to recommend. But the expert Socrates wants (and wants to be) will know what to recommend. Again, the Socratic expert would know that fine things are desirable and beneficial (p. 182). But if the fine were simply different things in different contexts, how could anyone rely on its always being desirable? Knowing the fine should give you the reassurance of knowing that you are right to praise what you praise as fine (cf. 286cd); but if all you know when you know the fine is that it varies with context, and you are not aware of some one good thing that the fine always is, then you will not have the confidence you need to face down Socrates' Questioner. What underlies Socrates' insistence on the unity of definition, then, is his sense of the lofty purposes to be served by the definition of the fine. What moves him is hope for the knowledge of good and evil.

APPENDIX: OTHER ACCOUNTS OF SELF-PREDICATION

Several accounts of self-predication have been proposed that differ from mine; but none of these can be right for the *Hippias Major*.

1. Socrates might mean that the form of the fine is itself one of those fine things that have a share of the fine. That assumption would help generate the Third Man Paradox (on which see Vlastos, TMA), and Plato may be committed to it elsewhere. But that is not a possible reading for the self-predications of the *Hippias Major*. Socrates is looking there for "what is fine always and for everyone" (292e2). The dative "for everyone" (*pasi*) harks back to the earlier datives in 292cd: ". . . I asked for the fine itself? For what when added to anything—whether to a stone [*lithōi*] or a plank or a man or a god or any action or any lesson—*anything* gets to be fine?" Also, in the argument, the dative at 292e2 ("for everyone") reaches proleptically to the usage at 292e8: "For Achilles as well?" Clearly, what is at issue is not whether a candidate for the fine is itself a fine thing, but whether everything in which it occurs will be fine. Hippias' proposal fails in this case because burying his father would not make a fine thing of the life of Achilles.

2. "Is fine" could be used equivocally, having one sense for most uses, and a special sense when it is used of the fine itself. No such special sense is marked in the *Hippias Major,* and Socrates' treatment of Hippias' answers militates against it. He shows that the things Hippias mentions are not strictly fine; he does not say that they are of the wrong ontological sort to be fine strictly. The interpretation I have given is univocal: "Socrates is strictly human" is read "Socrates is human insofar as he is Socrates"; and "the *G* is fine" reads "things are fine insofar as they are *G*." Since Socrates does not treat "is fine" as equivocal, and since we are able to interpret it without making it equivocal, charity requires that we do so.

3. On another interpretation, the self-predication of "fine" *would* say merely that *any* fine thing is fine.[8] But this is too weak for Socrates' purpose, which was to use the self-predication test against Hippias' answers. All the things Hippias says are fine are indeed fine in some respects. Why is that not enough for Socrates? Apparently he thinks self-predication requires that what is fine never be in any respect foul. Why *that* should be so, the present simple reading of self-predication does not go far enough to explain.

4. The self-predication could state a definition.[9] To say that something is fine, on this view, is to say that it is what it is to be fine. The only subject to which we could rightly attach "is fine" would be "the fine itself" (or an equivalent expression). Sentences like "a fine girl is fine" or "gold is fine" would be unsuccessful partial definitions of the fine. Hippias' mistake in offering them would be the mistake of proposing a partial in place of a general definition. He would intend that being a fine girl is what it is to be fine—obviously not for everyone (since it wouldn't do for Zeus or Socrates or a race horse), but for *girls* (or perhaps women). And being golden would be what it is to be fine for some other class of fine things. This is a plausible sort of gambit to ascribe to Hippias, especially if he was, as I suggested, influenced by Gorgias (p. 117).

This is not, however, the most likely reading of the text and has unfortunate consequences for the wider interpretation of the early dialogues. It would falsify, for example, such sentences as "courage is fine," to which Socrates is clearly committed (*Laches* 192c), unless (as is unlikely) *courage* is Socrates' definition for the fine. And it either makes "is fine" equivocal, or makes of every particular ascription of "is fine" a category mistake. For to say "Helen is fine" is on this view either to make the absurd claim that *being Helen* is what it is to be fine, or to use "is fine" equivocally.

The difficulty with the text is that neither Hippias nor Socrates understands Hippias' answers as giving such definitions. (See note 63.)

NOTES TO CHAPTER SIX

1. For more thorough general treatments of Socratic definition, see Santas, 1979: 97–135, and Guthrie, 1969: 425–442. Other useful discussions are by Robinson (1953: 49–60), Geach (1966), Nakhnikian (1971), Sharvey (1972), Beversluis (1974) and Irwin (1977A: 37–68).

2. The *Phaedo* autobiography appears to present the theory of logical causes Socrates applies in the *Hippias Major*. For a discussion of the place of the *Hippias Major* with respect to the *Phaedo,* see below, p. 170.

3. The expression "logical cause" is borrowed from Vlastos, who carefully and correctly, I think, distinguishes logical from other causes (RC: 91, ff.). See Sharvey (1972), Santas (1979: 110), Gallop (1975: 213).

4. The principle underlying this self-predication requirement is that causes generally are what they make things. Barnes calls this the Synonymy Principle and believes it must have a presocratic origin (1979: I, 119). Aristotle frequently is influenced by the principle, as at *Metaphysics* 1070a 4–9: "each substance . . . comes to be from a thing with the same name . . . for man generates man" (cf. *Generation and Corruption* 324a20, ff.). Elsewhere he asserts a very Platonic version of the principle: that in virtue of which things are *F* is itself most *F* ("as fire, being most hot, is also the cause of heat in other things"—*Metaphysics* 993b24–31). But see *Metaphysics* 1034a34 for a restriction on the principle.

5. The conception of strict predication is one I introduce as a hypothesis for interpreting Socrates and others. The hypothesis is that Socrates and his contemporaries try to understand any predication, if they can, as strict predication. Thus Protagoras would say, if the wind is cold for me, that it is cold, understanding "is cold" as unrestricted by its qualifier.

6. Anything strictly *F* would be *a* logical cause of things' being *F*. But the definition Socrates wants will identify not only *a* logical cause, but *the* logical cause for all fine things (p. 156; cf. p. 84 and note 167).

7. Aristotle, *Eudemian Ethics* I.8, *Metaphysics* IV.1 (see Owen, 1960). Wittgenstein, PI: Sections 66–67.

8. This is what Vlastos has called *Pauline Predication* (Vlastos, AS).

9. This is how I understand the intriguing proposal of Nehamas (1979).

SEVEN
Ontology

We know what Socrates says and does in the *Hippias Major* and similar dialogues of search. But what sort of theory prompts him to say and do those things? Because Plato represents Socrates as wary of stating a theoretical position, we can only speculate about what Socrates (or Plato, writing of Socrates) must have believed in order to have insisted on seeking definitions as he does. Plato's Socrates might have been moved in his search by a belief in all or part of the mature theory of Forms that dominates the *Phaedo* and *Republic*. Or he might have been moved by considerations that have nothing to do with ontology. We must ask whether Socrates' search for definitions, as Plato represents it, is generated by an ontological theory, or whether the reverse holds: that Socrates' search invites Plato to ontology. On the answer rides the great issue of Plato's development. We want to know from what beginnings Plato's ontology grew, and how far it had grown when he wrote the dialogues of search. We also want to know if the *Hippias Major* can be included in a good story of Plato's development. If it cannot, that will count against its authenticity.

My position is that we do not need to attribute any ontological theory to Socrates, either in the *Hippias Major* or in any other dialogue of search, to explain his asking the "what-is-it" question (*pace* Allen, 1970). The search, however, *invites* ontology by making a distinction that will grow into Plato's separation of Forms. Whether Plato had thought of the theory of Forms when he wrote the early dialogues is an unanswerable question; for all we know, he might have held the theory but kept it silent. This much is clear, however: the *Hippias Major* does not commit its author either to the mature theory of Forms or to any full-grown ontological position. Still,

161

the *Hippias Major* comes closer than any other dialogue of search to saying the sort of thing Plato says about Forms in the *Phaedo* and *Republic*. Therefore it is most likely a transitional piece, pointing from the early towards the middle dialogues (so Malcolm, 1968).

In what follows I shall distinguish two questions: First, how much of Plato's mature theory of Forms shows up in the *Hippias Major?* Second, are the concerns of the *Hippias Major* ontological? The two questions are independently interesting and should be kept separate. Whether Plato's mature theory of Forms is an ontological theory is a question on which I shall reserve judgment.

FORMS

Anyone who wants to tell the story of Plato's development is obliged to try formulating the centrally Platonic theory of Forms. But this is no easy matter: Plato himself did not do it in his written work, possibly because he had not settled all the details. (In particular, Plato appears to have lacked a full account of the relation obtaining between a Form and its instances, hence the uncertainty at *Phaedo* 100d on this score, the puzzles of the *Parmenides,* and the absence everywhere of a detailed account of the matter.)

Here nevertheless is a sketch of the theory of Forms.[1] Its chief burden is a distinction between two different sorts of things, Forms and everything else. For each Form (the Fine, for example) there is a set of shadowy entities (the many fine things) that are different from it, yet called after it (all are called "fine"). From these namesakes, the Forms themselves are supposed to exist apart, according to Aristotle, who notes with approval that Socrates did not believe in separating the Forms (*Metaphysics* 1078b30–32 and 1086b2–5, cf. 987b1, ff.). Plato is not explicitly helpful about separation; but he does distinguish Forms from their namesakes in a variety of ways. I shall note what he says with as little interpretation on my part as possible, so as to stay within the scope of this book:

1. One-over-many. Each Form is one; but the things called after it are many (*Phaedo* 78e, *Republic* 479a).

2. Logical causation. Forms are causes (*aitiai*) in that Plato seeks to explain the way other things are with reference to Forms (e.g., at *Phaedo* 100b, ff.).

3. Self-predication. Each Form *is* what it explains: the Fine, for example, which is that by which fine things are fine, is itself fine (implication of *Phaedo* 100c4). Moreover, the Form of the *F* is *F* in every circumstance; but the many things called after it are not (*Phaedo* 78e, *Republic* 479a,

Symposium 211ab). For our example, the Fine is fine in every circumstance, but none of the many fine things is always fine.

4. Being versus becoming. Each Form *is* and never comes to be; whereas the many things called after it come to be and never are (e.g., *Timaeus* 27d6–28a1).[2]

5. Knowledge versus opinion. Only Forms can be known; the other sort of things are at best objects of opinion based on perception (*Phaedo* 65de; *Republic* V, VI, esp. 479e; *Timaeus* 28a1–4).[3]

To this list must be added two ways in which tradition has marked off Platonic Forms, ways Plato does not explicitly state:[4]

6. Independence. Each Form exists whether or not the things called after it exist.

7. Priority. Each Form is ontologically prior to the many things called after it: they cannot exist unless it exists.

Finally, for what it is worth, we should record one possible interpretation of the Aristotle texts cited above which imply that Plato *separated* the Forms. What Aristotle meant is a matter for conjecture; he *might* have intended for Plato:

8. Transcendence. Forms are not immanent in the many things called after them, but transcendent. (Immanent Forms would exist in their namesakes; transcendent Forms would exist outside them, in another world.) This doctrine is also known as the Two-Worlds Theory.[5]

ONTOLOGY

The word "ontology" has had a variety of uses in philosophy.[6] Here I shall simply prescribe the use that best suits my discussion. Ontology, I shall say, is a distinctly philosophical matter. It shows up in the distinction between universals and particulars, in the "two-world" doctrine just mentioned, and in questions about how something is related to its properties. Ontology asks whether there are universals, for example, but it leaves to zoology the question of whether there are Loch Ness Monsters. And it does not care whether there is fraud in high places; that is the police's affair. As I am using the word, not every question about what there is is ontological. Ontology is peculiar to philosophers, and to philosophers of a certain stamp. To construe ontology more broadly would be to trivialize the question of whether Socrates leaned in that direction. Those who would enlarge ontology to cover every question about what there is would make ontologists of us all, and thus blur the history of philosophy.

I must therefore dismiss as irrelevant the considerable evidence at *Hippias Major* 287cd that commits Socrates to the *existence* of things like justice and the fine. Such commitments have nothing to do with ontology and are not controversial. Any discussion presupposes the existence of the subjects it discusses; but few discussions commit themselves to an ontological theory about their subjects. Most people who talk of forestry have no doubt that trees exist, but at the same time have not the inkling of an ontological theory about them: in talking of trees they do not adopt an ontology of physical objects continuous in space and time. Commitments to existence are not commitments to specific ontological theories.[7]

Socrates' search for the fine is no more ontologically significant than is the speech of some ordinary person inveighing against injustice. The latter speaks of injustice and would not scruple to admit (with regret) that it exists; but he need have no idea about whether injustice is a universal, or whether universals can be done without. If our speaker were a philosopher speaking of injustice, and moreover a philosopher engaged in ontology, then he would be obliged to have a theory that could accommodate injustice in some ontological way—as a universal, or what have you. That is what we must say about Socrates and the fine: if, having spoken of the fine, he turns for some reason to ontology, he must give an ontological theory for such entities as the fine. Whether Plato's Socrates does turn to ontology in the *Hippias Major* is the chief question of this Chapter. For now it is enough to note that in speaking of the Fine as a something (287d1) Socrates does not break ontological silence.

Socrates does ask what makes all fine things fine. This could be understood in two ways:

THE CRITERION READING. Socrates would on this reading want to know what a thing must be in order to be fine, much as a lawyer might ask of censored novels, "What (if anything) makes them obscene?" In both cases, the questioners want to know how judgments are to be justified; they expect to identify something we can roughly call a *criterion:* e.g., a characteristic or set of characteristics that occurs always and only where fineness occurs. One would naturally begin looking for this by collecting examples of things believed to be fine and asking what they have in common. (The word "characteristic" I shall use naively for anything like blue or brave or odd-numbered—without marking off the use of these words from their mention and without asking what sorts of things characteristics are.)

THE ONTOLOGICAL READING. Here the lawyer analogy is inappropriate. On this reading Socrates would want to know what it is for a fine thing to have the characteristic that makes it fine—whether the characteristic is *in* the fine thing or not, what sort of entity the characteristic is (whether it is a separately-existing universal), and what sort of entity the fine thing is (whether simple or complex). He would, in short, be seeking to establish an ontological foundation for judgments of fineness.

A philosopher who began by asking for criteria would be likely to turn to ontology, especially if his subject were as slippery as the fine. There appear to be many ways of being fine, different ways for different things, and this multiplicity is reflected in ordinary usage. A criterion satisfying Socrates' unity requirement is not likely to be induced from familiar examples. Descriptions of ordinary usage will not help either. What would help, if it could succeed, would be an ontological theory that guaranteed the unity of the fine—the theory, for example, that the Fine is an unchanging Form, which fine things come in various ways to resemble. If he were convinced by such a theory, our criteria-seeker would have to change the nature of his search: originally, he had wanted to know what characteristics a thing must have if it is to be fine; now he will want to know what entity the thing should resemble, and he will want to know what sort of resemblance is required. That would be one sort of ontological turn; others are possible.

In fact, if the criteria-seeker came to the crossroads I have just sketched, and saw ontology beckoning to one side, but chose instead to veer towards collecting criteria from ordinary language, he would have taken by refusal a sort of ontological position. We must therefore mark off yet a third reading of Socrates' question.

THE NAÏVE READING. On this reading Socrates would be a criteria-seeker who did not know that he had a choice. Not yet aware of the allurements of ontology, he would innocently examine proposed criteria. This is the reading best supported by the evidence of the *Hippias Major*. The question Socrates asks there is not an ontological question; neither is it the question of one who has repudiated ontology.[8]

THE SILENCE OF EARLIER DIALOGUES

Plato's earlier dialogues of search (the *Euthyphro, Laches, Charmides, Lysis,* and *Hippias Major*) all display parts of Plato's mature theory. They are silent, however, on its most distinctively Platonic features. To be precise, traces of the doctrines of the one-over-many (1), logical causation (2), and self-predication (3) occur in early Plato. The transcendence of Forms (8), however, is contradicted without being explicitly denied; and the companion dichotomies between being and becoming, knowledge and belief, do not show themselves at all (4, 5). Nor is there any sign in the

Hippias Major or elsewhere among early dialogues of the independent or prior existence of Forms (6, 7). In this Section I shall say what can be said about Plato's early silence on these important matters; in the remainder of the Chapter I shall defend the ontological innocence of the doctrines that are employed in the dialogues of search.

TRANSCENDENCE. If Plato's mature theory takes Forms to be entirely *outside* their instances, then the *Hippias Major* contradicts that part of the theory when it has Socrates say that forms are or come to be *present in* their instances (294a1, 294c4, 300a10, 303a5; cf. 289d4), that forms are *had by* their instances (300a9, 299e1), and are *added to* their instances (289d4, 293e4). Similar language, but not so intensively used, occurs in other presumably early dialogues: *Charmides* 158e7, *Laches* 189e, *Lysis* 217b, ff., and *Euthydemus* 301a.

In none of those contexts is a theory of transcendent Forms either stated or explicitly denied. We would think (following Aristotle) that a philosopher must choose between making forms separate (= be transcendent) on the one hand, and making them exist in (= be immanent) concrete particulars on the other. But Plato uses language suggestive of immanence even in the same dialogues as he uses language suggestive of transcendence (as we see from Ross's table—1951: 338–9). What are we to make of this? The less the better, I think. Plato seems not to be aware of the immanence-transcendence issue in earlier works like the *Hippias Major;* later, as at *Phaedo* 100d, he simply fails to face the problem squarely. The various expressions Plato uses to connect a form and its namesakes do not at any stage in his career clearly betoken an ontological choice. The language of immanence (e.g., "she has great beauty") is natural and easily explained in terms of ordinary locutions. The language of transcendence, when it occurs, is ambiguous or tentative.

On the issue of transcendence, then, Socrates in the *Hippias Major* appears naïve: what he says would be incompatible with making the fine transcendent; but he does not seem to be aware of the ontological issue.

THE DICHOTOMIES. The same should be said about the dichotomies between being and becoming, knowledge and opinion. Neither one is an object of ontological interest to Socrates in the *Hippias Major*. The exclusive dichotomy between being and becoming is incompatible with the linking of the two at 293c2, but is nowhere directly considered.

As for the knowledge-opinion distinction, nothing is said about it in the *Hippias*. A related distinction, between *being* and *being seen to be,* is employed in one argument (294c, ff.), but is not an exclusive dichotomy and is not used to mark off Forms from other entities.

INDEPENDENCE. The independent existence of Forms may be suggested to some readers by the catechism at 287c–d in which Socrates has Hippias agree that justice, wisdom, the good and the fine are, each of them, *something* (see note 56). Does Plato mean to confer a determinate ontological status on the fine when he says that it is something? The answer is surely negative. Even in middle period dialogues, "something" (*ti*) carries no ontological burden; and later, in the *Sophist,* Plato actually argues that it does not.

In middle period dialogues, Plato says of various Forms that they are somethings (as at *Phaedo* 65d4). But he does not say that being something is a distinctive mark of the sort of things that are Forms. For example, at *Phaedo* 74a9–12 he appears to separate the Equal from the equal sticks and stones, but not by saying that the Equal itself is something. Indeed, he says, "we say that equal is something," but to make his point he needs to add, ". . . I don't mean a stick to a stick or a stone to a stone, but something else, *apart* from all those things." Another passage supports the same point more strongly: what is opined is said at *Republic* 478b10 to be something (and so is not a thing that is not—478c6). But neither is it a thing that *is* (478b3). To say of an entity that it is something is not to place it in any ontological category. All it does is ensure that the thing is not nothing.

In the *Sophist,* laying a famous trap for Theaetetus, the Visitor insists, "each time we say this 'something' we say it of what is" (237d1–2). That, as the remainder of the *Sophist* argues, is a dangerous half-truth: there is a being that is by its own nature, and everything else is different from that; but even what is not (though different from what is-by-its-own-nature) nevertheless is something. It is what is not. To say of an entity that it is something is not to locate it on the ontological map but merely to give it such a status that an ontologist would have to find it a location. It is not nothing whatever. The Visitor's task in the *Sophist* is to show that what is not is something, and this he carries out by developing a way of saying that what is not "steadfastly is, having its own nature" (258c10).

In the catechism of the *Hippias Major* (287cd), "the fine is something" serves merely to prepare the way for Socrates' question. Socrates is about to ask what the fine is, but he must first establish that it is something, so that it is at least in principle definable. "Something" is here a pro-noun, a dummy standing in for whatever it is that (if the search is successful) the fine will turn out to be (Woodruff, 1978A: 107).

PRIORITY. The prior existence of Forms may be implied in the *Hippias Major* at 288a8, ff. (R. E. Allen, 1970: 121, 147). As emended by Schanz, the passage reads: "Shall I say that if a fine girl is a fine thing, there *exists* something because of which those things are fine?" On the ontological reading, this question would propose an inference from "A fine girl is fine" to "The fine has prior existence." Burnet's reading, which I adopt (note 67), is better Greek and gives a better sense: "Shall I say that if a fine girl is a fine thing, those things are fine because of *that?*" What refutes Hippias is not the ontological status of the fine, but its role as a logical cause. The same point is made more clearly in the summing-up at 289d1–5: "Do you *still* think that the fine itself by which everything else is beautified and seen to be fine when that form is added to it—that *that* is a girl or a horse or a lyre?" The trouble with Hippias' fine girl is that she does not explain, in the way a logical cause is supposed to explain, the many things that are fine. For one thing, she does not occur in every fine thing. The point is straightforward and has nothing to do with the ontological status of the fine. Of course, the fine is prior epistemologically (p. 138): you must know what it is before you know of anything else that it is fine. But that is not at issue here; conceivably, a fine girl could be prior in that way.

Neither in the *Hippias Major* nor in any of the accepted early dialogues is the doctrine of the ontological priority of Forms stated or implied. (For a full discussion, see Woodruff, 1978A.) It remains for us to consider the ontological significance of those parts of Plato's mature theory that do show themselves in early dialogues.

THE MODEST SEPARATION OF FORMS

Without engaging openly in ontology, the *Hippias Major* lays a partial foundation for Plato's theory of Forms. Here Plato has Socrates mark off a Form from its instances more systematically than in other dialogues of search. The marking off is not presented as part of an ontological theory, however, for it is not generalized to other Forms, and its basis is logical in character. It is a more modest separation of Forms than what we find in the *Phaedo*.

What elements of Plato's mature theory are to be seen in the *Hippias Major?* (i) The one-over-many doctrine is foreshadowed by Socrates' insistence on the unity of definition (above, p. 156). (ii) The doctrine of logical causation makes a strong showing in the *Hippias Major* among Socrates' requirements for definition (above, p. 151). (iii) Most promising ontologically is the requirement of self-predication, which is stated explicitly in the *Hippias Major* (above, p. 153).

All three of these govern a working distinction Socrates uses between the sorts of answers Hippias gives and a better sort of answer that comes from Socrates or the Questioner (293d6–e1). What is distinctively wrong with Hippias' answers?

Hippias refuses to recognize the distinction Socrates draws between the fine (*to kalon*) and a fine thing (*kalon*—287d9); later he says he understands it (e2); and then he violates it (e4). This appears to be the root of Hippias' errors. But what is the distinction at issue?

The received interpretation of this exchange is that Socrates is trying to establish the difference between universals and particulars, and that Hippias, in giving a particular where a universal was called for, shows his deep confusion (e.g., Tarrant *ad loc.*). But Hippias' confusion must be deep indeed if he thinks there is no difference between something he understands to be a universal, and something he understands to be a particular. Nehamas argues that Hippias *does* understand that the fine is a universal (287d1, 287e2), and that he intends "a fine girl" also as a universal, *"being a fine girl"* (1975: 299 ff.). I discuss the passage at length in the Commentary (note 63), arguing that neither Socrates nor Hippias shows in the passage any sign of anticipating the distinction between universals and particulars.

What Hippias displays in this passage is not the confusion of denying a difference between universals and particulars (that would be an unexpectedly sophisticated move for him to make), but a dialectical strategy. Hippias probably knows, as having some experience of Socrates (301b), that no one wins by seriously trying to answer Socratic questions. He therefore shifts ground. Instead of trying to say what the fine is, he tries to get away with mentioning something that is fine. He tries this three times. Had he an audience, as he is accustomed, he might have succeeded in turning aside Socrates' question with laughter (above, p. 125). As it is, he fails for three reasons: One, Socrates wants to know the *one* thing that makes all fine things fine, but Hippias is prepared to mention more than one thing ("ivory, too, is fine"—290c1–2). Two, Socrates wants to know what makes *all* fine things fine, but none of the things Hippias mentions occurs in every fine thing. If Hippias were right that a fine girl is a fine thing, she would satisfy a necessary condition for being what the fine is; for the fine, we know by the self-predication requirement, is itself fine. But the condition is not sufficient. An entity can be fine (as justice, for example, is fine) without being *the* fine. This is not a confusion of universals with particulars (justice is not a particular), but the mistaking of a necessary for a sufficient condition. Three, none of the things Hippias mentions satisfies even the self-predication requirement; none is, according to the strict usage, *fine.*[9]

Now we are in a position to summarize the disabilities of the things Hippias mentions. The fine Socrates wants to know about is *one,* occurs in *all* of the many fine things, and is itself *fine.* The things Hippias gives him are *many,* occur in only *some* fine things at best, and *fail to be strictly fine*. The working distinction of the *Hippias Major* may then be fully expressed by the three doctrines with which I introduced this section (p. 168): one-over-many, logical causation, and self-predication. We shall have to ask of each of these how far it carries us towards Plato's mature theory of Forms, and whether Socrates can hold it without yet subscribing to Platonic ontology.

The theme of my answer is that these three doctrines are nothing in the *Hippias Major* but working constraints on definition. They are not part of a general theory of definition or ontology, for nothing of the sort is given here. And they arise not from metaphysical lucubrations, but from the needs and practice of the elenchus itself. They are in fact the requirements discussed in Chapter Six above. That the fine is the logical cause of fineness is among its guiding properties (p. 144), and the other two requirements (unity and self-predication) are simply necessary conditions for that (p. 150). Socrates could have laid down these requirements without being a believer in the mature theory of Forms.

LOGICAL CAUSATION AND THE THEORY OF FORMS

The fine is that by which all fine things are fine. It is, in other words, the logical cause for things being fine. Logical causes must, we have seen, serve as grounds for explanation of a certain sort (p. 151). They must also satisfy the other two more formal requirements: they must occur in all the many cases to be explained, and they must themselves *be* whatever it is that they make other things be. Is this general doctrine of logical causation part of Plato's mature theory of Forms? Is it inseparable from the famous separation of Forms? My answer is no. Even though Plato treats logical causation in a context neighboring on the theory of Forms at *Phaedo* 100c, ff., the two doctrines are independent. Logical causes are not necessarily Forms.

What Socrates says on the subject in the *Phaedo* he says in a long speech known as the autobiography, which purports to tell the story of Socrates' eccentric turn in philosophy. There Socrates presents his account of causes as nothing new (100b1), so we should expect it to contain a doctrine Socrates either stated, or more likely applied, during the elenchus of Plato's early dialogues. And this is possible, for the autobiography (which ends at 102a1) does not commit Socrates to the mature theory of Forms, though it does use language (*auto kath' auto*—100b6) belonging to that theory. The autobiography no more explicitly separates the Forms than do the early dialogues. We are thus invited to interpret the *Phaedo*'s account of logical causes against the background of Plato's earlier dialogues, and no early dialogue but the *Hippias Major* furnishes the background we want, for none so clearly treats a Form as a cause. And neither the *Hippias* nor the autobiography presents logical causation as part of an ontological theory.

Even outside the autobiography, the *Phaedo* does not use the concept of logical cause to mark off Forms ontologically. The logical causes of greatest interest in the *Phaedo* are not Forms at all, but entities like fire (which makes things hot) and soul (which makes things alive—*Phaedo* 105b–d). This fire is *our* phenomenal fire, not the transcendent Form of *Timaeus* 51be; and soul also, though kin to the Forms (80b), is not said to be one of them.[10] They do not need to be Forms or even universals to be logical causes. All they need is to be by their own natures (cf. 104a3) what they make other things to be and to be unable to remain in things that acquire opposite properties. We may suppose then that even gold could be a logical cause, not of fineness, but of malleability or the like. For insofar as an object is made of gold, it is malleable, that being the nature of gold.

We may put the matter in this ontologically suggestive manner (though it is instructive to note that Socrates avoids making a general formulation of this sort): a logical cause must be a definite nature, which it imparts to everything in which it occurs (*Phaedo* 104a3). To say that is not yet to adopt an ontological theory of natures—a theory about what sorts of things have or are natures, and how natures are related to the things that have them.[11] Such a theory, for example, might insist that only entities of a certain kind—say, universals or properties or transcendent Forms—are natures. Or it might speculate about how Socrates and the nature of being human are related to one another—by participation, resemblance, identity, or what have you. Any thinking of this sort would be ontological, but none is reflected in the doctrine of logical causation.

ONE-OVER-MANY

The fine is one in contrast to many fine things. This contrast is implied in two ways by the argument of the *Hippias Major*. First, Socrates wants to be told *the* (presumably single) thing that makes all fine things fine (e.g., at 288a), but Hippias mentions three of the many things he thinks are fine, in an attempt to silence Socrates' Questioner. Hippias would continue in this vein indefinitely, had Socrates not stopped him by adopting a more unified line of inquiry (293d, cf. note 91). Second, Socrates rejects the last definition proposal because it violates his principle of the unity of definition (p. 78; cf. pp. 118–9). The proposal was that the fine is what is pleasant through sight and hearing (298a).

Both passages that insist on unity do so without explicitly appealing to ontological considerations. Socrates might have clung to the unity of definition on Parmenidean grounds, believing that the fine, if it is to *be,* must *be one.* But of Parmenidean influence on this theme in Plato's early thought there is no direct evidence. The unity of definition emerges as a requirement of the elenchus for the reason I have discussed above (p. 156): if the fine were not one but many different values, then a person who knew what they were would be unable to satisfy the Questioner that he knew enough to give praise and blame. That is enough to explain Socrates' adherence to the unity requirement. We need not attribute to him an abstract ontological or semantic theory on this score; and in the absence of a need, we should avoid speculation.

SELF-PREDICATION AS STRICT PREDICATION

Because a logical cause must be what it makes things, the fine must be fine. Hence arises the self-predication requirement stated most strongly at 292e: "And I asked him the way you asked me, for that which is fine always and for everyone." This I have explained as strict predication: the fine must be something that is fine, without restrictive qualification (above, p. 153, ff.).

Socrates uses the self-predication standard to eliminate Hippias' answers, thereby indicating roughly a class of things that are not strictly fine. But he does not turn from this to a distinction among ontological types. It remains for the *Phaedo* and the *Republic* to divide the things that are into those that are strictly what they are, and those that fail to be so. But even this distinction will not by itself separate the Forms, for not everything that *is* strictly, is a Form: fire is strictly hot and soul is always alive, yet neither is a Form (pp. 170–1 above, with note 10 on p. 180). Similarly, pleasure through sight may be strictly fine without being *the* fine. The self-predication requirement is necessary but not sufficient for Socratic definition.

What sort of entity must the fine be if it is to bear predicates like "fine"? The fine is not supposed to be a mass substance like gold that can be fine in one use and foul in another. It is a form or character (see note 85). But in what way could the form of the fine be itself fine? This question has puzzled a generation of Plato scholars and will not be resolved here. For the general problem in Plato, I refer readers to a recent promising study (Nehamas, 1979). For self-predication in the *Hippias Major* I shall attempt to provide some clarification.

One attractive possibility is that Socrates naïvely treats the form of the fine *on the model* of mass substances, but does not have a complete theory about what sort of thing a form is or in what way predicates are true of it. On this hypothesis he would suppose that "the fine is fine" just means something like "ice is cold" and "gold is malleable," but he would not be able to give an exact ontological account of what it means.

Another possibility emerges from Socrates' idea that forms are natures, first broached in the *Hippias Major* (293e4, cf. *Sophist* 257c7, etc.). He could say that what all the strict predications have in common is this: things strictly *are* whatever it is their natures to be. Then self-predication would require simply that what is defined as the fine be something whose nature it is to be fine. Socrates is human no matter what because that is his nature; fire is hot, ice is cold, and the fine is fine because those are their natures. What you are by your nature is not restrictively qualified. This we can say to illuminate strict and self-predication without making the false suggestion that early Plato had a theory about what it is to be or to have a nature. That suggestion would tell the story backwards; for later Plato became interested in natures, I believe, in the hope of explicating the strict, nature-guaranteed predications on which he had depended naïvely from the start.

The safest conclusion to draw about self-predication, or indeed about any predication of forms, is that it is something for which Plato has not yet developed a background of ontological theory in the *Hippias Major*.

Two questions remain: Does the *Hippias Major* borrow on this subject from mature Platonic works? Is the self-predication doctrine of the *Hippias Major* the same as the famously pernicious assumption of the third man paradox?

1. The similarity between Socrates' statement at 292e and the famous encomium on the fine at *Symposium* 211a has caught the attention of scholars (Tarrant *ad loc.*; Malcolm, 1968: 192): the Form of the Fine is there described as "being always, neither coming to be nor perishing, neither growing nor dwindling, and, further, it is not fine in this way but foul in that, nor fine at one time but foul in another, nor fine in one comparison but foul in another, nor fine here but foul there as being fine to some but foul to others." If self-predication in the *Hippias Major* were borrowed from such passages as this in the *Symposium,* the dialogue would surely be spurious. But the borrowing thesis is implausible for two reasons. First, the self-predication requirement develops naturally out of the elenchus in the *Hippias Major* (p. 153), not abruptly as it would in a pastiche. And

second, the statement in the *Hippias Major* is less elaborate than the one in the *Symposium:* only three of the five ways in which a thing may fail to be strictly fine appear in the *Hippias Major,* as Malcolm points out in his argument for assigning the dialogue a transitional role (1968: 193). What is adumbrated in the *Hippias Major* is grandly stated in the *Symposium,* which is more likely, therefore, to be the later dialogue. I cannot entirely discount the possibility that the *Hippias* writer simply abbreviated what he found in the *Symposium.* But imitators of the *Symposium* (and they are legion) have not been able to curtail or abbreviate their enthusiasm for the fine as this author clearly does.

2. We must now ask a question about self-predication that does not admit a definite answer. Is the doctrine as we have it in the *Hippias Major* the "notorious self-predication of forms" (as Malcolm calls it) that with other pernicious assumptions generates the third man paradox?[12] This paradox, which dooms the theory of Forms under one formulation, depends on the assumption that any Form, the *F,* is *F* in exactly the way *F* things are *F,* by participating in Form *F.* Whether this assumption was held by the mature Plato is an open question, and beyond the scope of this book. Certainly, he believed in the self-predication of Forms; but this belief has been interpreted in many ways, not all of which help bring on the third man.

For the earlier dialogues we can come nearer to an answer. Self-predication is a case of strict predication, and strict predication in the early dialogues is to be explained by an innocuous paraphrase: for "the *F* is *G*" we may say "*F* things, insofar as they are *F,* are *G.*"[13] So far as we can tell, this is a paraphrase and not a consequence of the self-predication; that is, the self-predication says no more than that. It is neutral, therefore, on the issue of whether the *F* is a thing at all, and similarly on the question of whether it is an *F* thing. All it does is to state a requirement of definition (p. 156). If Socrates intends anything loaded ontologically by self-predication, he keeps quiet about it. The safest hypothesis is that he does not. By that hypothesis the *Hippias Major* would be in innocent of the "notorious assumption" Malcolm found there. Other interpretations (including Malcolm's risky one) are consistent with the evidence. But charity requires us to avoid the risk. My safe hypothesis is enough to makes Socrates' arguments succeed, and to save him the embarrassment of the "notorious assumption."

What, then, is the distinction Socrates presupposes in the *Hippias Major* between the fine and the many fine things? The fine is strictly fine. But none of the many fine things Hippias mentions satisfies that condition. What is strictly fine is fine everywhere, that being its nature. But the girl is not fine everywhere, since she is foul compared to goddesses; she is, therefore, "no more fine than foul" (i.e., she fails to be strictly fine or foul); she is fine under one qualification and foul under another (see pp. 48–9). Failures like this are frequent in the early dialogues of search. Do they reflect the later Platonic doctrine that such failures belong to an ontological kind different from Forms?[14]

Socrates is silent on that matter in the early dialogues of search. We can, however, note that the things that fail in early dialogues to be strictly what they are supposed to be do not seem to constitute an ontological kind. They are, in the *Charmides,* respect (161b1), in the *Laches,* various forms of endurance (192e–193e), and in the *Euthyphro,* the god-loved (8a7, ff.). In the *Hippias Major,* they are a particular (the girl), a mass substance (gold), and a repeatable universal (the good life). What do these things have ontologically in common that would separate them from Forms? Nothing suggests itself. It appears, then, that early Plato does not use strict predication to suggest an ontological divide. The divide is simply logical, between what things are strictly (by their natures), and what they are only under some qualification. That is a distinction that can be used ontologically (as in the *Phaedo*); but I do not find it so used in the *Hippias Major.*

THE PLACE OF THE *HIPPIAS MAJOR* IN PLATO'S PHILOSOPHICAL DEVELOPMENT

We do not know for certain whether Plato ever changed his mind on philosophical matters, and we never shall, unless he thrusts his head up through the earth to tell us. His written works can at least be stretched to allow either interpretation: the unitarian view that Plato's theory of Forms is presupposed in dialogues that do not mention it, or the developmental view that Plato's theory emerged in a middle period, foundered on objections in the *Parmenides,* and was modified or abandoned in later work. We are not likely to establish a decision between these without agreement on just what principles constitute the theory of Forms. That happy condition is not in sight. Even if it were, we would be uncertain; for we do not know how accurately the dialogues represent Plato's actual *thought.* Speculation about Plato's unwritten doctrine threatens to undermine the entire project of strict textual interpretation.[15]

Fortunately, we need not assume an answer to the question of Plato's development here. All parties to the dispute recognize superficial doctrinal differences among the dialogues. We will merely characterize groups of dialogues here in terms of doctrinal characteristics that may or may not bear on an account of Plato's thought, and ask whether (and if so, how) the *Hippias Major* can be fitted into our picture. The picture itself, though not entirely uncontroversial, should be drawn in such a way that most Plato scholars can work with it.

First come small mostly inconclusive dialogues, zesty with the flavor of Socrates as he most likely was (*Euthyphro, Laches, Charmides* along with *Apology* and *Crito,* etc.). These are silent about Plato's theory of Forms, and their protagonist is a Socrates of acknowledged ignorance who does little but ask questions. After these comes a group of middle works (*Phaedo, Republic, Symposium,* etc.) with a new style, a new theory, and a new Socrates—one who expounds. The central theory of these works is the theory of Forms. What happens next is in more dispute and does not concern us, but the division into early and middle dialogues is widely accepted though not unchallenged.[16]

Where does the *Hippias Major* belong? Its style surely puts it early, with the *Euthyphro* group, but in content the *Hippias Major* seems more deeply implicated than they in Platonic ontology. There are three views on the matter: 1. The *Hippias Major* is too far advanced toward the theory of Forms to have an early position in Plato's work; it must therefore have been written by someone who knew the middle-period theory, presumably a student in the Academy (Tarrant, 1928; Moreau, 1941; Thesleff, 1976). 2. The *Hippias Major* is no more advanced than the agreed-upon early dialogues (Stallbaum, 1857; Grube, 1926; Allen, 1969; Guthrie, 1975). 3. The *Hippias Major* falls doctrinally between the *Euthyphro* group and the *Phaedo* group (Soreth, 1953; Malcolm, 1968; cf. Brandwood, 1976).

I shall argue that the first view is unsupported by the evidence, and that the second is unlikely. The *Hippias Major* goes beyond what we find in the *Euthyphro* group without stating or presupposing the full theory of the *Phaedo.*

1. Of those who reject the dialogue's authenticity, many do so because they cannot find a place for it in Plato's development; they think it comes doctrinally after middle dialogues but stylistically before them. Tarrant writes: ". . . we have in the *Hippias Major* an exercise upon various of the logico-metaphysical terms of the *Phaedo,* bringing its ontology to a *reductio ad absurdum*" (1928: lxv). This suggestion is rightly rejected by Malcolm (1968: 189, n. 3). The only speaker in the *Hippias Major* who voices anything like criticism of Platonic theory is Hippias himself, but the work's author cannot expect us to be seriously moved by what Hippias says about a theory he clearly does not understand.

Soreth (1953) tried to establish the priority of the *Hippias Major* to the *Phaedo* by an argument that seems to have persuaded no one (above, p. 66; cf. Cherniss, 1959: 100; Malcolm, 1968: 194, n. 3). Capelle tried to establish the reverse in a detailed reply to Soreth (1956). She calls attention to three passages which, as she reads them, recall middle Platonic doctrines. First, Hippias' criticism of Socrates' logic-chopping (301bc) is, she thinks, in opposition to Plato's method of division. Second, the strong self-predication requirement (as at 291d) recalls the mature Platonic theory of the Seventh Letter (343a). Third, expressions such as "the projecting" (294b2), "the each itself" and "the both itself" (303a9–10) recall the theory of Forms. Capelle is wrong on all three counts (*pace* Thesleff, 1976: 109). First, Plato's method of division is in no way foreshadowed in Socrates' arguments, so there is no reason to interpret Hippias' criticism as criticism of that. Hippias' attack on logic-chopping is easy to explain in any case (Commentary, note 172). Second, the self-predication requirement is, as we have seen, not untoward in an early work. Third, finding expressions suggestive of Forms is not enough; Capelle must show that they refer to Forms in Plato's mature sense. But this she cannot show for either passage (notes 119, 184). Capelle's arguments failing, we have no remaining reason to place the *Hippias Major* after the *Phaedo* in doctrine.

2. *The Break with the Euthyphro.* Does the *Hippias Major* belong with or after the *Euthyphro* group of searching dialogues? Its greater sophistication about forms suggests a later date (so Malcolm, 1968; Ross, 1951: 17). Only the *Hippias Major,* among dialogues earlier than the *Phaedo,* treats forms explicitly as causes and as self-predicating. Only the *Hippias Major* gives a full-dress argument against a set of partial definitions (above, p. 78). And only the *Hippias Major* supplies a missing link in one of Plato's mature arguments for Forms. For the *Hippias Major* first observes the deficiency of some of the things that are not forms. I shall return to this point, as *the* support for treating the dialogue as transitional. (See also Shiner, 1974: 28 and Grube, 1926B: 141).

How decisively does the *Hippias Major* break away from the *Euthyphro?* The two works are divided in a conflict first noticed by Marion Soreth (1953: 19–25). The *Euthyphro* seeks a definition that would make every pious action pious without qualification (and so never impious); whereas the *Hippias Major* shows that some fine things will turn out also to be foul. The strict purity of forms, in other words, rubs off on their instances in the *Euthyphro,* but not in the *Hippias Major.*

The *Euthyphro*'s argument requires not only that Piety itself never be impious, but also that Euthyphro's action—an instance of Piety—never be impious.[17] Euthyphro's second definition (the pious is the god-loved) fails that requirement; for by it the same action could be both pious and impious (loved by some gods and hated by others—8a7–12). But what is wrong with that? In the *Hippias Major* it is shown that some fine things will turn out to be foul (e.g., at 289c), and in the *Republic* it is taken for granted that none of the many fine things is any better. What goes for fine things should go for pious actions: there is no hope of Euthyphro's acting in a way that is untainted with impiety. Since the *Hippias Major* undercuts the *Euthyphro*'s search in this way, it must come later. So argues Soreth, and she is right on the main point (*pace* Malcolm, 1968: 194, n. 12). The *Euthyphro* seeks a definition that would make pious actions pious without qualification, but a requirement of that strength would be impossible for the *Hippias Major* or middle dialogues.

(Two reservations should be stated about the conflict. Neither dialogue budges from the Socratic principle that what is strictly *F* is so without qualification (p. 153). And if the *Euthyphro* imposes an impossibly strict standard of definition, that is the fault of Euthyphro himself. He it was, after all, who boasted that what he did was pious without taint of impiety. Socrates, in asking for a definition to support the boast, did not thereby agree that actions could be pious without qualification.)

The conflict nevertheless requires dating the *Hippias Major* after the *Euthyphro*. Had the fine-girl argument of the *Hippias* been in the air, Socrates could not simply have assumed the overly strict requirement in the *Euthyphro*. Why should the same thing not be both pious (in one way) and impious (in another)? Socrates does not appear to be aware of the question.

3. The Transition. We have seen that the *Hippias Major* need not be later than the *Phaedo* and that it is probably later than the *Euthyphro*. Now for the case that Plato's philosophy pivots on the *Hippias Major*. In earlier dialogues of search Plato shows no interest in assigning a distinct and privileged status to Forms. That, however, is the chief burden of the mature theory of Forms. The *Republic* gives an argument designed to win over lovers of sights and sounds, people who, without an inkling of the Forms, do not know what they are missing (476e, ff.). The argument leaves a gap; it relies on a general point not made in the *Republic* but supposed by it to be general knowledge: that any of the many fine things will be seen to be foul (479a). The missing point is argued in the *Hippias Major* for some fine things. We may, therefore, understand the *Republic* as generalizing from the three first arguments of the *Hippias* to the conclusion that *any* of the many fine things will be seen to be foul. Without the *Hippias Major,* we could not explain why Plato leaves the gap; with it, we can reasonably suppose Plato thought the point too well-known to require argument.

What are the many fine things? The cases treated in the *Hippias* are diverse: a fine girl, gold, the good life. They are not all objects of perception, since lives are not perceived. They are not all particulars, since neither gold nor the good life is a particular. What they have in common, I can say speculatively, is that none has more than a *part* of the fine. The girl, for example, has as much fineness as a girl can have, but she lacks the part reserved for goddesses.[18] Borrowing a mature Platonic expression, I shall say that the fine girl and other fine things merely *participate* in the fine. What the *Hippias Major* supports is a distinction between participants in the fine and the fine itself.

What are the many fine things of the *Republic?*[19] At first (476b), they appear to be fine universals (colors and shapes) as well as fine particulars (things made of them), that have in common their being fine to eye or ear. But the group should probably be enlarged to include all participants in the fine (476d2–4). What is a participant? Here we are on our own; the text is little help. I suggest that participants in the fine are just those fine things that are fine only with a qualification. Plato is here arguing that what delights lovers of sights and sounds belongs entirely in that group, and that members of the group are deficient in not being *strictly* fine. This deficiency Plato first observed in writing the *Hippias Major.* That he later came to build a general theory on that observation gives the *Hippias Major* its philosophical distinction.

NOTES TO CHAPTER SEVEN

1. An introduction to Plato's mature theory of Forms is to be found in Gallop, 1975: 93, ff. For more thorough discussions, see Ryle (1968: 320), Ross (1951), and Wedberg (1955: Chapter III). My purpose here is not to say what Plato's theory is, but to say what it is usually thought to be, so I can ask if *that* theory occurs in the *Hippias.*

2. What sort of dichotomy Plato intends is in dispute. It is certainly meant to be exclusive, but whether or not it is to be exhaustive as well is not clear from the evidence. See Shiner (1974: Chapter 10), with my review (1979).

3. Again, this dichotomy is not clearly required by the texts; I mention it here because it is part of the theory usually attributed to Plato. See Fine (1978).

4. For scholars who attribute the Independence Thesis to Plato, and for a well-argued case on the other side, see Rohr (1978).

For the Priority Thesis, see Allen (1970).

5. On the Two-Worlds Theory, and whether Plato held it, see Ryle (1968: 320) and Crombie (1963, Vol. II: 247, ff., esp. 319–325).

6. See MacIntyre (1968), and, for a representative dispute about the nature of ontology, Browning (1973) vs. Quine (1948).

7. This I take to be the point of Quine's doctrine of ontological relativity (1973). Until talk of trees is interpreted against a background of theory, it is not committed to any specific ontology.

On the difficulty of separating ontological from other questions, see Sellars, 1980: I.10.

8. Note that though one may pursue the naïve course naïvely, one cannot easily describe it naïvely. I have had no choice but to use ontologically

loaded words such as "criterion," "characteristic," and "occur in," audaciously stipulating that they are used here without theoretical trappings.

9. On strict prediction, see above, p. 153; on Hippias' failures, p. 47, ff. and 59.

10. Nehamas (1972: 483–4). *Pace* Vlastos (RC: 102, ff.).

11. To say that a logical cause is *in* something (as soul is in a living body, or fire in something hot) is not to adopt an ontology of immanent forms. See p. 166.

12. For a discussion of the Third Man with bibliography, see Vlastos (TMA).

13. See p. 155 above. The paraphrase treats self-predication as neutral by making it about F things. For an objection to this way of neutralizing self-predication, see Nehamas (1979: 96, n. 13). Nehamas' chief objection is that such paraphrases do neutralize Plato's ontological commitment to forms. But that is what is at issue.

14. See *Phaedo* 78d10–e4, with 47b8–9 and the contrasts at 78d3–7 and 74a9–12; *Republic* 479a5–8, with b9–10; *Republic* 538c6 with 538d9–e1; *Parmenides* 129a6–d6.

15. On the unwritten doctrine, see Vlastos (1973: 379–398) and Wippern (1972).

16. See Guthrie (1969: 459, ff.); for the challenge, see Kahn (1981).

17. *Euthyphro* 4e9. Euthyphro's goal is to show he knows enough to have no fear of impiety in doing what he now does. Cf. 5d1–2 and 7a8–9.

18. Such a division into parts does not compromise the essential unity of the fine. See *Sophist* 257cd and Woodruff, 1976: 108–110.

19. There are as many accounts of this passage as scholars who have treated it. A recent promising one (that disagrees with mine) is that of G. Fine (1978).

EIGHT
The Fine, the Good, and the Beneficial

Like most early Platonic dialogues, the *Hippias Major* carries no explicit message. There is no obvious lesson it drives home.[1] There is not even a single subject or theme to unify the piece. We could say equally well it is about Hippias, or about definition, or about the fine, or about Socrates himself. The elusiveness of Plato's purpose in writing such works frustrates scholars, but it is part of Plato's fascination for us. And despite its complexities, the *Hippias Major* is a unified work; the themes are related mutually (above, p. 130), and the arguments take an orderly sequence (above, p. 46).

I have already treated the most obvious of the many things accomplished in the *Hippias Major:* the revelation of Hippias' dangerously versatile character; the contrast of his easy public life against Socrates' urgent domestic dialogue with the Questioner; the development of standards for Socratic definition which lead towards the theory of Forms. I shall end with a speculative comment on what Socrates shows himself to believe about the fine.

Socrates says he does not know what the fine is, and I have shown why we should believe him (p. 141). What he does not know is the Socratic definition of the fine. But such ignorance is compatible with his knowing plenty about the fine. Indeed, he must know enough to know that the definitions proposed in the *Hippias Major* fail. Socrates' pursuit of the fine is guided by a set of antecedent doctrines, one of which reveals itself each time he rejects a proposed definition. We can therefore construct an account of the fine from the arguments of the *Hippias Major*. I list here the most prominent of Socrates' guiding doctrines on that subject, with the warning that these guiding doctrines must *not* be thought to constitute a definition:

a. The fine is fine (Proposals 1 to 3).
b. The fine makes fine things *be* (not be seen to be) fine (Proposal 4).
c. The fine is beneficial (Proposal 5).
d. The fine is good (Proposal 6).
e. The fine is common to all fine things (Proposal 7).

(The proposals cited by number are those shipwrecked on each doctrine about the fine. Numbers refer to the sequence described on p. 46.) Two of these beliefs come as no surprise; they are instances of the rules for definition: *a* for self-predication, and *e* for the unity of definition. Another, *b,* is also a matter of logic. But that the fine is good and beneficial, (*c* and *d*), is astounding. How could Socrates know that without knowing what the fine is? How can it be reconciled with Socrates' argument that the fine cannot be both good and the beneficial (p. 71–4)? And how can a Socrates who believes it be made consistent with the enthusiastic Socrates of Plato's middle dialogues?

THE BOUNDS OF IGNORANCE REVISITED

I aim to show here that Socrates can believe the fine to be beneficial without compromising his celebrated ignorance and without contradicting his other beliefs about the fine. Socrates does not think he knows the definition of the fine; the fine is something he pursues and pursues under a certain description, much as a lawman might chase a criminal he does not know, hoping a suspect matching his description will turn up and confess. What Socrates chases in the *Hippias Major* (indeed, what he chases whenever he chases anything) is something *beneficial*. Why else would he pursue it?

The bounds of Socrates' ignorance have been drawn in an earlier chapter (pp. 141, ff), where I argued that Socrates' prior beliefs about his *definienda* are grounded in the purpose of his search for definitions. The purpose of the *Hippias Major* is complicated by the doubling effect of the Questioner. Both Socrates and Hippias are on trial, Socrates as to whether he is competent to judge speakers like Hippias, and Hippias as to whether he is right to try to teach young Spartans. At issue in each case is whether the witness knows the fine practices that are good for young Spartans, whether, to put the matter in one word, he knows the fine. Any account of the fine that failed to present it in all its beneficial glory would fail the witness' purpose. If (*per impossible*) the witness knew that the fine were pleasure and proved himself an expert on pleasure, he would not have proved himself competent on what is good for young Spartans, not unless he could show also that pleasure is beneficial. If the hunt turned up a definition for the fine that did not make the fine beneficial, Socrates would have to say they had been hunting the wrong quarry, in some bafflement, like hunters who had followed lion tracks to a trembling rabbit. Socrates may therefore confidently insist that what he seeks to define is beneficial. That is why he pursues it.

Knowing that the fine is beneficial will not enable you to pick out fine things unless you already know what the good things are that something must produce if it is to be beneficial. But that must remain in question, unless the good is different from the fine.

THE FINE IS BENEFICIAL

Socrates talks of the fine often as something drab and sexless, the virtue of solid kitchenware or effective legislation, or even of his own serviceable body. *Kalon* is as *kalon* does, so his examples contend. Accordingly, a number of modern scholars make a utilitarian of Socrates—George Grote (1888: II.55) and his friend J. S. Mill (1863: Chapter 1), more recently Tarrant (1928: 68) and Guthrie (1971: 142–7). What it means to call Socrates utilitarian is not altogether clear; it may mean something demonstrably false. Both in history and in Plato's works, Socrates held that all and only fine things are beneficial, so argues a wealth of evidence. But (i) that belief is, so far as we know, not Socrates' definition of the fine. If it were, then the argument of *Hippias Major* 296d–297d would be either a fallacy as Joseph Moreau urges (1941: 35–7), or a Platonic criticism of Socrates as Irwin suggests (1977A: 165). Furthermore (ii), Socrates' belief that the fine is beneficial does not subordinate fineness to any other good as being instrumental.[2] If it did, then Plato's insistence on the autonomy of the fine and of fine things like virtues would be anti-Socratic; virtues and other fine things would be valued by Socrates only as instruments for some other more final good. But Socrates' belief that the fine is beneficial is neither instrumentalist nor a definition. I shall examine the evidence of Xenophon and Plato in turn. For once, they harmonize.

Xenophon's Socrates insists that fine things be beneficial (*Memorabilia* III.viii. 4, ff. and IV.vi. 8–9) and uses strikingly utilitarian examples of fineness (compare the manure basket, III.viii. 6, with the pot of *Hippias Major* 288a10). In the notorious beauty contest, Xenophon's Socrates argues for his superiority over a young boy by citing the utility of his less attractive features (*Symposium* 4,5). Nonutilitarian considerations intrude on a judgment of fineness in the *Oeconomicus* (VIII. 19, ff.), but this is exceptional. Xenophon's testimony on the historical Socrates has of course been doubted; but on this point he is fairly consistent, too clever to be making things up himself, and in remarkable agreement with Plato, as we shall see.

Does Xenophon make Socrates subordinate fineness to some other good by definition? Socrates is not, in the first place, giving in the *Memorabilia* the sort of definition Plato shows him seeking in the *Hippias Major*. In *Memorabilia* III. viii, Socrates is extricating himself from a trap laid by Aristippus. Aristippus challenged Socrates to say of something that it is good, planning to refute him by showing that whatever Socrates mentioned was sometimes bad. Socrates (here speaking remarkably like Protagoras in *Protagoras* 334a, ff.) claims that anything good or fine is good or fine *for something:* "But look, if you're asking me if I know something good that's not good for anything, I neither know nor care to know" (III.viii. 3). Socrates here gives identical accounts of the fine and the good; he cannot, therefore, be subordinating one to the other. And the accounts are not Socratic definitions; they do not (indeed, by the argument of 296d–297d, they could not) say what it is that makes fine things fine and good things good.

Plato's Socrates is much the same. In the *Hippias Major* he uses characteristically homely examples of fineness (288cd and 290e), and rejects a proposed definition because it conflicts with the hitherto unstated assumption that fine things should be not harmful, but beneficial (296cd). In the *Gorgias* he uses against Polus an account of the fine as the pleasant or beneficial (474de). Although in the *Hippias Major* he rejects a proposal for defining the fine as the beneficial, he still brings the argument back to that proposal suggestively at the close of the dialogue (295ce and 303e). A proposal in the *Euthyphro* meets a similiar fate, and turns out to state not the essence of what is to be defined but something merely true of it (a *pathos*—11ab). Although Socrates does not say outright in the *Hippias Major* that the fine is beneficial as *pathos* rather than *ousia,* his believing such a thing would explain the tension between his rejection of the proposed definition and his treatment of the fine as beneficial in such contexts as 296cd. To the evidence of the *Gorgias* and *Hippias Major* we must add a fiercely disputed passage from the *Protagoras:* "then are all actions directed at this, at living without pain and pleasantly, fine and beneficial?" (358a3–5 with 353c1–e1). As with most of what Socrates says in the heat of argument, we cannot be sure whether he says this because he believes it, or because he thinks his opponents believe it (cf. Taylor, 1976: 175–6.) Most persuasive of all the Platonic evidence on this score is Thrasymachus' attack on Socrates in the *Republic* (336cd; cf. Guthrie 1971: 142). There Thrasymachus implies that Socrates is known for giving utilitarian-type accounts of virtues, saying, for example, that justice is advantageous, but not saying for whom it is advantageous (336d with Thrasymachus' improved answer at 338c). As we have seen, Socrates tends to assume of each virtue he tries to define that it is fine (above, p. 111, n. 2); he takes similar pains in some cases to reveal his guiding doctrine that virtues are beneficial (*Charmides* 175e–176a, *Meno* 89a2, *Euthydemus* 278e–281d). Altogether, the case that Socrates held all fine things to be beneficial is highly persuasive.

Socrates does not apparently think that in accepting this link between the fine and the beneficial he has found a definition of the fine. The argument at *Hippias Major* 296d–297d firmly and soundly repudiates that sort of definition of the fine, as I have shown in the Commentary (pp. 71–74). The basis of that argument is another hitherto unstated Socratic doctrine: that the fine is good and the good fine. The importance of this for Socrates' axiology will be discussed in its place. Here I need only point out that Socrates' linkage of the fine with the beneficial not only stops short of defining the fine; it also avoids subordinating the fine to the good. For the good is also linked to the beneficial, and in exactly the same way: all good things are beneficial (*Meno* 87e, *Gorgias* 499d). We must therefore understand "beneficial" in such a way that fine things can be beneficial without fineness' being subordinated to the good. For the good is not subordinated to itself. No one could seriously entertain the idea that good things are valued merely as instruments for the production of good things. If good things can be beneficial without being mere instruments, then so can fine things.

This conclusion is welcome, for it smooths over a potential rift between Socrates and his most famous pupil. When George Grote found that Socrates was a utilitarian he saw on this issue "a material disagreement" between Plato and Socrates. Plato certainly abhorred the use of virtue-like qualities to obtain pleasure (*Phaedo* 68d–69d), and would have been at odds with a Socrates who reduced virtues to instruments. Moreover, what makes the virtues valuable is their fineness, and the fine was always valued by Plato in its own right. Plato's Socrates too is in love with the fine, rather than with what it produces. We find him in earlier dialogues surrounded by fine young men and boys, looking for fineness in their talk and in their souls, highly excited, hoping for a glimpse, as if the very sight of fineness would be its own reward. Later Plato paints Socrates gripped by a longing only arduous metaphysics could satisfy, and that with a vision of the fine itself, nothing more. The utilitarian conception of the fine, as something that produces good or pleasurable effects, by itself hardly justifies this enthusiasm. If the fine is valuable because it produces good, then the good is what Socrates should be excited about. Had the historical Socrates been satisfied with an account of the fine as merely instrumentally desirable, Plato would have represented him falsely throughout his work.

We have still not understood Socrates' way of linking the fine with the beneficial, however. Three problems remain. *First,* we have to ask how the fine and the good are related to one another if both are beneficial, and how they are both related to the sorts of benefits that fine and good things produce. That question admits a speculative answer, which I give in the next section. *Second,* we should like to give a formal account of the relation Socrates finds between the fine and the beneficial. This question is less tractable. Socrates seems to believe at least in a conditional: all fine things are beneficial. The connection must extend beyond that, however, and have some basis in the meanings of the two words, since it governs their proper usage and excludes a proposed definition (296d). But we know that the connection cannot be so strong as to constitute a definition itself (296d–297d). We must therefore be content to say that it is stronger than a conditional and weaker than a definition. A more precise account than that would go beyond the available evidence. *Third,* we need to explain Socrates' curiously incomplete use of "beneficial." This is the point on which Xenophon and Plato diverge: Xenophon's Socrates took care to say what a fine thing was beneficial for (*Memorabilia* III.viii. 3); whereas Plato's Socrates was given to using "beneficial" without completing it. (That, at any rate, is the implication both of Thrasymachus' attack at *Republic* 336d, and of Socrates' disapproving attitude towards Protagoras' account of the beneficial at *Protagoras* 334a–d.) In being beneficial, a fine thing should be fine relative to a use and a user, and so forth. Although Socrates recognizes that relativity occasionally (*Hippias Major* 295d, *Gorgias* 474d), he elsewhere requires that what is fine be so for everyone, and for all seasons (e.g., at *Hippias Major* 292e). How can the fine be conceived as beneficial and still be the same in every case? The problem here is how Socrates overcomes the apparent incompleteness of "fine," its tendency to depend for meaning on context. What benefits one person (a thief, for example) is likely to harm another (his victim). Different things are beneficial for different people, we think; therefore Socrates should find different things fine for different people as well. But fineness enshrines Socrates' most trusted values; it is what the virtues have. He must insist that it is one thing in every case, and that the word for it can stand alone, without qualification, and without danger of contradiction (above, p. 157).

He can do this, as we saw, if he uses "beneficial" in strict predication (p. 153). By the rules of Socratic logic, if exercise is strictly beneficial for one person, then it is beneficial without qualification, and there must be no one for whom it is harmful. So if there is anyone whom exercise drives to premature cardiac arrest, it is not strictly beneficial at all, not even for those whom it strengthens. That is because, as we saw, it cannot be the nature of something to be *F* if it is *F* in some contexts and the opposite of *F* in others. Natures do not shift with context. Since strict predication is limited to what is true of or by natures, it must therefore be context-neutral.

If fine things are beneficial without qualification (if, that is, they are strictly beneficial) they must be beneficial wherever they occur, and never harmful. That seems absurd on its face. Most of the benefits we want come at some expense to other people; and to say of something that it is beneficial —full stop—is to say nothing that would distinguish it from successful burglary. That must be the substance of Thrasymachus' objection (*Republic* 336cd). Socrates says that a virtue is beneficial. But where is the rest of the sentence? Is it beneficial for those who have the virtue? For others? For the ruling class?

Socrates does not need to say more to complete his sentence. When he calls a virtue beneficial he is not defining it, but stating one of its guiding properties (above, p. 144). He is asking for a definition of a virtue along with the assurance that anything that satisfies the definition will be strictly beneficial. Exercise, we saw, could not be strictly beneficial. But any genuine virtue is. That is the wonderful virtue of virtue. Though a virtue benefits particular people particularly, there is no one whom it harms; and everyone affected by it is benefited. When you have virtue, it benefits you by strengthening itself in you; it benefits others by your example, or more directly through teaching and punishment. It harms no one, if to harm a person is, as Socrates believes, to diminish his virtue (*Republic* 334b1, ff., cf. *Apology* 41cd). Socrates uses "beneficial" strictly of the things he deems fine. That would be unacceptably strange if his prime example of fineness— virtue—were not strictly beneficial. On this subject, his strict logic gives splendid results: the personal character he bids us seek and cultivate in ourselves and others is one of contagious goodness, a character that brings harm to no one, a character whose most striking feature is its ability to reproduce itself in those who are touched by it, like a smile, only more so. Who could quarrel with that?

THE FINE IS GOOD

Socrates says that the fine is good, and the good fine, and both are beneficial. To be beneficial, moreover, is to produce good things (296e7, with my note *ad loc.*). How can we make sense of this entanglement?

Separating the fine from the good in Socrates' thought would help, but runs against the texts. Socrates' proposal to define the fine as the beneficial is wrecked on this very point: the proposed definition turns out not to be compatible with the strong connection Socrates wants to maintain between the fine and the good (297c7–8). And in the *Gorgias* Socrates refutes Polus' attempt to divide the fine from the good (474c, ff.). In Xenophon too Socrates treats the fine and the good as very much the same sort of thing. Indeed, all the evidence supports attributing to Socrates the thesis that the fine and the good are the same thing. On the other side we have only the hypothesis that Socrates defined the fine as the beneficial (advanced, for example, by Moreau, 1941: 35–7). On such a view, the *Hippias Major* would be adopting a Platonic stance in rejecting the "Socratic" definition (as Irwin suggests, 1977A: 165). But that is highly unlikely; for the *Hippias Major,* as we saw, supplied part of our case that Socrates connected the fine with the beneficial in the first place. The best account of the evidence is that Socrates believes everything fine is beneficial (as I have urged) without accepting that as his definition.

What Socrates implies is that the fine is good, and that the good is fine. In the context these are strict predications and entail that fine things, in being fine, are good, and *vice versa*. Now fine things, for Socrates, are beneficial, and that means they produce good things. But the good things they produce are, in being good, fine. So we have the odd pair of results: in being beneficial, fine things produce fine things, and good things produce good things. To say that those are uninformative is an understatement. We had thought, when we were told that the beneficial was a guiding property of the fine, that we had something substantial to go on in our search. But now it appears that our quarry is antecedently known by an account that turns back on itself: the fine and good are beneficial; that is, fine and good things produce fine and good things. If that is the most substantial thing we know about our quarry we are in trouble. The fine reproduces itself; but so, perhaps, do many harmful things, vice, for example, to say nothing of mumps and mosquitoes. Socrates wants to marry the fine with the good, to explain "beneficial" in terms of the good and still to say something useful with "the fine is beneficial." That, it seems, is more than he can do.

That the fine reproduces itself does not, by itself, contribute to its definition. But it does add a desirable luster to the fine, and it shows how Socrates' conception of the fine harmonizes with the more enthusiastic one of Plato's middle dialogues. In the *Symposium* Socrates recalls Diotima's account of love. It is not so much a desire for the fine as it is a desire to procreate in fineness; and the ultimate lover's reward will be the begetting in himself of true virtue, which will in turn make him—the ultimate lover—an object of divine love (212a). The highest fineness, fineness itself, is presented here as useful for the reproduction of fine things. That accounts for the Platonic Socrates' sexually charged enthusiasm for it.

We are still left with an awkward gap. Not knowing what the good is, and therefore ignorant of the beneficial, how is Socrates to be guided in his search by knowing that the fine is beneficial? He does not know what it is to be beneficial, and indeed he cannot know that until he knows what it is to be good and fine—what it is that the beneficial produces. What use, then, can Socrates make of his knowing that the fine is beneficial? He can use it only with *beliefs* about what sorts of things are beneficial. Beliefs, as we have seen, may be good enough to live by; and a conflict among beliefs is enough to prove the believer's confusion (p. 245). But such slender guidance could not lead him to a definition with the assurance he wants. No wonder his search remained unsatisfied. "What's fine is hard." There, appropriately, the story of Socrates' quest comes to an end.

NOTES TO CHAPTER 8

1. Two suggestions have been made about the implicit lesson of the *Hippias Major:*

(1) Socrates (and the author) believe that the fine is the beneficial and reveal this by arguing badly against that definition. Socrates is not really stuck at the end: his favorite definition is not refuted. (Moreau, 1941.)

(2) Plato illustrates part of the theory of transcendent Forms in the *Hippias Major.* ("What this Dialogue shows, rather than asserts, is the higher-order or 'transcendental' character of Beauty. . . ." Findlay, 1974, p. 88.) The reader is supposed to learn from Socrates' failure to identify the fine with any lower-level character that the fine is a transcendental Form.

The first of these suggestions is impossible. The proposed definition is unacceptable and is soundly refuted in the *Hippias Major* in any case (pp. 71–74). The second suggestion cannot be ruled out. The evidence of the text neither supports nor undermines it. In such a case, with a proposition that cannot be tested, we are best advised to reserve judgment indefinitely.

2. Since Socrates' prime example of fineness appears to be virtue (p. 111, n. 2), this issue is closely related to the question of whether Socrates subordinates virtue as being instrumental for some other good. That has been aired recently in correspondence between Gregory Vlastos and Terence Irwin in the *Times Literary Supplement* consequent to Vlastos' February 24 review of Irwin's *Plato's Moral Theory.* Letters appeared in the issues of March 17, April 21, May 5, June 9, June 16, July 14, August 4, and September 22, 1978.

Bibliography

Other available translations are by Jowett's Editors (Fourth Edition, 1955), Fowler (in the *Loeb*), Croiset (in the *Budé*), and Apelt. The commentary of Dorothy Tarrant (1928) is helpful. The best and most recent discussion of the dialogue is in Guthrie's *History* (1975, Volume IV). The general bibliography that follows is not intended to be complete. It lists alphabetically and by date the works to which I have had occasion to refer.

Adam, J. and A. M. *Platonis Protagoras; with Introduction, Notes, and Appendices.* Cambridge: Cambridge University Press, 1893.

Adkins, Arthur W. H.
  1960: *Merit and Responsibility; A Study in Greek Values.* Oxford: Clarendon Press, 1960.
  1973: "ARĒTĒ, TECHNĒ, Democracy, and Sophists: *Protagoras* 316B–328D." *The Journal of Hellenic Studies,* XCIII (1973), 3–12.

Allen, R. E. *Plato's 'Euthyphro' and the Earlier Theory of Forms.* New York: Humanities Press, 1970.

Apelt, Otto.
  1912: "Die beiden Dialoge Hippias." *Neue Jahrbücher,* 19 (1907), 630–58. Repr. New York: Arno, 1976, in his Platonische Aufsätze, pp. 203–237.
  1918: *Platons Dialoge Hippias I und II, Ion; übersetzt und erläutert.* Leipzig: Felix Meiner, 1918.

Ast, Friedrich. *Platon's Leben und Schriften.* Leipzig: Weidmanischen Buchhandlung, 1816.

Barnes, Jonathan. *The Presocratic Philosophers.* London: Routledge & Kegan Paul, 1979.

Beversluis, J. "Socratic Definitions." *American Philosophical Quarterly,* 11 (1974), 331–6.

Bonitz, Hermann. *Index Aristotelicus.* Berlin: Reimer, 1870.

Brandwood, Leonard. *A Word Index to Plato.* Leeds: W. S. Maney, 1976. (Compendia; Computer-Generated Aids to Library and Linguistic Research, Volume 8.)

Browning, Douglas. "Quine and the Ontological Enterprise." *The Review of Metaphysics,* XXVII (1973), 492–510.

Burnyeat, M. F. "Examples in Epistemology: Socrates, Theaetetus and G. E. Moore." *Philosophy,* 52 (1977), 381–98.

Capelle, Annemarie. "Platonishes in grösseren Hippias." *Rheinisches Museum für Philologie,* 99 (1956), 178–90.

Chaintraine, P. "Xénophon, Économique, VIII, 19." *Revue Philologie,* 21 (1947), 46–8.

Cherniss, Harold.
>   1952: Review of Dupréel (1948). *American Journal of Philology,* 73 (1952), 199–207.
>   1959: "Plato 1950–1957." *Lustrum,* 4–5 (1959–1960), 5–648.

Classen, Carl Joachim. *Sophistik.* (*Wege der Forschung,* CLXXXVII). Darmstadt, 1976.

Croiset, Alfred. Translation of the *Hippias Major* in Volume II of the *Budé* series. 2d ed., corrected by Louis Bodin. Paris, 1965.

de Strycker, É.
>   1937: "Une énigme mathématiqué dans l'Hippias majeur." *Mélange Émile Boisacq,* Volume I, pp. 317–26. (Annuaire de l'Institut de Philologie et d'Histoire orientales et slaves de l'Université libre de Bruxelles, V (1937), 317–26.)
>   1941: "De irrationalen in den Hippias Major." *L'Antiquité Classique,* X (1941), 25–36.
>   1950: Review of Michel (1950). *L'Antiquité Classique,* XXI (1952), 531.
>   1953: Review of Soreth (1953). L'Antiquité Classique, XXIII (1954), 472–3.

Diès, A. *Autour de Platon; essais de critique et d'histoire.* Paris: Beauchesne, 1927.

Dillon, John. *The Middle Platonists; A Study of Platonism 80* B.C. *to* A.D. *220.* London: Duckworth, 1977.

Dodds, E. R. *Plato:* Gorgias; *A Revised Text with Introduction and Commentary.* Oxford: Clarendon Press, 1959.

Dover, K. J.
>   1974: *Greek Popular Morality in the Time of Plato and Aristotle.* Berkeley: University of California Press, 1974.

1978: *Greek Homosexuality*. Cambridge, Massachusetts: Harvard University Press, 1978.

Dupréel, Eugène. *Les Sophistes; Protagoras, Gorgias, Prodicus, Hippias*. Neufchatel: Griffon, 1948.

Findlay, J. N. *Plato; The Written and Unwritten Doctrines*. London: Routledge & Kegan Paul, 1974.

Fine, Gail. "Knowledge and Belief in *Republic* V." *Archiv für Geschichte der Philosophie,* 60 (1978), 121–38.

Friedländer, Paul. *Plato*. Trans. Hans Meyerhoff, from the 2d ed. of 1957. New York: Pantheon, 1964.

Fowler, H. N. *Plato; With an English Translation* (Loeb Series). Volume V New York: G. P. Putnam, 1926.

Gadamer, Hans-Georg. *Dialogue and Dialectic; Eight Hermeneutical Studies on Plato*. Trans. by P. Christopher Smith. New Haven: Yale University Press, 1980.

Gallop, David. Plato, *Phaedo*. Oxford: Clarendon Press, 1975.

Garcia Bacca, Juan David. *Hippias Major; Fedro*. Translated with Introduction and Notes. Mexico City: University of Mexico Press, 1945.

Gauss, Hermann. *Philosophisches Handkommentar zu den Dialogen Plato's*. Volume I.2 (Die Frühdialoge). Berlin: Verlag Herbert Lang, 1954.

Geach, P. T. "Plato's *Euthyphro:* An Analysis and Commentary." *Monist* 50 (1966), 369–382. Repr. in his *Logic that Matters* (Oxford, 1972), pp. 31-44.

Geffcken, Johannes. *Griechische Literaturgeschichte*. Heidelberg: Carl Winters, 1934.

Gigon, O. Review of Soreth (1953). *Gnomon,* 27 (1955), 14–20.

Gomperz, H. *Sophistik und Rhetorik*. Berlin: Teubner, 1912.

Gomperz, T. *Greek Thinkers; A History of Ancient Philosophy*. Trans. by Laurie Magnus. London: John Murray, 1901. (Orig. 1896.)

Grote, George.
  1872: *A History of Greece*. 4th ed. London: John Murray, 1872.
  1888: *Plato, and the Other Companions of Sokrates*. 2d ed. London: John Murray, 1888.

Grube, G. M. A.
  1926A: "Notes on the Hippias Major." *Classical Review,* XL (1926), 188–9.
  1926B: "On the Authenticity of the *Hippias Major*." *Classical Quarterly,* 20 (1926), 134–48.
  1927: "Plato's Theory of Beauty." *Monist,* 37 (1927), 269–288.

1929: "The Logic and Language of the *Hippias Major.*" *Classical Philology,* XXIV (1929), 369–75.

Guthrie, W. K. C. *A History of Greek Philosophy.* Cambridge: Cambridge University Press, 1962–
  1969: Volume III. *The Fifth Century Enlightenment.* 1969.
  1975: Volume IV. *Plato; the Man and His Dialogues: Earlier Period.* 1975.
  1975r: Review of Newiger (1973). *Gnomon,* XLVI (1975), 705–8.

Harrison, E. L. "Was Gorgias a Sophist?" *Phoenix,* XVIII (1964), 183–92.

Heath, Thomas Little. *A History of Greek Mathematics.* Oxford: Clarendon Press, 1921.

Heidel, William Arthur. *Pseudo-Platonica.* New York: Arno Press, 1976. (Orig. Baltimore, 1896.)

Hoerber, Robert G. "Plato's Greater Hippias." *Phronesis,* IX (1964), 143–54.

Horneffer, Ernest. *De Hippia Majoire Qui Fertur Platonis.* Göttingen Dissertation, 1895.

Irwin, Terence.
  1977A: *Plato's Moral Theory: The Early and Middle Dialogues.* Oxford: Clarendon Press, 1977.
  1977B: "Plato's Heracliteanism." *The Philosophical Quarterly,* 27 (1977), 1–13.

Johann, H. T. "Hippias von Elis und der Physis-Nomos Gedanke." *Phronesis,* XVIII (1973), 15–25.

Kahn, Charles. "Did Plato Write Socratic Dialogues?" *Classical Quarterly* (forthcoming).

Kerferd, G. B. "Gorgias on Nature or That Which Is Not." *Phronesis,* 1 (1955), 3–25.

Keuls, Eva C. *Plato and Greek Painting.* London: E. J. Brill, 1978.

Kühner, Raphael, and Gerth, Bernhard. *Ausführliche Grammatik der Griechischen Sprache.* Hannover & Leipzig, 1898.

Lacey, A. R. "Our Knowledge of Socrates." In Gregory Vlastos (1971), pp. 22–49.

MacIntyre, Alasdair. "Ontology." In Paul Edwards, *et al.,* eds., *The Encyclopedia of Philosophy* (New York, 1968), Vol. V, p. 542.

Malcolm, J. "On the Place of the Hippias Major in the development of Plato's thought." *Archiv für Geschichte der Philosophie,* (1968), 189–95.

Mejer, Jørgen. Review of Newiger (1973). *Classical World,* LXX (1976), 275.

Michel, P. H. *De Pythagore à Euclide; Contribution à l'histoire des mathématiques préeuclidiennes.* Paris: Les Belles Lettres, 1950.

Mill, John Stuart. *Utilitarianism.* London, 1863.

Moreau, Joseph.
1941: "Le Platonisme de 'L'Hippias Majeur'." *Revue des Études Grecques,* 54 (1941), 19–42.
1954: Review of Soreth (1953). *Revue des Études Anciennes,* 56 (1954), 191–2.

Nakhnikian, George. "Elenctic Definitions." In Vlastos (1971), pp. 125–157.

Nehamas, Alexander:
1972: "Predication and Forms of Opposites in the Phaedo." *The Review of Metaphysics,* XXVI (1972), 461-94.
1975: "Confusing Universals and Particulars in Plato's Early Dialogues." *The Review of Metaphysics,* XXIX (1975), 288–306.
1979: "Self-Predication and Plato's Theory of Forms." *American Philosophical Quarterly,* 16 (1979), 93–103.

Nestle, Wilhelm. *Vom Mythos zum Logos; Die Selbstentfaltung des griechischen Denkens von Homer bis auf die Sophistik und Sokrates.* 2d ed. Stuttgart: Alfred Kröner, 1942.

Newiger, Hans-Joachim. *Untersuchungen zu Gorgias' Schrift über das Nichtseiende.* Berlin: De Gruyter, 1973.

Ostwald, Martin. *Nomos and the Beginnings of the Athenian Democracy.* Oxford: Clarendon Press, 1969.

Owen, G. E. L. "Logic and Metaphysics in Some Earlier Works of Aristotle." In Owen and I. Düring, eds., *Aristotle and Plato in the Mid-Fourth Century* (Göteborg, 1960), pp. 163–190.

Penner, Terry. "The Unity of Virtue." *The Philosophical Review,* LXXXII (1973), 35–68.

Pohlenz, Max.
1913: *Aus Platos Werdezeit; Philologische Untersuchungen.* Berlin: Weidmanischen Buchhandlung, 1913.
1931: Review of Tarrant (1928). *Gnomon,* 7 (1931), 300–307.

Quine, W. V.
1948: "On What There Is." In his *From a Logical Point of View,* 2d ed. (Cambridge, Massachusetts, 1961), pp. 1–19.
1969: "Ontological Relativity." In his *Ontological Relativity and Other Essays* (New York, 1969), pp. 26–68.

Rawson, Elizabeth. *The Spartan Tradition in European Thought.* Oxford: Clarendon Press, 1969.

Rist, J. M. "Plato's 'Earlier Theory of Forms'." *Phoenix,* 29 (1975), 336–57.

Robinson, John M. "On Gorgias." In Lee, *et al.,* eds., *Exegesis and Argument* (Assen, 1973), pp. 49–60.

Robinson, Richard. *Plato's Earlier Dialectic*. 2d ed. Oxford: Clarendon Press, 1953.

Rohr, Michael David. "Empty Forms in Plato." *Archiv für Geschichte der Philosophie*, 60 (1978), 268–83.

Ross, David. *Plato's Theory of Ideas*. Oxford: Clarendon Press, 1951.

Ryle, Gilbert. "Plato." In Paul Edwards, *et al.*, eds., *The Encyclopedia of Philosophy* (New York, 1968), Vol. VI, pp. 314–333.

Santas, Gerasimos Xenophon.
> 1972: "The Socratic Fallacy." *Journal of the History of Philosophy*, 10 (1972), 127–41.
> 1979: *Socrates; Philosophy in Plato's Early Dialogues*. London: Routledge & Kegan Paul, 1979.

Schleiermacher, Friedrich. *Introductions to the Dialogues of Plato*. Trans. William Dobson. Repr. New York: Arno Press, 1973, from trans. of 1836 (orig. 1804–10).

Schmid, Wilhelm, and Stälin, Otto. *geschichte der Griechischen Literatur*. Munich: Beck'sche, 1940.

Sellars, Wilfrid. *Naturalism and Ontology*. Atascadero, California: Ridgeview, 1980.

Sharvey, Richard. "Euthyphro 9D–11B: Analysis and Definition in Plato and Others." *Nous*, 6 (1972), 119–137.

Shiner, Roger A. *Knowledge and Reality in Plato's Philebus*. Assen: Van Gorcum, 1974.

Shorey, Paul.
> 1922: "Plato *Euthydemus* 304E." *Classical Philology*, XVII (1922), 261–2.
> 1933: *What Plato Said*. Chicago: University of Chicago Press, 1933.

Smyth, Herbert Weir. *Greek Grammar*. (Revised by Gordon M. Messing.) Cambridge, Massachusetts: Harvard University Press, 1959.

Soreth, Marion. *Der platonische Dialog Hippias Maior*. (*Zetemata*, 6.) Munich: Beck'sche, 1953.

Sprague, Rosamund Kent, ed. *The Older Sophists; A Complete Translation by Several Hands of the Fragments in Diels-Kranz*. Columbia, South Carolina: University of South Carolina Press, 1972.

Stallbaum, Gottfried. *Platonis Opera Omnia*. 2d ed. Volume IV.1. Gotha: Hennings, 1857.

Stone, I. F. "I. F. Stone Breaks the Socrates Story." *The New York Times* (April 8, 1979), Section 6, pp. 22, ff.

Tarrant, Dorothy.
> 1920: "On the *Hippias Major*." *The Journal of Philology*, 35 (1920), 319–331.

1927: "The Authorship of the *Hippias Major.*" *Classical Quarterly,* XXI (1927), 82–7.

1928: *The Hippias Major Attributed to Plato; With Introductory Essays and Commentary.* Cambridge: Cambridge University Press, 1928. Repr. New York: Arno Press, 1973.

1938: "The Pseudo-Platonic Socrates." *Classical Quarterly,* XXXII (1938), 169–73.

1955: Review of Soreth (1953). *Classical Review,* n.s. V (1955), pp. 52–3.

Taylor, A. E. *Plato; The Man and His Work.* London: Methuen, 1926.

Taylor, C. C. W. *Plato* Protagoras. Oxford: Clarendon Press, 1976.

Teloh, Henry. "Self-Predication or Anaxagorean Causation in Plato." *Apeiron,* 9.2 (1976), 15-23.

Thesleff, Holger. "The Date of the Pseudo-Platonic *Hippias Major.*" *Arctos (Acta Philologica Fennica),* X (1976), 105-117.

Tigerstedt, E. N.

1965: *The Legend of Sparta in Classical Antiquity.* Stockholm: Almqvist & Wiksell, 1965.

1969: *Plato's Idea of Poetical Inspiration.* (Commentationes Humanarum Litterarum—Societas Scientarum Fennica—Volume 44.2) Helsinki: 1969.

1977: *Interpreting Plato.* (Stockholm Series in History of Literature, 17.) Uppsala: 1977.

Überweg, Friedrich. *Grundriss der Geschichte der Philosophie.* Darmstadt: Wissenschaftliche Buchgesellschaft, 1967–. (Orig. 1861.)

Untersteiner, Mario. *The Sophists.* Trans. Kathleen Freeman. Oxford: Blackwell, 1954. (Orig. 1948.)

Vlastos, Gregory.

1956: *Plato's Protagoras.* (Editor) Indianapolis: Bobbs-Merrill, 1956.

1971: *The Philosophy of Socrates; A Collection of Critical Essays.* (Editor) Garden City, New York: Anchor, 1971.

1973: *Platonic Studies.* Princeton: Princeton University Press, 1973.

AS: "An Ambiguity in the *Sophist.*" In Vlastos, 1973: pp. 270–322.

RC: "Reasons and Causes in the *Phaedo.*" In Vlastos, 1973: pp. 76–110.

TMA: "Plato's 'Third Man' Argument (*Parm.* 132A1–B2)." In Vlastos, 1973: pp. 342–365.

Webster, T. B. L. *Studies in Later Greek Comedy.* 2d ed. New York: Barnes & Noble, 1970.

Wedberg, Anders. *Plato's Philosophy of Mathematics.* Stockholm: Almqvist and Wiksell, 1955.

Wilamowitz-Moellendorff, U. von. *Platon.* 2 vols. Berlin: Weidman, 1919.

Williams, Michael. *Groundless Belief.* Oxford: Blackwell, 1977.

Wippern, Jürgen. *Das Problem der ungeschriebenen Letre Platons.* Darmstadt: *Wege der Forschung* (186), 1972.

Wittgenstein, Ludwig. *Philosophical Investigations.* 3d ed. Trans. by G. E. M. Anscombe. New York: Macmillan, 1968.

Woodruff, Paul.

1976: "Socrates on the Parts of Virtue." *Canadian Journal of Philosophy,* Supplementary Volume II (1976), 101–116.

1978A: "Socrates and Ontology: The Evidence of the *Hippias Major.*" *Phronesis,* XXIII (1978), 101–117.

1978B: "The Socratic Approach to Semantic Incompleteness." *Philosophy and Phenomenological Research,* XXXVIII (1978), 453–468.

1979: Review of Shiner (1974). *Journal of the History of Philosophy,* XVII (1979), 79–81.

"Zeller-Nestle": Zeller, E. *Die Philosophie der Griechen in ihrer geschichtliche Entwicklung.* Ed. by W. Nestle. Leipzig: O. R. Reisland, 1920–23.

The following bear significantly on topics covered in the Hippias Major, but were too recently published to be treated in these pages:

Annas, Julia. *An Introduction to Plato's Republic.* Oxford: Clarendon Press, 1981.

Kerferd, G. B. *The Sophistic Movement.* Cambridge: Cambridge University Press, 1981.

Moline, Jon. *Plato's Theory of Understanding.* Madison, Wisconsin: The University of Wisconsin Press, 1981.

Teloh, Henry. *The Development of Plato's Metaphysics.* University Park, Pennsylvania: The Pennsylvania State University Press, 1981.

General Index

Able (*dunaton*), 67, 69
Achilles, 61*n107*
Aeacus, 61*n108*
Aesthetics, 110
Agathon (good), 74, 110, 145, 187
Aischron (foul), 44*n48,* 69*n-131*
Anaxagoras, 39*n23,* 102, 152
Anaxandrides, 100
Apelt, Otto, 95
Apotome, 87*n187*
Appropriate. See *Prepon*
Argument from opposites, 174–75, 178–79
Aristippus, 184
Aristocracy, 39*n27*
Aristotle, 93, 95
Arrēta (Irrational numbers), 87*n187*
Aretē. See Virtue
Ast, Friedrich, 94
Athena Parthenos, 57*n90*
Attribute. See *Pathos*

BE (general rule for *both* and *each*), 80, 83–84, 85, 86, 87
Beauty, 110
Being: vs. becoming, 163, 165, 166, 179*n2*
Belief. *See* Opinion
Beneficial. See *Ōphelimon*
Bias, 37*n6,* 128
Both, 79–80

Callicles, 132

Causes, 152. *See also* Logical cause, Productive cause
Chrēsimon (*useful*), 67, 69*n-134*
Chytra, 53*n73*
Circularity in definitions, 151
Comedy in the *Hippias Major,* 99–101, 106, 127–28
Craft, 40*n29*
Craftsman analogy, 37*n8*
Criterion, 164

Daedalus, 37*n10*
Daimonion (of Socrates), 81*n-157,* 98
Dardanus, 61*n111*
Dative, 45*n55,* 70*n137,* 152, 158
Definite article: omission of, 64*n116,* 73, 75*n142,* 75*n143*
Definition, 45*n56,* 59; sequence of proposals, 46. *See also* Gorgian definition, Socratic definition
Democracy, 60*n104*
Democritus, 134*n2*
Dithyramb, 60*n105*
Dunaton (able), 67, 69

each, 79–80
Eidos (form), 55*n85,* 56, 57*n86,* 76*n146,* 85. *See also* Forms
Elenchus, 137–8, 141
Elis, 36*n2*
Epideixis (display speech), 38-*n15,* 89*n197,* 123

199

Essence (*ousia*), 55*n85*, 86*n-176*, 122n14, 184; vs. attribute (*pathos*), 71, 86*n181*
Euboulia (sound judgment), 40
Eudicus, 42*n45*
Eunomia, 39*n27*, 41*n35*
Examples: in the *elenchus*, 146–47

Fine. See *Kalon*
Form (*eidos, idea*), 55*n85*, 56, 57*n86*, 76*n146*, 85
Forms, 54*n83*, 87*n184*, 122*n15*, 166–173 *passim*, 178; theory of, 48, 55*n85*, 161–63, 170–76 *passim*, 179*n1*, 189*n2;* and definition, 149
Foul (*aischron*), 44*n48*, 69*n131*
Freedom of speech, 41*n35*, 60*n-104*

Good. See *Agathon*.
Georgian definition, 50*n63*, 58-*n91*, 67*n123*, 78, 116, 117, 157, 158
Gorgias, 37*n13*, 38*n15*, 40, 53-*n74*, 60*n104*, 60*n105*, 65*n-117*, 94, 116–17, 121*n10*, 132, 121*n8;* influence on Hippias, 121*n12*, 124, 135*n1*, 158
Grote, George, 95, 113, 135*n13*, 185
Guthrie, W.K.C., 64, 71

Heracles, 61*n110*
Hippias, 134*n1;* characterization, 35, 97, 109, 127–32, 138; versatility of, 35, 36, 130, 181; earnings, 36*n4*, 39-*n25*, 85*n171*, 100; on virtue, 40, 42*n36;* answers, 42*n45*,

47–48, 56, 59–60, 65*n117*, 169; rhetoric of, 82*n162*, 124, 125–27, 132–3; doctrines of, 125; superficiality of, 130–1
Hoi polloi (ordinary people), 41*n33*
Hypothesis, 82*n161*, 87*n182*

Immanence, 166, 180*n11*
Incompleteness, 48, 56, 59–60, 62, 63, 67, 69*n134*, 110–11
Instrumentalism, 183–87, 189*n3*
Irony, 35, 36*n4*, 37*n10*, 64*n113*, 89*n200*, 128–29, 134*n6*, 147*n1*
Irrational numbers, 87*n187*
Irwin, Terence, 147*n4*
Isonomia, 39*n27*

Justification, 141

Kalon (fine), 35, 36*n1*, 56, 67*n-123*, 68*n128*, 74, 76*n148*, 84, 98, 109, 111, 130–31, 140, 142, 183; translation of, 110; puns on, 36, 43*n46*, 98; used of feminine subject, 53*n70*
Knowledge: vs. opinion, 140, 143, 163, 165, 166, 179*n3*

Lamachus, 100
Law, 41*n32*, 81*n158*, 81*n159*. See also *Nomos*
Logical attributives, 110–111
Logical cause, 45*n55*, 50*n63*, 62, 64, 65*n119*, 70*n137*, 72, 73, 74*n140*, 76*n148*, 77*n149*, 78, 82*n167*, 150–153 *passim*, 159*n3*, 165, 168, 170–71, 180*n11*
Logos, 88*n194*
Middle Comedy, 100

Moral virtue. *See* Virtue

Nature (*physis*), 55*n85*, 64*n-115*, 14, 171, 173, 174
Nehamas, Alexander, 50*n63*, 180*n13;* on Hippias' confusion, 49; on self-predication, 160*n9*, cf. 158
Neoptolemus, 42*n43*
Nestor, 42*n43*
Nomos (law), 40*n30*, 124

One (the number), 86*n177*
One-over-many, 115–117 *passim*, 162, 165, 168, 170, 171
Ontology, 45*n56*, 118, 163–65, 176, 179*n6.*
Ōphelimon (beneficial), 71, 87-*n190*, 145, 182–189
Opinion: vs. knowledge, 140, 143, 148*n7*, 165, 166, 179*n2*
Ousia. See Essence

Partial definition. *See* Gorgian definition
Participation, 171, 178
Particulars, 178; vs. universals, 169
Part-whole problem, 82*n170*
Pathos (attribute), 82*n169*, 86-*n176*, 86*n181*, 184
Pelops, 61*n111*
Phainesthai (to be seen), 54*n80*, 57*n87*, 65*n118*
Pheidias, 57*n89*
Physis. See nature
Pittacus, 37*n6*, 128
Pleasure, 77
Polus, 184
Predication. *See* Self-predication, Strict predication

Prepon (appropriate), 63, 66*n-120*, 67
Presence (of a form), 66*n120*
Priority of definition, 89*n198*, 138–41, 146, 148*n7*
Prodicus, 38*n15*, 38*n17*
Productive cause, 72, 74*n140*, 75*n142*, 76*n144*, 152
Progress, 36*n4*, 125
Protagoras, 38*n15*, 38*n19*, 40, 101, 132, 159*n5*, 184; discussed, 115–116, 121*n8*

Quadratrix, 134*n3*
Qualities, 82*n165*
Questioner, 43*n47*, 46*n60*, 81*n-153*, 81*n157*, 83, 85*n173*, 86*n178*, 87*n189*, 97, 107–108, 124, 135*n8*, 151, 182

Rhetoric, 40, 116, 124, 125–27, 132–33; Socrates vs. Hippias, 44*n49*, 89*n200;* vs. philosophy, 88*n192;* and virtue, 89*n-196;* laughter in, 134*n5*

Schleiermacher, 94, 95, 108–09
Self-predication, 153–56, 157–59, 162, 165, 168–74 *passim*, 177, 180*n13*, 182
Skill (*technē*), 37*n5*, 40*n29*
Smikrologia, 88*n194*
Socrates, 78, 118–119, 122*n15*, 122*n17*, 122*n18*, 145, 176, 182–3
Socratic arguments, 137–38
Socratic definition, 62, 64, 71, 73, 74, 138, 139, 141, 142, 145, 149, 172, 181, 159*n1*
Socratic Fallacy, 139, 141
Something (*ti*), 167
Sophia (wisdom), 37*n5*, 70*n-*

135, 70*n136*
Sophists, 38*n15*, 81*n156*, 111, 113–15, 131
Sparta, 36*n3*, 39*n27*, 41*n35*
Strict predication, 82*n163*, 147, 153–56, 159*n5*, 172–75, 186, 188
Synonymy principle, 159*n4*

Tantalus, 61*n111*
Tarrant, Dorothy, 98, 135*n8*
Technē (skill), 37*n5*, 40*n29*
Thales, 37*n6*
The fine. See to kalon
Thesleff, Holger, 98
Third Man Paradox, 157, 173–74, 180*n12*
Thrasyllus, 95
Thrasymachus, 132
Ti (something), 167
To kalon (the fine), 44n50, 57-n86; definitions of, 46; vs. *kalon*, 46*n61*, 49, 64*n116*, 129, 169
Transcendence, 163, 166

Trojan Dialogue, 42*n42*
Two-worlds theory, 163, 179*n5*

Unity of definition, 78–80 *passim*, 117, 156–57, 168, 172, 182
Unity requirement, 157, 165
Universals, 45*n58*, 49, 163, 164; vs. particulars, 169
Unwritten doctrine, 180*n15*
Useful (*chrēsimon*), 67, 69*n134*
Utilitarianism, 142, 183–87

Virtue, 88*n192*, 116, 187, 189*n3;* teaching of, 40, 42-*n36*, 89*n196*, 115, 116–17, 118, 121*n10*
Vlastos, Gregory, 189*n3*
Vocabulary, 98–99

Wisdom, 37*n5*, 70*n135*, 70*n136*

Xenophon, 93, 96, 142, 183–84

Zethus, 61*n111*

Index Locorum

Title	Citation	Page Number
	ARISTOPHANES	
Acharnians	l. 572	100
Clouds	l. 1321	60*n104*
	ARISTOTLE	
De Sophisticus Elenchis	XXV	154
Metaphysics	1025a6–13	96
Poetics	1452a24	96
Politics	1261b27–30	82*n170*, 96, 156
Rhetoric	1361b7	156
Topics	102a6	65, 96
	135a13	65, 96
	145a21	78, 80*n152*, 96
	146a21–23	96
	GORGIAS	
Peri Physeos		117, 121*n11*, 122*n14*
DK 82B23		65*n117*
	HERACLEITUS	
DK 22B82		54*n79*
	HOMER	
Iliad	II. 188	60*n104*
	PLATO	
Apology		119, 120*n3*, 176
	19d–20c	118

Title	Citation	Page Number
	21b	118
	21d	136
	29de	118
	30a5–7	143
	33c5	98
	40a	81*n157*, 98
Charmides		96, 149, 165, 176
	154de	102
	158e	139
	159c	111*n2*, 145, 146
	161a	68
	161b	54*n83*, 46, 64*n113*, 175
	175e–176a	185
	176cd	137
Cratylus	384b1	89*n200*
Crito		176
	49ab	143
	50a	98
	52b	118
	52e5–6	39*n27*
Euthydemus		113, 115
	227e	156
	278d	118
	278e–281d	185
	281e	70*n135*
	301a	56
	392c	154

Title	Citation	Page Number
Euthyphro		87*n190*, 93, 94, 96, 102, 149, 165, 176, 177, 178
	4e4–5a2	43
	4e9	180*n17*
	5a3ff	44*n52*
	5c	47, 58*n93*, 144
	6d9–11	54*n81*, 55*n85*, 152
	6e4	82*n166*
	7a	58*n93*
	7c10–d5	66*n121*
	8ab	54*n83*, 138, 175, 177
	10d	111*n2*
	11a	71, 86*n181*, 184
	11e4	46, 64*n113*
	15e	136, 138
	16a	139
Gorgias		93, 102, 113, 142, 143
	452de	88*n192*
	463a	114, 118, 151, 118, 151
	466b4	88*n192*
	474c	188
	474de	68*n127*, 68*n130*, 74*n140*, 81, 142, 184, 186
	486bc	88*n192*, 88*n194*
	497b7	88*n194*

Title	Citation	Page Number
	497e	45n55
	499c6–7	78
	499d	185
	509a4–7	143, 148n7
Hippias Minor		94, 95, 102, 113
	363a8	124
	363b	42n45, 58n99
	369b8–369c8	85n172, 85n174, 88n192
	369c6	124
Ion		35, 94, 96, 151
	523c	128
	541e	135n11
Laches		96, 142, 149, 165, 176
	188ab	137
	190e	47
	192ab	143
	192c	111n2, 146, 159
	192e–193e	54n83, 175
	194c2	46, 64n113
Laws	670d7	88n191
	815b6	39n27
	816e	101
	908d	120n5
	935e	101
Lysis		93, 96, 165
	217c–e	153

Title	Citation	Page Number
Meno		102, 143
	71a	140
	71e–72a	47
	72ab	157
	72c8	152
	79ab	47
	79d	51
	80e	82*n161*, 144
	87d	111*n2*
	87e	185
	89a2	185
	97b	148*n7*
	100b	140
Parmenides		162, 175
Phaedo		93, 102, 105, 149, 153, 161, 162, 168, 172, 175, 176, 177, 178
	65d4	167
	68d–69d	185
	68e	78
	74a9–12	167
	74b8–9	54*n83*
	77a4	65
	78d10–e4	54*n83*
	96a6–102a1	152, 159*n2*, 170
	100a3	82*n161*
	100c	170

Title	Citation	Page Number
	100d7	45*n55*, 55*n85*, 152, 162, 166
	101a7	73
	102bc	65*n119*
	103ab	152
	104a	156, 171
	105b–d	86*n177*, 155, 171
Phaedrus		102, 126
Philebus		102
	11b4	65
	12d8–e2	82*n64*
	26e7	75*n141*
	27a8–9	75*n141*
	49a–e	101, 131, 132
	51a	80*n152*
	51b3	55
Protagoras		96, 113, 126, 133, 142
	309c10	120*n7*
	314c	105*n5*
	318e	40, 42*n36*
	334a–d	45*n57*, 116, 184, 186
	337c–338b	98, 125, 126, 133
	342–47	105*n6*
	347a	125
	348c5	68*n127*
	353ab	98, 184
	360d	142

Title	Citation	Page Number
	360c1–2	152
	361e4	120*n7*
Republic		93, 102, 113, 142, 149, 161, 162, 172, 176
	335bc	45*n57*
	336cd	68*n127*, 185, 186, 187
	339c	70
	349d12	45*n59*
	350e2	135*n8*
	354b	140
	365a6	74*n139*
	372c1–2	58*n98*
	395c–e	101
	420cd	57*n90*
	422a	135*n11*
	435c8	89*n200*
	476b–d	120*n6*, 179
	478bc	167
	479a	153, 177, 178
	479b9–10	54*n82*
	486a4–6	88*n194*
	493a–d	114, 118
	497d10	89*n200*
	505c6	65
	506e	76*n145*
	538d9–e1	54*n82*
	606c	101

Title	Citation	Page Number
Sophist		102
	216c	114
	218d	114
	223c	114
	230bc	118, 137
	231c	114
	232e	114
	234c	120*n5*
	237d1–2	167
	240c	114
	247bc	85*n175*
	257cd	154, 173, 180*n18*
	258c10	167
Symposium		102, 105, 126, 174, 176
	192c7	74*n139*
	211a	173, 174
	212a	188
Theaetetus		102
	152d	116
	154e2–3	85*n174*
	185e4	44*n49*
	201d8	82*n170*
Timaeus	30c4	76*n146*
	50d	76*n145*
	51be	171

PROTAGORAS

| DK80B1 | | 116 |

Title	Citation	Page Number
	SOPHOCLES	
Antigone	1.450	41
	XENOPHON	
Memorabilia	I.ii.58	60*n104*
	III.viii	53*n75*, 55, 183, 186
	IV.iv.	39*n27*, 41*n32*
	IV.vi	111*n2*, 183
Oeconomicus	VIII.19	53*n75*, 96, 184
Symposium	iv-v	68*n128*, 110, 184